Soundings on Cinema

THE SUNY SERIES

HORIZONS OF CINEMA

MURRAY POMERANCE | EDITOR

Also in the series

William Rothman, editor, *Cavell on Film*

J. David Slocum, editor, *Rebel Without a Cause*

Joe McElhaney, *The Death of Classical Cinema*

Kirsten Thompson, *Apocalyptic Dread*

Francis Gateward, editor, *Seoul Searching*

Michael Atkinson, editor, *Exile Cinema*

Soundings on Cinema

Speaking to Film and Film Artists

Bert Cardullo

STATE UNIVERSITY OF NEW YORK PRESS

Published by
State University of New York Press, Albany

For information, contact State University of New York Press, Albany, NY
www.sunypress.edu

Production by Marilyn P. Semerad
Marketing by Anne M. Valentine

Library of Congress Cataloging-in-Publication Data

Cardullo, Bert.
  Soundings on cinema : speaking to film and film artists / Bert Cardullo.
     p. cm. — (SUNY series, horizons of cinema)
  Includes index.
  ISBN 978-0-7914-7407-5 (hardcover : alk. paper)
  ISBN 978-0-7914-7408-2 (pbk. : alk. paper)
  1. Motion pictures producers and directors—Europe—Interviews.
2. Motion pictures—Europe.   I. Title.

PN1998.2.C3643 2008
791.4302'3309224—dc22   2007030823

10 9 8 7 6 5 4 3 2 1

Contents

Illustrations

Preface

This book began as a wildly ambitious adventure over three decades ago, a few years after I had graduated from college: try to interview, or at least meet, as many of the world's most esteemed filmmakers as possible. Through various contacts—familial, academic, journalistic—unflagging persistence, and some great good luck, I was able to do so. But my "adventure" took much longer than I had expected, for the usual reasons: money, time, other commitments, and so on. In any event, meeting up with filmmakers got easier after I became the movie critic of *The Hudson Review* in 1987. And *Soundings on Cinema* is the result of hours of conversation with the likes of Michelangelo Antonioni and Robert Bresson, to name just two of my subjects in the pages to follow.

The conversations with Antonioni, Vittorio De Sica, and Federico Fellini were all conducted, as much as possible, in English; when each director had to use Italian, I translated later with the assistance of my mother, a native speaker. The same goes for the interviews with Jean Renoir and Bresson: mostly in English, with a smattering of French, which I was able to translate on my own. Ingmar Bergman, Aki Kaurismäki (who graciously provided me with my introduction to the reclusive Bergman), and, of course, Mike Leigh all spoke only in English; and Hans-Jürgen Syberberg spoke exclusively in German, which I myself subsequently translated. In the cases of the interviews with Kaurismäki, Bergman, and Leigh, each man either was already familiar with my writings on his work or requested copies in advance of our meeting. When those writings were negative, in whole or in part, as in the instances of *Autumn Sonata* and *Vera Drake*, the filmmaker happily happened to agree with my assessment (Bergman) or wanted very much to contest it—in person (Leigh).

Soundings on Cinema is organized along national lines, and, although I have limited my nations to those of Europe, I have otherwise tried to be inclusive in my selections. Finland, Italy, Germany, France, England, and Sweden are represented here. I would have liked to include other continents and other countries along with their best directors, and I tried. But Gutiérrez Alea of Cuba, for example, regrettably passed away several weeks before our scheduled meeting; Ousmane Sembène of Senegal canceled on me three times; and Agnès Varda simply refused all requests for an interview. Still, I managed to conduct nine interviews with some of the men who figured (and figure) most in the making of the movies; in any case, restrictions on length would have prevented me from including all the filmmakers I would have wanted. It must be said, moreover, that the subject of African or Latin American cinema—like the subject of Asian cinema—deserves a representative collection of interviews unto itself.

The European filmmakers I have included, the reader will note, are important not because they are "mere" directors, but because they are *writer*-directors or cinematic *auteurs*. Each of them has written, or collaborated in the writing of, every script he has directed; some are even complete *auteurs* in the sense that they perform almost every function that goes into the making of a film, including editing and musical scoring. Why is such authorship so important? For the obvious reason that it puts a work of film art on the same level as any other work of art (not so negligible a reason when you consider the relative youth of the cinema as an art form): as primarily the product of one person's vision, supervision, and execution. *Auteurism* is also significant for the less obvious reason that, as it is properly understood, it correctly privileges the well-wrought script, the carefully chosen word, as the place where every narrative film of quality must begin. That so many narrative films do not so begin—that they limit *auteurism* to signature visual style or stylistic flourish—is the reason so many of them finally fall short of cinematic wholeness, let alone excellence.

A word on the pairings: Each interview is accompanied either by an overview of the director's career, a section on a particular film of his, or a series of interconnected reviews of films by the *auteur* in question. My intent in doing this, of course, is to "bounce" my writings off a director's own words, to juxtapose what I think of his work against what *he* thinks of his work. We do not always agree, but, why must we? Where I am bold enough to differ, say, with Leigh, I hope that our disagreement is a productive or "teaching" one. Where I am (at the tender age of twenty-five) cheeky enough to challenge De Sica, in conversation if not in writing, I trust that his exasperated response to my question is telling as well as comic.

As for the three groupings themselves, they are, aside from being geographically representative of Europe, artistically inclusive as well. Among the Italian neorealist directors, for example, are those who go beyond realism into realms that can only be called "romantically fantastic" in the case of Fellini and "sculpturally spatial" in the case of Antonioni. In the grouping "Anglo-Nordic Temperaments," Syberberg's theater of film is juxtaposed against Bergman's film as music. Finally, among the French, there is one director, Renoir, to whom one cannot easily ascribe a specific narrative style or tone—and there is another director, Bresson, whose style and tone remained the same throughout his career (as they have remained the same, thus far, in the work of his Finnish admirer, Kaurismäki).

I have tried to make the interviews themselves as artistically inclusive as possible. That is, my questions focus on practical matters related to filmmaking (which, lest we forget, is variously known as a technology, an industry, an entertainment, and an art) as much as they do on historical, aesthetic, and critical-theoretical issues raised by the films themselves. Among those practical matters, furthermore, the reader will note that as much attention is given to acting, design, and cinematography as to directing, writing, and editing (with some attention paid to finance and audience-reception, as well). Naturally, this is because film is the most "total" of the arts, containing or embracing all the others: literature, painting, sculpture, architecture, photography, music, theater, and dance. Hence any interview of a film artist should itself aspire to be as aesthetically comprehensive as it can.

Soundings on Cinema is the culmination, then, of my lifelong love affair with the cinema, even though I somehow managed to marry into the theater (as the reader will see, for instance, in the chapter devoted to Syberberg). That love affair, from the start, has been premised on my belief, or rather knowledge, that not only is film the most democratic of the arts in addition to being the most "total"—making all faces equal and making "travel," through time as well as space, available to people of every social class at the same low price. Film is also the only narrative art form almost instantaneously available, through subtitling, throughout the world. Its immediate international character is what drew me to it, and therefore it is ultimately what made this book possible.

Soundings on Cinema was also made possible in the end through the generosity, confidence, and even forbearance of my editors at *The Hudson Review*, Paula Deitz and the late Frederick Morgan. It was completed during a Fulbright research fellowship in Istanbul, Turkey—a country, poised between East and West, where I remain today. It was improved by my editor, Murray Pomerance, together with the two anonymous readers of the original manuscript. It is dedicated to Barbara Ann Wittenberg, the woman who accompanied me during the early part of my great adventure—and the one who got away.

PART 1

Italian Neorealism
and Beyond

Actor-Become-Auteur

The Neorealist Films of Vittorio De Sica

VITTORIO DE SICA HAS BEEN considered one of the major contributors to neorealism, a movement that altered the content and style of international as well as Italian cinema. Despite these contributions and numerous citations of praise for such films as *Sciuscià* (*Shoeshine*, 1946), *Ladri di biciclette* (*Bicycle Thieves*, 1948), *Miracolo a Milano* (*Miracle in Milano*, 1951), and *Umberto D.* (1952), which are his best known and most beloved in addition to being his best pictures, De Sica has become a neglected figure in film studies. He may be seen as a victim of (postmodernist) fashion, for today emphasis is frequently placed on technical or stylistic virtuosity, and films of social content are looked upon—often justifiably—as sentimental or quaint (unless that content is of the politically correct kind). The works of De Sica that were once on everybody's list of best films have, to a large extent, therefore been relegated to the ranks of "historical examples" on the shelves of museums, archives, and university libraries. Then, too, the director who was lionized during the Italian postwar era was later dismissed as a film revolutionary who had sold out to commercialism. Except for *Il giardino dei Finzi-Contini* (*The Garden of the Finzi-Continis*, 1971) and *Una breve vacanza* (*A Brief Vacation*, 1973), De Sica's films after the neorealist period have been considered minor or inferior works in comparison to those of his contemporaries.

In Italy, it must be said, one encounters very favorable reactions to his work; yet behind these reactions there are always attempts at qualification. Scholars there approach a discussion of De Sica with awe and respect but also with the proviso that he was, of course, too sentimental. The fact that the first full-length study of De Sica's work was not published

3

Vittorio De Sica, 1963, on the set of *Ieri, Oggi, Domani,* a.k.a. *Yesterday, Today, and Tomorrow.* © Embassy Pictures Corporation. *(Courtesy of Photofest)*

by the Italians until 1992—Lino Miccichè's edited collection titled *De Sica: Autore, Regista, Attore (De Sica: Author, Director, Actor)*—attests to his countrymen's ultimate indifference toward a major director who has been demoted to the rank of interesting but minor filmmaker. The French initially had no such indifference, being the first to hail De Sica as a "genius." During the 1950s and 1960s, French film critics and historians preoccupied themselves with De Sica to such an extent that they produced the only full-length studies of the Italian director ever to be published in any country: Henri Agel's *Vittorio De Sica* (1955, rev. 1964) and Pierre Leprohon's book of the same name (1966). The waves of acclaim from France have by now subsided, however.

In Great Britain and America, as in Italy, De Sica is known and studied as a "link" in the Italian postwar movement of neorealism, such as he is represented in two basic British works on Italian cinema: Vernon Jarratt's *Italian Cinema* (1951) and Roy Armes's *Patterns of Realism* (1971). In America, aside from interpretive articles or chapters on individual films, movie reviews, and career surveys in general film histories as well as specifically Italian ones, a single-authored full-length critical study on the works of De Sica is nonexistent. John Darretta's *Vittorio De Sica: A Guide to References and Resources* (1983) is certainly valuable for its biographical information; filmography complete with synopses and credits; annotated bibliography of criticism in Italian, French, and English; and chronological guide to De Sica's careers on the stage and on the screen. But Darretta's critical survey of the director's films is limited to 8 pages in a book that otherwise runs to 340.

Perhaps this lack of scholarly attention derives from the fact that De Sica was at once the Italian screen's most versatile artist and its greatest paradox. As a star performer in well over a hundred films, he embodied the escapist show-biz spirit at its most ebullient, wooing a vast public with his charm and drollery. Yet De Sica the director aspired to, and frequently achieved, the highest cinematic standards, challenging the audience to re spond to his unflinching social insights and psychological portraiture. De Sica's most disarming trait as a screen star was his nonchalance, which could shift irresistibly to a wry narcissism with the flick of a well-tonsured eyebrow. Particularly in his many postwar comedies, De Sica tended to play lovable frauds—smoothies whose looks and manner were a little too studied to be true (though he did prove himself capable of a solid dramatic performance as an amoral poseur-turned-partisan in Rossellini's look back at Italian neorealism, *Il Generale della Rovere* [1959], which was set during the darkest moment of the Nazi occupation of Rome). Yet when he relinquished his own close-ups to venture behind the camera, De Sica became the utter opposite of this extroverted entertainer. De Sica's signal trait as a filmmaker was his own compassionate self-effacement, which caused him to intervene as unobtrusively as possible to tell the stories of the powerless and marginal creatures who populate his best work.

This intriguing dichotomy is what distinguishes De Sica from the brace of other successful actor-directors who have enriched film history in all eras. From von Stroheim and Chaplin through Welles and Olivier to Kevin Costner and Kenneth Branagh in the present, most actors who have turned to directing have done so in part to protect and enhance their own luster as performers. As such, their filmmaking styles tend to reflect the persona each projects on screen as an actor—the theatrical flourish of an Olivier, say, or the high-spirited pop lyricism that Gene Kelly projected in *Singin' in the Rain* (1952). However, after his first forays as a director, De Sica only appeared in his own films with reluctance. Perhaps this was because, as a director, he guided his professional cast and amateur actors of all ages in exactly the same way: He acted everything out according to his wishes, down to the smallest inflection, then expected his human subjects to imitate him precisely. Therefore, for De Sica actually to perform in a movie he was directing himself would, on a certain level, be redundant. In any event, the visual spareness and emotional force that are the key traits of his best, neorealist work behind the camera have no discernible connection to the sleek routines of that clever mountebank who enlivened four decades of Italian popular movies.

The post–World War II birth or creation of neorealism, it must be said, was anything but a collective theoretical enterprise. The origins of Italian neorealist cinema were far more complex than that. Generally stated, its roots were political, in that neorealism reacted ideologically to the control and censorship of the prewar cinema; aesthetic, for the intuitive, imaginative response of neorealist directors coincided with the rise or resurgence of realism in Italian literature, particularly the novels of Italo Calvino, Alberto Moravia, Cesare Pavese, Elio Vittorini, and Vasco Pratolini (a realism that can be traced to the veristic style first cultivated in the Italian cinema between 1913 and 1916, when films inspired by the writings of Giovanni Verga and others dealt with human problems as well as social themes in natural settings); and economic, in that this new realism posed basic solutions to the lack of funds, of functioning studios, and of working equipment.

Indeed, what is sometimes overlooked in the growth of the neorealist movement in Italy is the fact that some of its most admired aspects sprang from the dictates of postwar adversity: A shortage of money made shooting in real locations an imperative choice over the use of expensive studio sets, and against such locations any introduction of the phony or the fake would appear glaringly obvious, whether in the appearance of the actors or in the style of the acting. It must have been paradoxically exhilarating for neorealist filmmakers to be able to stare unflinchingly at the tragic spectacle of a society in shambles, its values utterly shattered, after years of making nice little movies approved by the powers that were within the walls of Cinecittà.

In fact, it was the Fascists who, in 1937, opened Cinecittà, the largest and best-equipped movie studio in all of Europe. Like the German Nazis and the Russian Communists, the Italian Fascists realized the power of cinema as a medium of propaganda, and when they came to power, they took over the film industry. Although this meant that those who opposed Fascism could not make movies and that foreign pictures were censored, the Fascists helped to establish the essential requirements for a flourishing postwar film industry. In 1935 they founded the Centro Sperimentale in Rome, a film school headed by Luigi Chiarini, which taught all aspects of movie production. Many important neorealist directors attended this school, including Rossellini, Antonioni, Zampa, Germi, and De Santis (but not De Sica); it also produced cameramen, editors, and technicians. Moreover, Chiarini was allowed to publish *Bianco e nero* (*Black and White*), the film journal that later became the official voice of neorealism. Once Mussolini fell from power, then, the stage was set for a strong left-wing cinema.

The Axis defeat happened to transform the Italian film industry into a close approximation of the ideal market of classical economists: a multitude of small producers engaged in fierce competition. There were no clearly dominant firms among Italian movie producers, and the Italian film industry as a whole exhibited considerable weakness. The very atomization and weakness of a privately owned and profit-oriented motion-picture industry, however, led to a *de facto* tolerance toward the left-wing ideology of neorealism. In addition, the political climate of postwar Italy was favorable to the rise of cinematic neorealism, since this artistic movement was initially a product of the spirit of resistance fostered by the Partisan movement. The presence of Nenni Socialists (Pietro Nenni was minister of foreign affairs) and Communists in the Italian government from 1945 to 1947 contributed to the governmental tolerance of neorealism's left-wing ideology, as did the absence of censorship from 1945 through 1949.

Rossellini's *Roma, città aperta* (*Open City*, 1945) became the landmark film in the promulgation of neorealist ideology. It so completely reflected the moral and psychological atmosphere of its historical moment that it alerted both the public and the critics—on the international level (including the United States) as well as the national one—to a new direction in Italian cinema. Furthermore, the conditions of its production (relatively little shooting in the studio, film stock bought on the black market and developed without the typical viewing of daily rushes, postsynchronization of sound to avoid laboratory costs, limited financial backing) did much to create many of the myths, or mythic truths, surrounding neorealism. With a daring combination of styles and tones—from the use of documentary footage to the deployment of the most blatant melodrama, from the juxtaposition of comic relief with the most tragic human events—Rossellini almost effortlessly captured forever the tension and drama of the Italian experience during the German occupation and the Partisan struggle against the Nazi invasion.

If, practically speaking, Rossellini at once introduced Italian cinematic neorealism to the world, De Sica's collaborator Cesare Zavattini—with whom he forged one of the most fruitful writer-director partnerships in the history of cinema—eventually became the theoretical spokesman for the neorealists. By his definition, neorealism does not concern itself with superficial themes and synthetic forms; in his famous manifesto "Some Ideas on the Cinema" (1952), Zavattini declares that the camera has a "hunger for reality," and that the invention of plots to make reality palatable or spectacular is a flight from the historical richness as well as the political importance of actual, everyday life.

Although inconsistently or irregularly observed, the basic tenets of this new realism were threefold: to portray real or everyday people (using nonprofessional actors) in actual settings, to examine socially significant themes (the geniune problems of living), and to promote the organic development of situations as opposed to the arbitrary manipulation of events (i.e., the real flow of life, in which complications are seldom resolved by coincidence, contrivance, or miracle). These tenets were clearly opposed to the prewar cinematic style that used polished actors on studio sets, conventional and even fatuous themes, and artificial, gratuitously resolved plots—the very style, of course, that De Sica himself had employed in the four pictures he made from 1939 to 1942 (*Rose scarlatte* [*Red Roses*, 1939], *Maddalena zero in condotta* [*Maddalena, Zero for Conduct*, 1940], *Teresa Venerdì* [1941], and *Un garibaldino al convento* [*A Garibaldian in the Convent*, 1942]).

Unfortunately, this was the cinematic style that the Italian public continued to demand after the war, despite the fact that during it such precursors of neorealism as Visconti's *Ossessione* (*Obsession*, 1942) and De Sica's own *I bambini ci guardano* (*The Children Are Watching Us*, 1943) had offered a serious alternative. Indeed, it was as early as 1942, when *Ossessione* and *I bambini ci guardano* were either being made or released, that the idea of the cinema was being transformed in Italy. Influenced by French cinematic realism as well as by prevailing Italian literary trends, Visconti shot *Ossessione* on location in the region of Romagna; the plot and atmosphere (based on James M. Cain's novel *The Postman Always Rings Twice* [1934]) were seamy in addition to steamy and did not adhere to the polished, resolved structures of conventional Italian movies. Visconti's film was previewed in the spring of 1943 and quickly censored, not to be appreciated until after the war.

Around the same time, Gianni Franciolini's *Fari nella nebbia* (*Headlights in the Fog*, 1941) was portraying infidelity among truck drivers and seamstresses, while Alessandro Blasetti's *Quattro passi fra le nuvole* (*Four Steps in the Clouds*, 1942)—coscripted by Zavattini and starring De Sica's wife at the time, Giuditta Rissone—was being praised for its return to realism in a warmhearted story of peasant life shot in natural settings. De Sica, too, was dissatisfied with the general state of the Italian cinema, and, after the relative success of his formulaic films, he felt it was time for a new challenge. Like Zavattini, who had by now achieved a measure of screenwriting success, De Sica wanted to do some serious work in which he expressed his ideas about human problems and human values.

The title of his new film had already been the heading of one of Zavattini's famous newspaper columns, and the subject matter of the story would be deemed scandalous when it reached the screen. *I bambini ci guardano* examines the impact on a young boy's life of his mother's extramarital affair with a family friend. The five-year-old Pricò becomes painfully aware of the rift in his family life, and his sense of loss is made even more acute when his father sends him away from Rome to live—first in the country with his unreceptive paternal grandmother, then at a Jesuit boarding school. His mother's love affair leads finally to the suicide of Pricò's ego-shattered father; and, at the end of the film, when his mother (draped in mourning dress) comes to the school to reclaim her child, Pricò rejects her. The last time we see him, he is walking away by himself, a small, agonized figure dwarfed by the huge, impersonal lobby of the school.

The cause of the marital rift leading to the wife's infidelity in this film is never revealed; the concern of De Sica and his screenwriters is purely with the effect of the rupture on the little boy. And it is this concentration on a child's view of the world—here the world of the petit bourgeois family almost apart from the social, economic, and political forces that combine to influence its workings (a world similarly explored, *sans* children, in *Ossessione*)—that gives a basically banal, even melodramatic tale a profounder aspect. Except for René Clément's *Forbidden Games* (1952), there has never been such an implacable view of the antagonism and desolation that separate the lives of adult and children.

I bambini ci guardano owes much to the remarkable performance of the boy, Luciano De Ambrosis, himself orphaned just before work on the picture began, and whose acting experience was limited to a walk-on in a Pirandello play. De Sica's uncanny directorial rapport with his five-year-old protagonist would, of course, later prove vital in the making of *Sciuscià* and *Ladri di biciclette*, which share with *I bambini ci guardano* the theme of childhood innocence in confrontation with adult realities. Arguably, De Sica would become the most eloquent director of children the screen has ever known, with the possible exception only of François Truffaut. And *I bambini ci guardano* gave the first evidence of that extraordinary dual perspective that De Sica conveyed in his films about children. At the same time, he managed both to simulate a child's vantage point on the baffling adult sorrows that surround him and to subtly establish an authorial detachment—expressed in the spare neutrality of his mise-en-scène, even the physical distance he so often maintains between the camera and his subject—which somehow makes the predicament of his characters doubly moving. It is as though De Sica's camera eye were a passive witness to tragedy rather than the active force in the shaping of a fictional story—this "passivity" being one of the grand illusions of the neorealist movement to come and one fostered by the frequent use of nonprofessional actors photographed in actual locations, as opposed to the artificial confines of the movie studio.

As in his subsequent neorealistic films, De Sica's cinematographer (Giuseppe Caracciolo) is not called upon in *I bambini ci guardano* to exhibit striking angles or exhilarating movement: The compositions rarely startle the viewer through their ingenuity; the use of the camera is clear-eyed rather than ingenious. *What* De Sica focuses on at a given point is more significant than the way in which he focuses his attention. The way is never neglected, it simply is not exploited; for it is to De Sica's purpose to move with unelliptical life as closely as he dares without vitiating motion-picture technique altogether. To subordinate the essentially cinematic as he does is itself a technique of ineffable skill; and to efface his signature as a director from the style of a film argues a modest purity of aim that is refreshing.

De Sica tried out such a detached or reserved mise-en-scène for the first time in *I bambini ci guardano*, whose simplicity of composition and subdued editing style markedly contrast with the formulaic, studio-dictated cinematic style of his previous four films. The tone of De Sica's fifth picture also strongly differs from that of *Rose scarlatte, Maddalena zero in condotta, Teresa Venerdì,* and *Un garibaldino al convento,* for there is no comedy in *I bambini ci guardano;* what relief we get from Pricò's suffering comes only in the form of his own heightened or mature perception and sensitivity—indeed, his name is a shortened form of the Italian word for precocious. Not only is there no comedy in the movie, there is a tragic ending that signaled a change in De Sica's artistic vision. The alienation evident at the start of *I bambini ci guardano* does not disappear; on the contrary, the gap in communication between the mother and her child widens. After the suicide of his father, moreover, as I have noted, Pricò is not reunited with his remaining parent: Instead, he turns his back on her and returns down a long corridor to his tiny dormitory room. The discordant ending is one of the most powerful in all of De Sica's work—challenged only by the final scene of *Sciuscià*—and it contrasts markedly with the comic endings of this director's first four movies, where the strife and confusion of the fictional world are replaced by happy harmony and romantic union.

I bambini ci guardano, then, proved to be a key work, thematically as well as stylistically, in De Sica's directing career: It cemented his collaborative artistic relationship with Cesare Zavattini, and it marked the beginning of his breakthrough as a filmmaker of more than provincial stature. In its thematic attempt to reveal the underside of Italy's moral life, shared with *Ossessione*, this film was indicative of a rising new vision in Italian cinema. In exhibiting semidocumentary qualities by being shot partially on location at the beaches of Alassio and by using nonprofessional actors in some roles, *I bambini ci guardano* was—again along with *Ossessione* as well as the aforementioned pictures by Blasetti and Franciolini—a precursor of the neorealism that would issue forth after the liberation of occupied Rome. De Sica's fifth film was not a financial success, however, and its negative reception was in part engineered by those who saw it as an impudent criticism of Italian morality. The unfavorable reaction to *I bambini ci guardano* was also influenced, of course, by the strictures of the past: During the era of Mussolini's regime and "white telephone" movies (trivial romantic comedies set in blatantly artificial studio surroundings), an insidious censorship had made it almost impossible for artists to deal with, and for audiences to appreciate, the moral, social, political, and spiritual components of actual, everyday life.

After the Second World War, a different kind of "censorship" obtained: that of the lira. For, in 1946, viewers wanted to spend their hard-earned lire on Hollywood movies through which they could escape their everyday lives, not on films that realistically depicted the effects of war—effects that they already knew only too well through direct experience. As a result, De Sica's first wholly neorealistic picture, *Sciuscià*, was a commercial disaster. Mostly negative movie reviewers cited the difficulty of understanding the performers' mixed accents and dialects, and neither the newspapers nor the Italian government appreciated what they called De Sica's capitalizing on the misfortunes of the poor as well as sensationalizing the conditions of prison life. Shot in three months under the primitive circumstances of postwar production, *Sciuscià* had a different reception, however, in other countries. It proved an artistic triumph particularly in France and the United States, where it won a "special award" at the 1947 presentations of the Academy of Motion Picture Arts and Sciences (since the Oscar for best foreign film did not yet exist). This was the film, then, that marked the beginning of De Sica's international recognition as a major director and that stands as a landmark in his professional relationship with Cesare Zavattini.

Sciuscià was conceived out of the experiences of vagrant orphans in poverty-stricken, postwar Rome, where, chief among Italy's cities, they organized their enterprises (many of them illegal) in the wake of the Allied liberation. Often these youngsters were seen trailing after American soldiers calling out "Sciuscià, Gio?"—their phonetic equivalent of "Shoeshine, Joe?"—for G.I.s were among the few able to afford even this minor luxury in a country filled with unemployment following the cessation of hostilities. A magazine published a photo spread on two of the shoeshine boys, nicknamed "Scimietta" (Little Monkey), who slept in elevators, and "Cappellone" (Big Hat), who suffered from rickets in addition to having a large head; and their pictures attracted a small-time, American-born producer, Paolo William Tamburella, who suggested to De Sica that a story about such street waifs would make a touching and topical movie. Immediately, Zavattini took up the suggestion, and he and De Sica walked the streets of Rome absorbing the atmosphere, in order to achieve maximum fidelity in the final motion picture.

The filmmakers even got to know the two boys, Scimietta and Cappellone, who tried to earn enough money shining G.I. boots on the Via Veneto so that they could rush to the nearby Villa Borghese stables for an hour of horseback riding. They became the models for Giuseppe and Pasquale of *Sciuscià*, and, for a brief moment, De Sica considered drafting Scimietta and Cappellone to play themselves in the movie, since there were no equivalent Roddy McDowells or Dean Stockwells working at the time in the Italian cinema. He decided, however, that they were too ugly—a decision that tellingly reveals the limits of realism, neo- or otherwise, and that points up yet again that realism is one among a number of artistic styles, not reality itself. Zavattini artfully adapted the shoeshine boys' lives and love of horses to the screen, while Rinaldo Smordoni and Franco Interlenghi were chosen from among the throngs of an open casting call to play Little Monkey and Big Hat.

In order to drum up money to realize their dream of owning a horse, the two boys become party—albeit innocently—to a robbery. When they acquire the animal, a white stallion named Bersagliere, no conditions adhere to its joyful ownership: The horse belongs to both of them, involves each youngster totally, and symbolizes their common pastoral longing for a life of pureness and beauty. They are soon apprehended by the police, however, and, when they refuse to implicate the real thieves, Giuseppe and Pasquale are sent to jail as juvenile delinquents. There they are tricked into turning against each other, and, in *Sciuscià*'s climax, Giuseppe slips to his death from a bridge in an attempt to escape attack by an angry, vengeful Pasquale. As the latter falls to his knees, screaming, next to his friend's body in the river bed, their beloved horse has long since symbolically galloped off into the darkness.

As was the usual practice in Italian films, the script of *Sciuscià* was the joint work of several professionals—Sergio Amedei, Adolfo Franci, and Cesare Giulio Viola—in addition to the team of De Sica-Zavattini. And, although *Sciuscià* was shot in real locations as much as possible (excluding the final bridge scene, which was shot in the studio because the producer did not have the money to wait for good weather), there was nothing improvised about its script, which was worked out to the smallest detail. There were those in the late 1940s who liked to proclaim that motion pictures like *Sciuscià* were pure, unadulterated Life flung onto the screen—which, of course, is nonsense, and even an unintended insult to De Sica's powers as a great, instinctive movie dramatist. In fact, De Sica the director cannily exploits every resource of the cinema in which he had been working for fifteen years—not hesitating to underscore *Sciuscià*'s pathetic tragedy with heart-tugging music by the redoubtable Alessandro Cicognini—in order to give his audience the emotional frissons latent in the story he chose to bring to the screen.

For all its hybridization, however, what endures from *Sciuscià* is De Sica's palpable empathy for these street children and the plight of the entire generation they represent. As an artist with no particular ideological axe to grind, moreover, he manages always to give a human or personal dimension to the abstract forces that frame this drama. The grainy, newsreel quality of Anchise Brizzi's photograhy, the sharp cutting, and the seemingly spontaneous naturalness of the acting (particularly of Smordoni and Interlenghi as the two boys) all sustain the feel of an exhausted Roman city, bereft of its pride. This same weariness affects the authorities in the prison scenes, which have an almost documentary air of moral as well as physical squalor.

The very title of this film—the Italian-English neologism coined by the shoeshine boys of Rome—is a clue to its all-embracing intentions. *Sciuscià* may be the pathetic story of Giuseppe and Pasquale, but the tragedy of post–World War II Italy is reflected in their sad tale. Even as the American G.I.s in the film see the image of their own security and prosperity in their shined shoes, so too does Italian society find the image of its own disarray and poverty in the story of these beautifully paired boys. *Sciuscià* is an illumination of reality—a "shining" of reality's "shoes," if you will—and of the basic problems facing a defeated nation in the wake of war: for the ruled, how to survive amidst rampant poverty at the same time as one does not break the law; for the rulers, how to enforce the law without sacrificing one's own humanity or that of the lawbreakers. As with so many of his contemporaries, the convulsive times awakened profound feelings in De Sica of which he may not previously have been aware; without question, he had traveled a huge aesthetic and emotional distance since the making of *Maddalena zero in condotta* only six years before.

Buoyed by the artistic success, if not by the commercial fiasco, of *Sciuscià*, De Sica turned next to *Immatella Califano*, a story by Michele Prisco about the love between a young Neapolitan girl and a black American soldier. But this project was rejected because of existing social taboos, although Alberto Lattuada managed to film a similar story in *Senza pietà* (*Without Pity*, 1947), which centered on a black G.I. who had fallen in love with a white prostitute and deserted the American army. It was Zavattini who found the spark that returned De Sica to directing after he had resumed his acting career in several commercial vehicles. The spark in question was Luigi Bartolini's minor novel *Ladri di biciclette* (1948).

Zavattini thought that the book's central situation, if little else, would appeal to his colleague, and De Sica was indeed seized by it immediately, although very little from Bartolini's original narrative found its way to the screen in the end. This time, constructing the screenplay turned out to be an especially tempestuous process: Sergio Amidei, for one (who had contributed to the script for *Sciuscià*), dropped out early because he found the story implausible. Surely, Amidei insisted, the protagonist's comrades, stalwart union members all, would have found him another bicycle after the first one was stolen. Fortunately for posterity, De Sica did not agree (or care), and neither did his coscenarist Suso Cecchi D'Amico. The final scenario, as minutely conceived as that for *Sciuscià*, was a close collaboration among D'Amico, De Sica, and Zavattini.

Raising the money to produce *Ladri di biciclette* was a predictable struggle, considering *Sciuscià*'s financial failure in Italy. De Sica's French admirers declared that they would be thrilled to *distribute* the picture once it was completed, and Gabriel Pascal of England passed on the project altogether, while David O. Selznick proclaimed from Hollywood that he would finance *Ladri di biciclette* on the condition that Cary Grant be cast in the lead. De Sica had suggested Henry Fonda or Barry Fitzgerald, but neither was considered "box office" at the time. In the end, De Sica's customary threadbare budget was scraped together from three local producers, and work could begin at last on the casting. For the central role of Ricci, De Sica chose Lamberto Maggiorani, a struggling factory worker from Breda who had brought his sons to Rome to audition for the part of the young Bruno. The role of Bruno went instead to Enzo Staiola, the eight-year-old son of a flower vendor, whom De Sica had noticed in a crowd gathered to watch the shooting of a street scene for *Ladri di biciclette*. Bruno's mother was played by Lianella Carell, a journalist from a Rome newspaper who had come to interview the filmmaker. The three major parts, then, went to nonprofessionals, although De Sica did use a professional actor to dub the role of Ricci. Actually, the only performer to appear in the movie with previous acting experience was Gino Saltamerenda (Baiocco), who had played "Il panza" in *Sciuscià*.

Ladri di biciclette can only be fully appreciated after being placed in its sociohistorical context: that of the traumatic, chaotic postwar years when a defeated Italy was occupied by Allied forces. In Rome after World War II unemployment is rife, and transportation is limited mainly to overcrowded streetcars. An unemployed workman, Ricci, gets a job as a bill poster on the condition that he himself provide a bicycle for getting around the city; he therefore retrieves his own bicycle from a pawnshop by pledging his and his wife's bedsheets. But while he is pasting up a glamorous poster of an American pin-up girl during his first day of work, Ricci's bicycle is stolen: an utter disaster, for here we have a man who has thus been deprived of a rare chance to earn tomorrow's bread for his family.

He spends an entire day scouring the city with his little boy, Bruno, hunting for the thief, with the story working continually on two levels: the father's relationship to the world, described in his search for the stolen bicycle; and the son's relationship with his father—for the child, the only one of which he is aware. Indeed, De Sica developed the film's rhythm by a *pas de deux* of man and boy in their scouting expedition through the city, the boy nervously anxious to keep in time with his father's mood and intention, the boy's relationship with his father serving as a barometer of the effects of the agonizing search on this man's soul. The adjustments of temper and tempo; the resolve, haste, anger, and embarrassment; the flanking movements, the frustrations, and the periodic losses of direction: These constituted a form of situational ballet that gave the picture its lyricism.

When at last Ricci finds the thief, however, he can prove nothing and is even attacked in the street by a gang of the man's supporters, intent on protecting one of their number. At that point, Ricci spots an unattended bicycle outside a house and tries to steal it. But he is immediately caught and shamed. In this climactic moment of frustration at committing an act that is fundamentally alien to him, the father commits another alien act by striking his son, who runs away from him. They are temporarily estranged, but nightfall finds the two of them reunited yet powerless—save for the loving bond that sustains them—against the bleak threat that tomorrow holds. At the end of the picture, the tracking camera simply halts and ambivalently observes both Riccis as they walk away into, or are swallowed up by, a Roman throng at dusk.

Bicycle Thieves (1948), a.k.a. *Ladri di biciclette*. Directed by Vittorio De Sica. Shown from left: Enzo Staiola (as Bruno), Lamberto Maggiorani (as Antonio Ricci). *(Courtesy of Photofest)*

Ladri di biciclette established beyond any doubt Vittorio De Sica's international reputation as a major director. But, once again, the movie received far greater acclaim in France, America, and England than it did in Italy. Like *Sciuscià*, it won a special Academy Award for best foreign film, as well as awards from the New York Film Critics, the British Film Academy, and the Belgian Film Festival. At home, however, *Ladri di biciclette* exacerbated the hostility that De Sica had aroused with *Sciuscià* for promulgating an unflattering view of his country—although, ironically, both films received Silver Ribbons there. Italian critics and politicians railed against the negative image of Italy that was being exposed to the world by neorealist filmmakers such as De Sica. Works such as *Sciuscià*, *Ladri di biciclette*, and later *Umberto D.* were labeled in the press "stracci all'estero" (rags for abroad), the extreme antithesis of the white telephone movies produced before the war.

Accordingly, the initial, indifferent reception of *Ladri di biciclette* upon its release in Italy at the end of 1948 was absolutely devastating to De Sica. The international enthusiasm for the picture did prompt its rerelease in his native country, however—which at least was successful enough to allow the director to pay off the debts left over from *Sciuscià*. Italian audiences, it seems, were reluctant to respond without prompting to an indigenous neorealist cinema intent on exploring the postwar themes of unemployment, inadequate housing, and neglected children, in alternately open-ended and tragic dramatic structures populated by mundane nonprofessional actors instead of glamorous stars. (In fact, one reason for neorealism's ultimate decline was that its aesthetic principle of using nonprofessional actors conflicted with the economic interests of the various organizations of professional Italian actors.) It was the unexceptional, not the extraordinary, man in which neorealism was interested—above all in the socioeconomic interaction of that man with his environment, not the exploration of his psychological problems or complexities. And to pursue that interest, neorealist cinema had to place him in his own straitened circumstances. Hence no famous monument or other tourist attraction shows that the action of *Ladri di biciclette* or *Sciuscià* takes place in Rome; moreover, instead of the city's ancient ruins, we get contemporary ones: drab, run-down city streets; ugly, dilapidated houses; and dusty, deserted embankments that look out on a sluggish, dirty Tiber River.

Zavattini was one of the few who always felt that *Ladri di biciclette* fell somewhat short of perfection, despite its registering of a visually austere rather than a picturesquely lush Rome. The movie's pathos strayed a little too close to pulp fiction for his taste, with De Sica a touch too canny in making his audience cry—aided once again by the mood music of Alessandro Cicognini. Still, Zavattini viewed his work on this project as a present to his good friend and trusted colleague. And De Sica, for his part, felt an immediate urge to reciprocate by turning for their next film to a subject that his collaborator had long held dear. The idea of Zavattini's fable or fairy tale for children and adults alike had gone through many stages: his early story "Diamo a tutti un cavallo a dondolo" ("Let's Give Everybody a Hobbyhorse," 1938); a treatment or outline in 1940 with the actor-director Totò in mind; a novel called *Totò il Buono* (*Totò the Good*) that was published in 1943; a working script titled *I poveri disturbano* (*The Poor Disturb*); and eventually the final screenplay of *Miracolo a Milano* in 1951, which Zavattini prepared in tandem with Suso Cecchi D'Amico, Mario Chiari, Adolfo Franci, and De Sica himself.

The film opens on a painting by Pieter Brueghel over which, as it comes to life, the words "Once upon a time" are superimposed, followed shortly afterward by the discovery by an old woman, Lolotta (played by Emma Gramatica), of a naked child in the cabbage patch of her garden. This is the orphan Totò, and we follow his adventures as he grows up, becoming, through his natural optimism and innocent ability to locate a glimmer of poetry in the harshest reality, a prop or support to everyone with whom he comes into contact. After his foster mother's death, Totò is living in a shantytown on the outskirts of Milan when oil is discovered on the squatters' stretch of land. The rich, headed by the industrialist Mobbi, move in to exploit the situation, and the homeless people are forced to fight the police hired to evacuate them. Aided by a symbolic white dove that possesses the power to create miracles—the dove being a gift from the departed Lolotta, who is now her foster son's guardian angel—Totò had endeavored to improve the earthly life of the poor, if only by making the elusive winter sun appear and beam down on them. But dove or no dove, the squatters are finally no match for the fat cats of this world, so Totò's only resource is to have his dispossessed charges snatch up the broomsticks of street cleaners and miraculously fly to a land "where there is only peace, love, and good."

Miracolo a Milano is understandably regarded as one of the outstanding stylistic contradictions of the neorealist period: Neorealist in action—the struggle to found, and maintain, a shantytown for the homeless—this movie undercuts that action at nearly every moment with unabashed clowning both in performance and in cinematic technique (special effects abound). However, this blend of stark verism and comic fantasy, which featured a cast that mixed numerous nonprofessionals (culled from the streets of suburban Milan) with professional leads, was not in the end such a thematic departure from De Sica's earlier neorealist films as it might at first seem: The familiar concern for the underprivileged was strongly there, as were the harsh social realities seen once again through the eyes of a child who grows up yet remains a boy full of wonder and faith; and a seriocomic tension may underlie all of *Miracolo a Milano*, but it can also be found in the "teamwork" between both big daddy Ricci and little boy Bruno in *Ladri di biciclette*, as well as between the old man and his small dog in *Umberto D.*

As for the Leftist criticism that the picture's use of the fanciful, even the burlesque or farcical, increasingly overshadows its social commentary about the exploitation and disenfranchisement of the underclass in an industrialized nation, one can respond that there is in fact an element of despair and pessimisim, of open-ended spiritual quandary, in the fairy-tale happy ending of *Miracolo a Milano.* For this finale implies that the poor-in-body but pure-in-soul have no choice but to soar to the skies and seek their heaven apart from the hopeless earth—which is to say only in their imaginations. For his part, De Sica (unlike the staunchly leftist, even Communist, Zavattini) liked to downplay the satirical overtones of *Miracolo a Milano*, characteristically maintaining that he wanted to bring to the screen, apart from any political considerations, a Christian or simply humanist sense of solidarity: the idea that all men should learn to be good to one another.

Not everyone was content to see the movie in such simple terms, however. The Vatican condemned it for depicting the birth of a child from a cabbage, while some right-wing critics, assessing the angle of the squatters' flight at the end over the Cathedral of Milan—not to speak of the clash between the fedora-hatted rich and the grubby but kindly have-nots—figured that they were heading east, that is, towards Moscow! Predictably, from the Left came the accusation, as we have already seen, that the excess of whimsy in *Miracolo a Milano* had sweetened the bitter pill of neorealism beyond recognition. Cinephiles from abroad turned out to be less ideologically prickly: *Miracolo a Milano* shared the 1951 Grand Prix at Cannes and also won the New York Film Critics' award for best foreign film of the year.

It is not surprising that *Miracolo a Milano* baffled so many when it was first screened, including those who thought they liked it, for the Italian cinema had never really produced anything remotely like it before. The sheer irrational magic of René Clair in combination with the irrepressibly bittersweet charm of Charlie Chaplin had, up to now, not found its equivalent among indigenous filmmakers. *Miracolo a Milano* consciously springs from the legacy of Clair and Chaplin but transposes it to a forlorn urban landscape that could only be identified with Italian neorealism. Indeed, for all its look back at earlier film comedy, De Sica's ninth film actually points forward to a new brand of Italian moviemaking: With its grotesque processions of fancily as well as raggedly dressed extras against an almost abstract horizon, *Miracolo a Milano* is "Felliniesque" two or more years before Fellini became so.

Furthermore, for all its undeniable quaintness, the movie now seems more topical than ever with its warring choruses of real-estate speculators and its huddled masses longing to become selfish consumers themselves. Thus Zavattini's social conscience is linked to a sublime anarchy all its own, particularly once the squatters' village is graced by the heavenly dove that can grant any wish. By this means, a black man and a white girl may exchange races out of mutual love, yet a tramp tries to satisfy his desire not only for millions of lire but also for many more millions than anyone else. A glorious, richly meaningful anomaly in De Sica's directorial career, *Miracolo a Milano* remains more miraculous than ever, enhanced by both the consummate cinematography of G. R. Aldo (a.k.a. Aldo Graziati) and a melodious score by the ever canny Alessandro Cicognini.

By now the Zavattini-De Sica team had reached a peak of mutual understanding, whereby the director and his writer could carry their neorealistic approach to its most concessionless expression: to insert into a film ninety minutes of a man's life in which nothing happened. This was Zavattini's avowed ambition, and he chose to fulfill it in a picture about the loneliness of old age: *Umberto D.*, which was dedicated to another Umberto, De Sica's father (though the content of the movie has little to do with his father's biography). De Sica endured considerable sacrifice to make *Umberto D.*, which as usual nobody wanted to finance; he supplied part of the budget himself, while turning down an offer from Angelo Rizzoli to direct Giovannino Guareschi's 1948 novel *Il piccolo mondi di Don Camillo* (*The Little World of Don Camillo*, filmed in 1952 by Julien Duvivier), which would have earned him a small fortune. In the title role, De Sica cast another of his inspired nonprofessionals, this time a celebrated philologist from the University of Florence, Carlo Battisti, whom he had encountered walking along a Roman street on his way to a lecture (after searching in vain for an actor in homes for the aged and organizations for the retired). And for the first time on a De Sica film, Zavattini wrote the script all by himself. *Umberto D.* would turn out to be the director's favorite among his works, as well as the film that many critics consider to be his finest.

The titular character of *Umberto D.* is a retired government clerk, whose struggle against loneliness, destitution, and humiliation is the movie's subject. This isolated old man, subsisting on his meager pension, is seen shuffling around his shabby room—where an entire reel is devoted to his preparations for bed. The only other human character of importance is the housemaid, Maria, illiterate and pregnant out of wedlock but for a while the companion of Umberto in his misery. She is observed preparing for yet another eventless day, in detail similar to that found in the scene where the elderly pensioner gets ready to go to sleep. The minutiae of drab, everyday lives are penetratingly depicted here, and they exert a powerful fascination. Then there is the old man's closest companion—his dog, Flick, in reality the only steady companion this pensioner can find. Although the film's tone is decidedly more austere than that of *Ladri di biciclette*—partly because De Sica and Zavattini shifted their attention here from the poor who are young to the poor who are old—there are many parallels to be drawn in the portrayal of the central friendship: Ricci loses and then refinds his son, Bruno, even as Umberto loses his dog but eventually discovers it in the pound, destined for the gas chamber; Ricci hits his son and as a result is temporarily estranged from him, while Umberto loses his dog's trust when, having failed to find it a better home, he contemplates their double suicide under a passing train rather than have them resort to a life of beggary.

All the incidents of *Umberto D.* are seamlessly woven into a beautifully observed texture of simple, indeed marginal existence, which nonetheless is never guilty of a calculated, sentimental onslaught on the senses. Umberto, after all, is not an immediately lovable or charming old cuss; and the servant girl is almost shameless in her lack of regret over, or aspiration for, her life. Moreover, De Sica and Zavattini eliminate any moment of false drama, of false climax, that the conveniences or contrivances of fiction might have tempted them to impose on their subject. It was Zavattini's intention, especially, to find dramatic relevance in "undramatic" detail—in things, facts, and people so delicately registered as to be imperceptible save to that second awareness evoked from most spectators without their being able to define it. The moment when Umberto has taken a taxi to the animal shelter to search for his dog is an excellent example of this. He has no change with which to pay the driver and therefore must ask some stallholders in the market outside the pound to break his bill; but they refuse, and he has to buy a tumbler he does not want in order to get the requisite coins. Umberto then tosses the tumbler into the gutter and pays the taxi driver. This is a trivial yet agonizing interruption, and the filmmakers were right to emphasize or dramatize it, for in trying to find his dog, Umberto is doing something on which his whole life appears to depend.

So rehearsed, the film may easily be construed as an artless and unbuttered slice of life, a testimony to "naturalism": ostensibly a method of expressing reality without inhibition, without overtones, and as far as possible without style. Nothing could be further from the case, however. Like *Sciuscià* or *Ladri di biciclette*, and with justification even more subtle, De Sica's *Umberto D.*—a masterpiece of compassion—might be termed "*super*-naturalism" if this compound had not been preempted for another kind of experience entirely. Indeed, De Sica's balance between the lifelike and the cinematic in this picture is tenuous; if he had actors less responsive to the naked untheatricality he is commonly after, his muted formalism might suffer from the risks he takes. But he can afford to dwell at length on the faces and motions of Umberto D. and Maria precisely because Carlo Battisti and Maria Pia Casilio are sentiently, gravely, *inside* life—not coasting along on its surface.

Actor-Become-Auteur 21

Maria, while subordinate to Umberto D., is by an inspired implication complementary: She is neglected youth; he is discarded old age. The girl has her involuntary burden-to-be; the man has his voluntarily assumed burden, Flick. (Girl and man are further subservient to the loud concerns of society, as exemplified by the middle-aged landlady, who is handsome in a brassy way, venal, pseudorespectable, and heartless—living in a world of opera and ormolu, broken-down technology and broken promises.) In *Sciuscià* the horse was a symbol, if you like, of the unattainable, a dream of freedom and empowerment. The bicycle in *Ladri di biciclette* was an occupational necessity that became a projection of man's self-respect. Flick, neither ideal necessity nor economic one, may be felt to represent the last thing a man will surrender: his love for a fellow living creature.

After the release of *Umberto D.* in January 1952, Giulio Andreotti, state undersecretary and head of the Direzione Generale dello Spettacolo (a powerful position that had direct influence on government grants as well as censorship and that led ultimately to the Right-wing Andreotti's own corruption, exposure, and disgrace), published an open letter in *Libertas* (a Christian Democrat weekly) bitterly deploring the neorealist trend in the Italian cinema and its negative image of the country—a letter that was quickly reprinted in other journals. Andreotti took direct aim at De Sica, who was castigated for exhibiting a subversively "pessimistic vision" and exhorted to be more "constructively optimistic." (De Sica later stated that if he had to do *Umberto D.* again, he would change nothing except to remove the "uplifting" final shots of children playing—precisely the kind of "positive" conclusion for which Andreotti seemed to be calling.)

It was this atmosphere of interventionist government criticism that hampered the exportation of neorealist films during the 1950s; indeed, the "Andreotti Law" of 1949 had established wide government control over the financing and censorship of films, including a right to ban the export of any Italian movie that Andreotti himself judged "might give an erroneous view of the true nature of our country." In November 1955 the "Manifesto of Italian Cinema" was published in response to Andreotti's *Libertas* letter by the French journal *Positif*—a manifesto that spoke out against movie censorship and was signed by the leaders of Italian neorealism, with the names of De Sica and Zavattini prominent among the signatures. By this time, however, postwar neorealism was rapidly waning as the burning social and political causes that had stimulated the movement were to some extent alleviated or glossed over by increasing prosperity. In a society becoming ever more economically as well as politically conservative, nobody wanted to throw away his capital on yet another tale of hardship and heartbreak on the side streets of Rome.

To be sure, neither De Sica nor Zavattini harbored any illusions that a film as intimate and melancholy as *Umberto D.* would be universally admired; still, the complete indifference to its release on the part of the Italian public, together with the howls of contempt from the cultural bureaucrats, left them dumbstruck and furious. Although De Sica managed to get *Umberto D.* screened out of competition at Cannes in 1952, the Italian government did its best to keep the picture a secret on foreign shores. At a prestigious London showcase of new Italian cinema inaugurated by Queen Elizabeth, for example, *Umberto D.* was conspicuous by its absence. Andreotti and the other Italian officials to the contrary, however, what is really subversive about *Umberto D.* has nothing to do with politics, at least not in the literal sense of the world. The insuperable tragedy of the film's elderly hero lies not in his material poverty, grave though it is, but rather in his spiritual poverty, in the utter silence that defines his solitary days and nights. *Umberto D.* tells of a hunger of the soul far more devastating, in the end, than any deprivations of the body, for they at least kill relatively quickly. And for all the specificity of its Roman setting, this story could take place virtually anywhere, in any time period.

As in the case of *Miracolo a Milano* vis-à-vis Fellini, De Sica exerted a profound influence on the next generation of filmmakers with his unembellished portrait of modern-day alienation: Without the example of *Umberto D.*, later portraits of alienation such as Antonioni's *La notte* (*The Night*, 1961) and Bergman's *Tystnaden* (*The Silence*, 1963) seem almost inconceivable. De Sica's astringent detachment, his strict avoidance of sentimentalism, is another sign of things to come in the cinema: Throughout he nobly resists the temptation to turn this slightly rigid, forbidding old man into a grizzled darling for the ages. (Even De Sica, however, is powerless before Signor Umberto's little spotted dog as his master agonizingly teaches him the tricks of the begging trade.) Yet, despite the fact that De Sica's own active career lasted another two decades, this was his last indisputable masterpiece, which may make the most poignant aspect of *Umberto D.* the discreet little professional drama beginning to unfold off-screen. Moreover, it was the complete commercial failure of this movie—despite winning an award from the New York Film Critics upon its release in America in 1955—that sounded the first death knell for the content and style of neorealist cinema, even if the dauntless De Sica would attempt to return to the aims and means of neorealism one last time with *Il tetto* (*The Roof*, 1956).

With *Il tetto*, De Sica attempted to recapture the full flavor of postwar neorealism not only by shooting on location in Rome but also by using a (photogenic) nonprofessional cast and treating the socially significant theme of inadequate or insufficient housing versus the primal human need for shelter. He chose for his leading characters Gabriella Pallotta, a seventeen-year-old salesgirl from a children's clothing store in the capital, and Giorgio Listuzzi, a former soccer player from Trieste. In *Il tetto*—regarded by many as the last strictly neorealist film—they appear as impoverished newlyweds, who, to escape from the two-room apartment they share with a swarm of relatives, decide to take advantage of a loophole in the city housing code by building their own shanty on a patch of wasteland: If it goes up in a day and the roof holds, the land is theirs, and the Roman police are powerless either to evict them or to demolish their makeshift dwelling. Based on a true story, the script was written by Zavattini, and, like *Miracolo a Milano*, *Il tetto* takes root from his belief in the solidarity as well as the essential goodness of humble people—a theme that De Sica is careful to flesh out with a wealth of behavioral detail placed amidst the austere beauty of Carlo Montuori's black-and-white cinematography.

Il tetto earned a respectful reception just about everywhere it was shown, but what pleasantly surprised De Sica was its reasonable success at the Italian box office. The picture's faint note of optimism managed for once to silence the Andreottis of the Right, though its sympathies were obvious. *Il tetto* even boasted something like a happy ending for a change, reflecting the changing economic times and the rising expectations of the movie audience. Moreover, there *are* memorable sequences in the film, as genuinely compassionate and moving as any in De Sica's earlier works: for example, the scene in which the couple has to share a bedroom with the husband's parents and young sister.

Still, although neatly executed, *Il tetto* could not help but have a faint air of déjà vu clinging to it, in addition to featuring a husband and a wife whose plight lacks a consistent intensity. As Arlene Croce pointed out from the United States, in spite of its honorable intentions, the script's "descent from poetry to journalism proves almost fatal; De Sica is unable to lift the level of *Il tetto* above that of a human-interest editorial. The human beings are never seen in their uniqueness, only in their generality" (*Film Quarterly*, Winter 1959). Writing after the film's first showing at the Cannes Festival, Lindsay Anderson, for his part, felt that De Sica and Zavattini had "reached a point in their works in which they are exploiting rather than exploring the effects of poverty" (*Sight and Sound*, Summer 1956).

From Stanley Kauffmann's compelling point of view, *Il tetto* exposed the latent fallacies in cinematic neorealism:

> Zavattini has said that he dislikes conventional screen stories be-cause they impose dead formulas on living social facts and create "metaphorical" situations. The logical outcome of this belief is to use nonactors, which is what this team has done. But analysis shows, I believe, not only the sterility of such neorealist theory, but also

that the virtues of memorable De Sica-Zavattini pictures like *Shoeshine, Bicycle Thieves, Miracle in Milan,* and *Umberto D.* derive from the very elements the filmmakers claim to abhor: metaphor and contrivance. As such, these films represent a triumph of their makers' art over their own denial of it. The choice propounded by the neorealists is between "living, real characters" (to quote Zavattini) and the arts of acting and writing, but the choice is spurious. De Sica and Zavattini have not, despite their theory, given up the latter for the former because the two are not mutually exclusive. (*The New Republic,* 11 May 1959)

Yet, in *Il tetto,* according to Kauffmann, they tried again, more obstinately then ever, to make that false choice, and they forced the issue so far as "to produce their first dull movie." If the scenarist Zavattini had been more concerned with character development and narrative texture than with avoidance of "metaphor," if the director De Sica had invested one-quarter of the rehearsal time to appropriate professionals that he gave to eliciting verisimilitude from nonactors, *Il tetto*—in Kauffmann's view—might then have been a moving film.

Nonetheless, working behind the camera as well as on screen in a career of unique breadth, Vittorio De Sica left much that will endure, including a handful of the greatest moving pictures any director has ever made. "To explain De Sica," André Bazin believed,

We must go back to the source of his art, namely his tenderness, his love. The quality shared in common by his best films is De Sica's inexhaustible affection for his characters. This tenderness is of a special kind and for this reason does not easily lend itself to any moral, religious, or political generalization. . . . "I am like a painter standing before a field, who asks himself which blade of grass he should begin with." De Sica is the ideal director for a declaration of faith such as this. To paint every blade of grass one must be the Douanier Rousseau. In the world of cinema one must have the love of a De Sica for all creation itself. (from "De Sica: Metteur en Scène," 1953; published in English in *What is Cinema?,* vol. 2 [University of California Press, 1971])

This seems like a more sentimental statement on Bazin's part than it is. What he means, I think, is that no subject or character becomes truly important or remarkable until awakened by art. For this reason, De Sica's love is not greater than art; his art *is* the love. And it deserves far more critical attention than it has hitherto received.

An Interview with Vittorio De Sica

The following interview took place in July 1973 in Rome, after De Sica had made a comeback of sorts with both *The Garden of the Finzi-Continis* and *A Brief Vacation*.

BERT CARDULLO: Signor De Sica, could we limit our discussion, for the most part, to your neorealist period?

VITTORIO DE SICA: Yes, that is all I really have time for today, I'm sorry to say.

BC: All your neorealist films are in black and white, but you've since worked in color as well. Do you like working in color?

VDS: No, it's distracting, though audiences seem to demand it. For me, reality is essentially black and white and all of the shades in between; color is limited only to the surface, and surfaces don't interest me.

BC: How did you manage, in films like *Shoeshine*, *Bicycle Thieves*, *Miracle in Milan*, and *Umberto D.*, to get such superior performances out of nonprofessional actors? And did you find it difficult to direct those nonprofessionals?

VDS: Not at all! In many ways they are more flexible and more intensive in their reactions than professional actors. At first, of course, when they feel the eye of the camera fixed on them, they become very self-conscious, stiff, and absurdly awkward. They cannot even sit down without upsetting the chair.

My method to get them back to their natural selves again is simply to live with them for days, even for weeks on end, till they treat me as a friend and forget all about "acting." My experience as an actor helps me enormously to time the take and to catch them just at the right moment.

These untrained people actually have an advantage, not a handicap. In the hands of a director like me, this material can be molded like plastic. Give them the barest necessary hints, and they will act naturally. On the other hand, it is easy for an experienced actor to overact. He cannot forget his metier; he is the "matador" of the scene.

I have a little theory of my own, why actually the results achieved with these ordinary people are often much more satisfactory than highly polished performances by actors. Let's give the image on the screen the value of 100 percent. The man appearing in it by his mere presence as a living being covers 50 percent of the value, his nonprofessional acting is worth a further 30 percent, and the remaining 20 percent are contributed by the spectator's own imagination.

This balance is immediately disturbed if and when the professional actor—this admirable monster—contributes not 30 but 50 percent. The two other factors remaining unchanged, the image value mounts to 120 percent, and that is what makes the screen image often appear "larger than life," quite beyond the frame of reality.

But I don't want to be misunderstood. This does not mean that I would want to make any future films without actors. Exactly as there are pictures crying out for a cast of "ordinary people," there are others absolutely requiring professional actors only. The postwar film I cowrote, *Natale al campo 119*—Pietro Francisci directed it—is a very good example of the latter type. All of this said, you know, I have to add that Italians really don't have to learn to act. They are born performers—all of them.

BC: I have heard you talk, with reference to neorealism, about "being faithful to the character." What exactly did you mean by this expression?

VDS: "Being faithful to the character" is perhaps simply an exaggeration of the time-honored principle of acting that gives an overwhelming importance to the so-called *physique du rôle*. Only, in my neorealist pictures, the process of interpretation is reversed: It is not the actor who lends the character a face which, however versatile he may be, is necessarily his own, but the character who reveals himself, sooner or later, in "that" particular face and in no other. It is not surprising if this face belongs, more often than not, to someone who exercises a profession far removed from that of acting. In *Bicycle Thieves*, for example, the people who acted the boy's parents were a workman from the Breda district and a female journalist from Rome who had come to interview me.

BC: Is it true that you found the actor for the role of the boy in *Bicycle Thieves* only after you had begun shooting?

VDS: Yes, finding the actor for his father was relatively easy, but finding the child was difficult. So, in desperation, I decided to start shooting anyway. I began with the scene in which Maggiorani goes with a friend who says he can help him to find the bike. During a pause, while I was talking to Maggiorani, and becoming irritated with the people who were pushing around me, I noticed among them an odd-looking, eight-year-old child with a round face and a weird nose and large, expressive eyes. He had just the right kind of expression: half comical, half tragic, and far from the Hollywood conception of child beauty. It was Enzo Staiola. I felt that our Neapolitan Saint Jannarius had sent him to me. Indeed, it was proof that everything was all right. There are days in a man's life when he feels that everything is going in his favor, and that first day's shooting of *Bicycle Thieves* was one of the most satisfying of my life.

BC: Could you comment a bit on the origins of neorealism, what became known as the "crisis" of neorealism, etc.?

VDS: Yes, but I feel I can only do so by way of my films themselves. The Americans entered Rome on June 5, 1944. The prodigious decade of the Italian cinema thus began. The tumultuous days that followed did not allow one to make plans for filming. There were no more cameras, film stock, or studios. We were all separated. Everyone lived for himself and by himself. Yet the neorealist cinema was being born, a vast collective movement in which we were all to participate.

It is not as if one day I was sitting at a café on the Via Veneto with Visconti, Rossellini, and others, and we suddenly looked at each other and said: "Let's create neorealism!" We came to know each other gradually. Somebody told me that Rossellini had started working again. "A film about a priest," they said. That was all.

Another day, I saw Rossellini and Sergio Amidei, the scriptwriter, sitting on the steps of a building in the center of Rome.

"What are you up to?" I asked.

They shook their heads sadly. "We're looking for money. We can't go on with the film."

"What film?" I inquired.

"The story of a priest. You know, Don Morosini, the one the Germans shot."

BC: What were you doing for a living at the time?

VDS: I had become a journalist. I had been asked to join the editorial committee of a film magazine, which lasted only four or five issues: But by the third number I had already left, for the magazine was becoming too political and calling for the shooting of this person and then that one. Instead of shooting people, I argued, we should be shooting film. In the first number I wrote a column entitled: "What Films Do You Want to Make?" I knew very well what film I wanted to make and wrote the first draft of *Shoeshine*, illustrating it with a photograph.

In those difficult times, my thoughts turned more to the children than to the adults, who had lost all sense of proportion. This was truly the moment when the children were watching us. They gave me the true picture of how our country was morally destroyed. They were the *Sciuscià*, the shoeshine boys.

I knew two of them, Scimmietta (Little Monkey) and Cappellone (Big Hat); I followed them around Rome, got to know their habits and practices, and witnessed all their transactions. Scimmietta slept in a lift in Via Lombardia, and he was lucky to have a grandfather who loved him. This family warmth saved him. Cappellone was nobody's child, completely alone in the world, with his big head deformed by rickets. Eventually he stole and ended up in jail. They were twelve and thirteen respectively. Scimmietta wore a weird cloak and nothing underneath except a pair of torn short pants. As soon as they earned three or four hundred lire from shining shoes, they ran to the nearby Villa Borghese park and hired a horse.

The drama of this story, just as life had shaped it, pointed out its own natural conclusion. I told the story to Zavattini, who immediately sensed the melancholy poetry of it, and he prepared the script—making of that horse, by the way, an exquisitely poetic touch. The question really was whether we should use actors or not. As I have indicated, I have no particular prejudice in this matter. There are some characters who demand professional actors, while there are others who can come to life only through a certain face, which is only to be found in real life.

Indeed, it was difficult to find two boys for *Shoeshine*. Cappellone and Scimmietta would not do: they were too ugly, almost deformed. Hundreds of parents brought me their children, the same exhausting procession that, as you know, was repeated when we were making *Bicycle Thieves*. The younger of the two, Rinaldo Smordoni, was found first. The other, Franco Interlenghi, was found in the street. The son of a modest Roman caretaker, he preferred the streets to any other entertainment. Both these boys had a natural acting talent.

BC: *Shoeshine* didn't cost much to make, did it?

VDS: No, less than a million lire, but it was a financial disaster for its producer. Production costs and lack of money were a determining factor in making me—and certainly Rossellini in *Open City*—take such actual life as my subject matter so that reality could be elevated to the plane of poetry. Poetic social realism, that's what neorealism really is—not naturalism, which itself can be poetic but is often just sordid, ugly, dirty.

DC. You were once described as "the poet of suffering."

VDS: I'd rather be known as the poet of truth, the creator of a poetry of real people and the truth of human relationships.

BC: But that poetry is what caused the so-called crisis of neorealism.

VDS: Well, it was only a momentary crisis due chiefly to disorientation caused by certain political—and erroneous—interpretations of our pictures, the content of which was *social*, insofar as we dealt mostly with the problems of the poor. The courage we had in saying and showing what we were, in the hope of promoting improvement and contributing toward a better world, was interpreted by some as the wrong kind of courage.

The crisis was also due in part to the fact that neorealism came into being in a period of strong passions—the immediate postwar era—and later we could not expect that same climate of emotional turbulence and stark truth. But regardless of this, let me assure you that neorealism, as a school of filmmaking, did and will survive for deeper merits, both human and poetic.

The portrayal of the realities of mankind does not call for cardboard backgrounds. What is needed is that absent-minded eyes become more attentive and aware, that they look more in depth than upon the surface, so that the relationships among people may be shown and understood, with love and with the soul of a poet. To see is very useful to an artist. Most men do not want to see, because often the pain of others troubles them. We neorealists, on the contrary, wanted to see. Our one aim was *to see*.

Neorealism, moreover, will never die. We shall have changes and variations, new applications to varying styles, yes. But neorealism will remain a revolutionary movement, a just and useful movement, in this wonderful art of the cinema, which is the art that comes closest to life and to mankind.

BC: You wouldn't want to confine the art of making films to neorealism, would you?

VDS: No, not at all. The British cinema, for instance, gave us examples of nonrealistic pictures—made more or less at the same time as the films of Italian neorealism—which will have a long life in the history of the cinema. I wish I could list them all, but I will gratefully mention a few of exceptional beauty and importance, such as the works of Laurence Olivier, Carol Reed, David Lean, and Anthony Asquith.

BC: You have said, in the past, that you didn't like being called a "neorealist."

VDS: I said that only because people were trying to see in my neorealist films certain political teachings instead of a single Christian sense of solidarity—which I believe should be felt by all of us, regardless of whatever political beliefs we may profess. You know, it is difficult, if not impossible, to argue with people who attribute to me ideas and intentions borrowed from their own mental makeup. I accomplished in my neorealist pictures what I wanted to accomplish, without any *"arrière-pensée."*

BC: Could you apply what you just said to *Shoeshine*, *Bicycle Thieves*, and *Miracle in Milan*?

VDS: In *Shoeshine*, my objective was to bring out man's indifference to the needs of other men. The indifference which created that tragedy was suffered and created once more in *Bicycle Thieves*, but there it was developed in a less cruel mood, in an atmosphere of pathetic human solidarity.

I had no intention of presenting Antonio, in *Bicycle Thieves*, as a kind of "Everyman" or personification of what is called today "the underprivileged." To me he was an individual, with his individual joys and worries, with his individual story. In presenting the one tragic Sunday of his long and varied life, I attempted to transpose reality to the poetical plane. This indeed seems to me one of the most important features of my work, because without such an attempt a film of this kind would simply become a newsreel. As I have made clear, I never saw any future in neorealism if it did not surmount the barrier separating the documentary from drama and poetry. But, of course, logic has always been an enemy of poetry. It takes a great artist to blend them harmoniously, and therefore I am not surprised if strict logicians point with an accusing finger to flaws in my work.

To those, however, who reproached me with excessive pessimism, because at the end of the film Antonio finds himself still without a bicycle, I should like to put the question: How many times in your life have you found yourself in a hopeless situation at the end of a day, without being broken by it? I frankly believe that people who find the screen reality of *Bicycle Thieves* so cruel as to dub the film "black" and "hopeless" have never lived through hardships themselves—such hardships, I mean, as are experienced daily by millions of Antonios all over the world. Or perhaps they do not understand the mentality of an Italian, who never takes things as seriously as people farther north.

As for *Miracle in Milan*, it is a fable suspended halfway between whimsy and reality—a fable that is intended more for grown-ups than for children, but still nothing but a fable. In *Miracle in Milan*, I took a holiday from my usual style, but I think that the picture nevertheless expresses the artistic credo and the moral convictions from which I have never deviated, namely, "Love thy neighbor as thyself." I sought to make *Miracle in Milan* speak in simple human language comprehensible to the greater part of mankind, a language that overflows from the heart and that, I hope, reached the heart of the public.

BC: What about the suggestion made by Italian newspapers at the time that *Miracle in Milan* tended to excite political animosities?

VDS: Oh, here we go again! Look, I have no interest in politics. I am a member of no party; I am not a propagandist of any ideology. *Miracle in Milan* is inspired by nothing but a Christian feeling of human solidarity. In it, I speak the natural language of a man who does not close his eyes to the sufferings of his fellows, the language that Christianity has been speaking for the last twenty centuries. And I am proud of the fact that, shortly after *Miracle in Milan* was released, the Vatican radio station called me an "enlightened interpreter of the word of Christ and of the Gospel." I realize that I have spoken much about myself today, so let me add that all my Italian colleagues at the time employed, more or less, the same methods I used. I know the passion that moved Visconti and Blasetti. I admire the marvelous spontaneity of Rossellini. I think they had the same poetic vision of reality as I had and that at the foundation of their art lay that identical human solidarity which guided and inspired my own films from *Shoeshine* to *Miracle in Milan*.

BC: Was *Umberto D.* met with any political intolerance?

VDS: I was quite prepared to face it once again, after all the politically-inspired attacks on *Miracle in Milan*—even some accusing me and Zavattini of subversion! But the story of that poor old-age pensioner, his tragic solitude, his irremediable sadness, and his pathetically inept attempts to keep his heart singing, seemed to me so universal a theme that anyone would understand it. *Umberto D.* did not make any money, but I really believe it was a good film. If I had to remake it, I would make it exactly as it now stands. The same for *Bicycle Thieves*. In *Umberto D*. I should cut only one scene, that of the children who are playing in the last sequence.

BC: Was this film in any way based on the character of your father?

VDS: Umberto De Sica was my father's name, but Zavattini said that he never thought of my father while he was writing the screenplay.

BC: Let me risk asking you one more "political" question, connected with what some see as your last, and *the* last, neorealist film, *The Roof*. This film seems more polemical than your other neorealist ones, especially given the fact that we see the Italian flag ironically displayed under the credits. What's your view of the politics of *The Roof*?

VDS: Once again, *The Roof* deals with the postwar *social* problem of inadequate or insufficient housing, which is still an issue for us; I leave the politics to the politicians and the bureaucrats. As for the flag, you misread it because you're not a native Italian: in Italy, you see, it is customary to place a flag of Italy atop a house when it is completed, which is where the flag under the film's credits is sitting.

BC: Were you already thinking in "neorealistic terms," let us call them, when you made *The Children Are Watching Us*?

VDS: It would perhaps be presumptuous of me to pretend that I was already thinking in terms of neorealism, but it is true that I had realized what possibilities there were in taking the camera outside the studios, into the open air, wherever one would be able to capture the way people really live. So in 1942 Zavattini and I collaborated in the making of *The Children Are Watching Us*.

BC: You regard this, then, as your first serious film?

VDS: Yes, but I knew it then, and I still admit it, that *The Children Are Watching Us* was a compromise between the old formula and the new. Still, for Zavattini and me it was a decisive experience. For a year we did nothing else.

BC: Almost all your neorealist films had multiple screenwriters, always including Zavattini and sometimes including you. Yet most critics would maintain that the ideal film artist should wholly write what he goes on to direct.

VDS: I disagree. Directing is not the same thing as writing; it is the creation of life on the screen. Here's my proof: If *Shoeshine* had been directed by someone else, from the very same script, don't you think it would be a different picture from the one I made? Equally good, perhaps, but different.

BC: How do you reconcile much of your acting career with your serious ambitions as a film director? For the first fifteen years of your acting career, at the very least, you were the idol of all the teenaged signorinas, the attractive, witty, elegant leading man of innumerable Italian screen comedies—some of them quite amusing and polished. The public admired and even loved your slick man-about-town figure, but hardly anybody suspected, beyond your indubitable acting talent, that you had within you the spark of inspiration that distinguishes the genuine creative artist.

VDS: In the first fifteen years or so of my acting career I made something like thirty-five pictures, and I don't regret it. I felt at my best in those directed by Mario Camerini. But even so, for fifteen years I played comic parts with my ideas of tragedy deeply hidden. That's the only explanation I have for the serious side of my directing career. Anyway, he is not a good humanist who is not also a good humorist.

BC: You once told another interviewer that, though you greatly valued René Clair and Charlie Chaplin, they in no way influenced you. Did you really mean that?

VDS: Yes and no. In the case of *Miracle in Milan*, the story is always poised midway between reality and fantasy, so I tried to express it in the style best suited to that kind of story. In this style, I had two masters, Clair and Chaplin, towering above me with all the force of their genius; their example drew me on and yet, at the same time, acted as a restraint and a warning to me: It was a dangerous attraction. I had to understand the difficult enterprise of embarking, on my own account, on a path that was at least equi-distant from both of them. Whether this was a new or a well-chosen departure point, it is not my place to say.

BC: Who, in your opinion, contributed most to the renaissance of film art after World War II?

VDS: Charlie Chaplin again, of course. And not only since the end of the war, but since 1910 the cinema owes to him its greatest inspiration.

BC: And, of course, he did more than merely make amusing movies.

VDS: Oh, yes. Look, many people regard film as a soporific, good only for putting to flight the lassitude, the ill-humor, the lowness of spirits that men experience in the evening after a day's work. But such films, like all drugs, are habit-forming, and the dose must be constantly increased if they are to have the desired effect. One soon reaches the dangerous, fluctuating, controversial boundary that divides the legitimate from the illegitimate use of drugs. Truly good films—like Chaplin's—should stimulate as well as soothe, should appeal to the mind as well as to the senses, should kindle thought as well as the emotions.

BC: This leads to my final question, Signor De Sica: What's wrong—and right—with Hollywood?

VDS: The postwar public wanted escapism, and that is what it got in a succession of mediocre films. Audiences had experienced all the realism they could stomach, and to use that word on Sunset Boulevard was the quickest way to be shown to the door.

There was a time, you know, when I thought Hollywood would never change; and it took a long time before the bosses realized the public mood had changed. But since about 1950 there has been a dramatic evolution of American motion pictures which has made them much more of an art form. It began for me, I believe, with the making of *A Streetcar Named Desire* and *On the Waterfront*. I sat up in my seat when I saw them; Hollywood was holding a mirror to life and reflecting it in sharp and vivid focus, instead of just entertaining us with extravagant musicals and spectaculars.

I didn't really believe the trend could last. These two pictures, I said, were oddities, rarities. But, as things transpired, they presaged a new and adult era which was to be sponsored and—even if cautiously— encouraged by the big wheels of Hollywood.

BC: What caused this intelligent change of heart in Hollywood?

VDS: We don't need to delve too deeply into causes. Our times are explosive, and people today have developed an analytical approach to life. Television itself had a cataclysmic effect on the American film market. Hollywood was rudely aroused from its torpor when in 1947 television was unleashed, and the public was subjected to a repetitive barrage of old films. In my view television, far from being the bogeyman it was made out to be, did Hollywood a signal service. The continual showing of low-grade films sharpened the public's critical faculty. The cry now was not for escapism but reality. Unless Hollywood could deliver the goods, it was doomed.

BC: Hollywood still has something to learn, though, doesn't it?

VDS: I believe so, yes. Even now, in their treatment of realistic subjects, there is still a bit of the old tendency to gloss over life as it really is. Many times I have been disappointed over what could have been an intelligent, well-made film, which in the end does not quite manage to come to terms with reality.

But there is a wind of change sweeping the executive corridors of Sunset Strip. Young producers, directors, and scriptwriters are being given their head now, in the early-to-mid 1970s. Thus we have men of power and perception such as John Cassavetes and Mike Nichols turning out first-rate pictures.

Hollywood is realizing that filmmakers must be given freedom of expression and interpretation. I feel certain that there will be a complete emancipation from the formulas of a dead past, and I feel that such a day will come soon.

Filmography of Feature Films

Red Roses, 1939
Maddalena, Zero for Conduct, 1940
Teresa Venerdì (a.k.a. *Doctor Beware*), 1941
A Garibaldian in the Convent, 1942
The Children Are Watching Us, 1943
The Gate of Heaven, 1946
Shoeshine, 1947
Bicycle Thieves, 1948
Miracle in Milan, 1951
Umberto D., 1952
It Happened in the Park, 1953
Indiscretion of an American Wife, 1953
The Gold of Naples, 1954
The Roof, 1956
Anna of Brooklyn, 1958
Two Women, 1961
The Last Judgment, 1961
Boccaccio '70, 1962
The Condemned of Altona, 1962

Il Boom, 1963
Yesterday, Today, and Tomorrow, 1963
Marriage Italian Style, 1964
A New World, 1966
After the Fox, 1966
"The Witches," 1966 (episode of *A Night Like Any Other*)
Woman Times Seven, 1967
A Place for Lovers, 1968
Sunflower, 1970
"The Couples," 1970 (episode of *The Lion*)
The Garden of the Finzi-Continis, 1971
We'll Call Him Andrew, 1972
A Brief Vacation, 1973
The Voyage, 1974

"The Cinema Is a Woman"

The Artistic Achievement of
Federico Fellini

I WAS GOING TO BEGIN THIS CHAPTER with some facts about Federico
Fellini's life. But any such account, I quickly realized, must be ap-
proximate. For Fellini enjoyed obfuscation; and his own recollections
about his past varied according to whim. Indeed, his enemies often
labeled him a *"buggiardo,"* a big liar; and his wife, Giulietta Masina,
herself said that Federico blushed only when he told the truth. Yet his
many friends generally discerned in him a rare sincerity. Both qualities—the obfuscatory or evasive, the sincere or revelatory—course
through Fellini's interviews, and these qualities are not unrelated to the
intermingling in his films themselves of fantasy and verity, reality and
illusion. "You could call hallucination a deeper reality," Fellini told more
than one questioner. "In any event, I see no line between the imaginary
and the actual" (from Dan Yakir, "The Italian Inquisition," *Heavy Metal*,
December 1984).

Fellini once even told the novelist Alberto Moravia, in a *Vogue* interview (1 March 1970), that he had tried to eliminate the idea of history
from his *Satyricon* (1969), "the idea that the ancient world *really* existed. . . .
I used an iconography that has the allusiveness and intangibility of dreams."
In reply to the next, logical question, the director said that his movie
dream of Petronius was a dream dreamed by himself, and then Moravia
asked, "I wonder why you dreamt such a dream." Fellini replied: "The
movies wanted me to." Exactly, just as his alter ego Guido in *8½* (1963)
was begging the movies to command a dream from *him*.

Fellini's reply to Moravia's question contains all the truth and fakery
and truth about fakery that have made Fellini, the artist and the man, one

of the most appealing of modern film figures—one who, in his simulta-
neous dealing with truth tellers and pretenders, realists and dreamers,
reprised the two distinctive directions in which, from the beginning, the
cinema itself had developed. Fellini's own life in art was spent in the
service of both reality and nonreality largely because he knew, as one of
the few film masters who also understood theatricality (perhaps since his
own self was so histrionic), that theater without artifice is a fake ideal and
a naïf's idea of the truth.

This much is known with certainty, or a degree of certainty, about
Fellini's early existence. He was born in 1920 in Rimini, a small town on
Italy's Adriatic Coast. (The seaside would turn out to be important in
many of his pictures.) For several years he attended a boarding school,
run by Catholic priests, at Fano—also on the Adriatic. During those
school years, at the age of seven or eight, Federico ran away to follow a
traveling circus until his truancy was discovered and he was returned
(after one night? within several days?) to his parents. This incident seems
to have left an indelible impression on Fellini's mind, for, even as priests,
together with nuns, were to find their ritualistic place in many of his
films, so too did the circus become for him a source of inspiration for his
work as a movie director.

During his last year in Rimini—1937—which was also his last year
of high school, Fellini and several of his friends were frequent truants,
leading the idle, empty (but fantasy-filled) street life he was later to depict
so vividly in *I vitelloni* (1953). Like Moraldo in this film, Fellini escaped
from the hopeless limbo of Rimini shortly thereafter, making his way to
Florence, where he worked as an illustrator for a comic-strip story magazine. This experience itself would provide the background for his movie
The White Sheik (1952), which chronicles a provincial bride's misadven-
tures in Rome with the man of her dreams—not her new husband, but
instead a star of the *fumetti* (enormously popular magazines telling romantic stories in photo-strip form). After six months or so, Fellini moved
on again, to Rome, where he drew cartoons and caricatures for the satirical publication *Marc' Aurelio*, in addition to becoming one of the writers
for a radio serial based on this magazine's most popular feature story
("Cico and Pallina," Italy's answer to Dagwood and Blondie).

Soon tiring of this work, Fellini joined his friend, the music-hall
comedian (and later character actor in films) Aldo Fabrizi, on a 1939
odyssey across Italy with a vaudeville troupe for which he performed a
variety of duties, such as sketch artist, wardrobe master, scenery painter,
traveling secretary, and bit player. Years later, Fellini would tell an interviewer that this was "perhaps the most important year of my life. . . . I

was overwhelmed by the variety of the country's physical landscape and, too, by the variety of its human landscape. It was the kind of experience that few young men are fortunate enough to have—a chance to discover the character of one's country and, at the same time, to discover one's own identity (from Tay Garnett, *Directing* [1996]). Back in Rome by the early 1940s, he began not only a new career as a gag writer for comic movies but also his courtship of the young actress Giulietta Masina. Her distinctive personality—puckish, vulnerable, yet resilient—clearly fired Fellini's imagination, and together they were to forge a unique alliance in the Italian cinema of their time.

By the end of the war, Fellini was married to Masina and working as a coscenarist and assistant director for the leading neorealist filmmaker Roberto Rossellini on such pictures as *Rome, Open City* (1945) and *Paisan* (1946). Following several assignments in the late 1940s as a coscreen-writer or assistant director for Pietro Germi and Alberto Lattuada, Fellini took his first stab at directing with *Variety Lights* (1950), a collaborative effort with Lattuada from Fellini's original story about a troupe of actors not unlike the vaudevillians with whom he had traveled the country a little over a decade before. Then he made five feature films on his own, all of which show two dominant influences: the neorealistic Rossellini and the reimagined materials of Fellini's life.

His long-standing romance with the circus and the theater appears not only in *Variety Lights* but also in *La strada* (1954); as already noted, Fellini's impatience with small-town life can be found in *I vitelloni*, his comic-strip experience in *The White Sheik*; and his realist's compassion for the exploited of postwar Italy is on display in both *Il bidone* (1955) and *The Nights of Cabiria* (1956). In this phase of his career, Fellini was, above all, an observer, constructing his films through juxtaposition: that is, through setting details of reconstructed reality side by side to point up a common denominator, or (more often) to expose the ironic relationship between unlike things. This method of construction is the one associated with neorealism, which Fellini himself defined in one interview as "the opposite of manufactured effects, of the laws of dramaturgy, spectacle, and even of cinematography" (from Charles Thomas Samuels, *Encountering Directors* [1972])—in other words, the presentation of the world in as natural a manner as possible, without arranging things in order to create plots or entertainments.

What distinguishes Fellini from the neorealists, however, is an insistence on the primary force of human imagination. His characters are not solely motivated by externals—the theft of a bicycle, social indifference, child abandonment or neglect—as Vittorio De Sica's were. Nor, like

Ermanno Olmi, does Fellini invert neorealism by studying only the human accommodation to such external circumstances. Instead, he denies the pure externality of events, choosing instead to show what he has repeatedly avowed in interviews: that reality and imagination interpenetrate. Thus Fellini's characters never face a fact without dressing it up: If, as in *I vitelloni*, they are in an empty piazza during the small hours of the night, they actively deny the implication that all human activities must pause; if, as in *The Nights of Cabiria*, they are stepping in place on a treadmill, they are nonetheless always on parade, decked out and boisterous.

It is, in fact, this "force of human imagination," as I have described it, that unites what many commentators otherwise consider the two halves of Fellini's career: the quasirealist and the baroque bordering on rococo. The second half begins with his first big international success, *La dolce vita* (1959), where, for the first time, his subject was upper-class, well-to-do Italy—the problems in lives of *luxe* and leisure—and Fellini's treatment of this subject was much more symbolic in method, as well as much more elegant in manner. To be sure, he is still the observer here: through the eyes of Marcello the journalist (Fellini's original ambition when he arrived in Rome), who, like Moraldo from the *I vitelloni* quintet, left his hometown to seek a glorious future in the eternal city. But now the film director is like a gifted rube reporter of naughty high life, for *La dolce vita* moves away from his early experience, out of which he had been creating, into a new social environment where he can only watch and never actively participate or assimilate. (Consequently, the most authentic moment in the film is the visit of Marcello's father, who brings to the Italian capital the touch of the small town in which his son grew up.)

La dolce vita, then, can be called a "transitional" work that will be followed by, and has some connection to, Fellini's masterpiece, *8½*. The director himself intimated as much when he told an interlocutor,

> I had a vague idea of *8½* even before *La dolce vita*: to try to show the dimensions of a man on all his different levels, intermingling his past, his dreams, and his memories, his physical and mental turmoil—all without chronology but giving the impression that man is a universe unto himself. But I couldn't resolve it and so made *La dolce vita* instead. (From Derek Prouse, "Federico Fellini," in *World Film Directors*, Vol. II [1988].)

One gets the feeling that, like Guido's artistic crisis in *8½*, Marcello's mounting spiritual crisis, which links the film's disparate incidents, might well have become Fellini's own had he allowed himself, as does his protagonist, to surrender to the frenzied Roman life around him.

After a three-year silence, Fellini made that picture about a protagonist whose crisis had become his own: *81/2*, whose movie director cannot settle on a subject for his next film. (Thus, in the seven years after 1956, he made only two features, having made six in his first six years.) The screenplay was written by Fellini and three collaborators, but, quite clearly, the job of these coscenarists was to help Fellini put on paper some material from his innermost self, a script from which he could make a cinematic journey alone. The result was the film world's best work about an artist's desperation as an artist, a quasiconfessional comedy-cum-drama about the torment of the modern artist who is bursting with talent but can find nothing on which to expend it.

The result was also the revelation that Fellini was the epitome of the romantic, not the realistic, artist. Observation and synthesis were not really his mode: It had to have happened to *him* before he could transmute it into art. It was around 1800 that the subject matter of art became the maker himself, that the work ceased to be regarded as primarily a reflection of nature, actual or improved. The mirror held up to nature became transparent, as it were, and yielded insights instead into the mind and heart of the artist. This mode has long survived the formal romantic era, has survived realism and naturalism, has in fact become intensified in our own self-regarding twentieth and twenty-first centuries. Many films exemplify romanticism in the most serious sense—the artist as pilgrim, as both warrior and battlefield—but none more thoroughly than Fellini's *81/2*.

Now the self-as-subject process of art-making is a ravenously gluttonous one and can—from time to time or even permanently—exhaust the artist, as it did Fellini. But some artists feel truthful only when they deny synthesis and deal solely with themselves. And through Fellini's career we can see this autobiographical impulse growing. As he relied more and more on his inner travails, less and less on what he had seen and could invent out of it, two things happened: The periods between his films grew longer, and Fellini's style—ornate, extravagant, flamboyant, grotesque, bizarre—became an increasingly prominent part of his work. His first complete acceptance of the "new" Fellini, whose subject is himself and whose art lies in the transformation of self-knowledge through cinematic style, is *81/2*.

The operative term here is *transformation*, since I do not mean to characterize Fellini's use of romantic self-exploration as narcissistic or solipsistic. Indeed, a man who sees himself as a performer, which Fellini does on film as in conversation—who sees that the best of himself is in the theatricalization of that self—may in our day be closer to authenticity than those who delude themselves into believing that they are not self-conscious. This leads me to the most significant aspect of *81/2*, the aspect that individuates Fellini's use of romantic self-exploration. This film about a man's need to make a film ends up as, in effect, the very film that the man is going to make (the number 8½ being the total of Fellini's previous output of features and short films, as well as the perfect working title for a film whose subject—indeed, its very making—is in question). The artistic scion that this ambivalence suggests is, of course, Pirandello, especially his *Six Characters in Search of an Author*. Here, too, there are characters that have appeared to an author and can be dealt with only by being theatricalized, *performed*. Pirandello's people were imagined, Fellini's remembered or relived, but their needs are the same: self-actualization by any other name.

Juliet of the Spirits (1965) is the second manifestation of this new Fellini, or Fellini, part 2. Like *8½*, it explores an interior landscape, but this time of a woman, played by Giulietta Masina. This was Fellini's first use of color—a medium that, as he indicates in several of his interviews, he had previously scorned—and *Juliet of the Spirits* was also the last film of his to win nearly unanimous critical approval or popular success until *Amarcord* in 1973. The reasons are not hard to locate, for, visually dazzling and indirectly autobiographical as *Juliet of the Spirits* may be, it has no coherent plot. Fellini himself agreed when he told Lillian Ross in a *New Yorker* profile that

> the story of this film is nothing. There *is* no story. . . . Movies now have gone past the phase of prose narrative and are coming nearer and nearer to poetry. I am trying to free my work from certain constrictions—a story with a beginning, a development, and ending. It should be more like a poem, with meter and cadence. (October 1965)

A *romantic* poem, one might add. The trouble with such poetry, in Fellini's case, is that the farther removed it became from his own past, his own self, the lesser it became—to the point that, in the manner of opera before the twentieth century, the story is a mere scaffolding for stylistic display or visual fireworks. Certainly this was the problem that afflicted *Satyricon* and *Casanova* (1976), as well as, to a lesser extent, *Orchestra Rehearsal* (1979), *City of Women* (1980), *And the Ship Sails On* (1983), and *Ginger and Fred* (1985), all of which, to one degree or another, depend for their being entirely on the way they are made, on their look, apart from any depiction of character or accretion of drama.

So desperate was Fellini to return to his senses, or his self, during this period that he made two quasidocumentaries in an effort to anchor himself in some kind of reality at the same time as he tried to confront

Casanova (1976), a.k.a. *Il Casanova di Federico Fellini*. Directed by Federico Fellini, here shown on the set. Universal Pictures. Photographer Pierluigi Praturlon. *(Courtesy of Univeral Pictures/Photofest)*

the ghosts of his youth: the circus and clowning in the case of *The Clowns* (1970) and the Italian capital in the instance of *Roma* (1972), what the city meant to him as a provincial youth, how it seemed when he arrived, and what he thought of it at middle age. Fellini even thematically connected these two films by calling the circus and the city, like the cinema itself, each "an old whore who knows how to give many kinds of pleasure"—and who, like women in general, represented to him not only myth and mystery but also the thirst for knowledge and the search for one's own identity (Fellini quoted in Gideon Bachmann, "The Cinema Seen as a Woman," *Film Quarterly* [Winter 1980–1981]).

The pleasure in *The Clowns*, for one, consists at least in part in the recognition of familiar Fellini hallmarks apart from, say, the appearance of the earth-mother whore in several pictures and the use of silent openings (as in *81/2*) as well as abrupt endings (like the freeze frame at the end of *I vitelloni*). First is the lighting—theatrical as ever. Often a character is first seen with his face completely shadowed before he "enters," in a kind of visual summary of Fellini's own theatrical personality (which enjoyed attention at the same time that, as the interviews of Fellini-the-artist make clear, it wanted to guard its privacy). Then there is Fellini's relating of the human face to Daumierlike caricature, as when, after the boy Federico sees his first circus, he perceives how many of his fellow townsmen look like clowns.

In *The Clowns*, as always, there is Fellini's eye for deep composition—a mind screen of the imagination, as it were. One example: After some schoolboys departing on a train insult a stationmaster in Fellini's hometown, the pompous little official begins jumping up and down with rage. In a shot down the platform, as the train pulls away, Fellini shows us not only the hopping-mad midget in the foreground but also, in various planes in the background, several fat men doubling up with laughter. The sanctification of memory touches this wonderful shot—wonderful in part because the fat "pots," made to seem fatter by their multiplication and their doubling up, are calling the diminutive "kettle" black—in the sense that it is silent: The sound under the shot is the narrator's voice, accompanied by music.

The search in *The Clowns* and *Roma* for his own identity, as Fellini put it, led to his temporary recovery from our age's gravest disease for artists: the inability to synthesize new subject matter out of experience, the shattering of creative confidence by the immensity of modern consciousness. As other artists have done in other arts, Fellini finally faced matters that had been haunting him all his adult life, nagging to get into his work, and he gave them a whole film in *Amarcord*—"whole" because his total surrender to the ghosts of his past provided him the best chance to use his supreme (and supremely unique) visual style since the monumental *8 1/2*. *Amarcord*—a word that, in the dialect of Fellini's native Rimini, means "I remember"—is rich with memory, desire for memory, memory of desire; and the director never exhibited better than he does here his startling eye for the quintessentially right face, his maestro's ability to build and develop and finish sequences like music, his firm conviction that life is more lifelike when you touch it up a bit.

In *Amarcord*, Fellini remembered 1930s Rimini so feelingly and so well that, like all memoirs made with good art, we possess it at once. It becomes our past, too. Many of us will recognize how the people in such a town become characters in an integrated drama being performed for one's self when young and how, for everyone, the figures of the past, pleasant and unpleasant, become rarefied through the years into talismans. In any event, the viewer recognizes the fundamental verity of the film: that memory is the only place toward which life heads certainly. And he or she recognizes a secondary verity as well: that, in transferring the recesses of recall to the screen with the knowledge that his past was no longer verifiable fact, it was an all-obsessing dream, Fellini established anew the primal commonwealth of cinema and dream, movies and memory, psychic exploration and filmic fabrication. As Fellini himself put the matter in an interview, "Think what a bale of memories and associations we all carry about with us. It's like seeing a dozen films simultaneously!" (Fellini quoted in Prouse, *World Film Directors*).

That last exclamation should give the reader some idea of Fellini's sense of humor, evident (as one might guess) not only in his interviews but also in his films. Indeed, what distinguishes him from other directors of his eminence is precisely his humor. Bergman proved his short supply of it in his few comedies. Antonioni rarely even attempted to be funny. And Kurosawa had humorous touches, but they were almost always grim, not high-spirited. Fellini alone of this group looked on the world's woes, on human travail, with a mischievous eye. Comedy, of course, is by no means automatically synonymous with shallowness, something the filmmaker proved in *8½*, which was a cascade of bitter, funny, scintillating, sometimes deeply probing jokes on himself: for the silliness of his situation, of his century, of the plight of art, and for the absurdity of ever having been born.

Intervista (1987) Fellini's penultimate picture—has the context of *8½* without its center. (His final film, *The Voice of the Moon* [1990], which may come closer to being surreal than any of his other works, did not gain an American distributor.) The framework is a visit to Cinecittà, the large film studio complex outside Rome, by some Japanese television people who have come to interview Fellini as he prepares a picture based on Kafka's *Amerika* (a film that the director had at one time actually contemplated making). *Intervista* was thus yet another pseudodocumentary, like *The Clowns* and *Roma*, which proved how desperate Fellini was to find a film subject, a subject to film other than (literally) himself—how much in fact he had become, in a reversal of the Pirandellian scheme, an author in search of sundry characters. Fellini himself put a bold face on the picture when he described it, in conversation, as "the ultimate result of my way of making cinema: where there is no longer a story or a script, only the feeling, precisely, of being inside a kind of creativity that refuses every preconceived order" (Fellini quoted in Peter Bondanella, *The Cinema of Federico Fellini* [1992]). Nevertheless, this affectionate divertissement, which characteristically balances illusion and reality, can be seen as a self-homage from an artist who had earned the right.

Even as Fellini appeared as himself in *Intervista*, so too did Anita Ekberg, who had acted years before in *La dolce vita*. Her presence raises the subject of Fellini's view of women, here and elsewhere in his oeuvre—

particularly in light of his famous comment to Gideon Bachmann in late 1980 that "the cinema [is] a woman," that "going to the cinema is like returning to the womb; you sit there, still and meditative in the darkness, waiting for life to appear on the screen." Fellini's view of women was never as empathetic as Antonioni's, whose moral protagonists were often females. And even when Fellini used a female protagonist, as in *La strada*, *The Nights of Cabiria*, and *Juliet of the Spirits*, she was a woman who accepted her life as determined by men. His women, then, are figures, often secondary ones, in a man's world: Fellini's own. This quality may in time date him, but it cannot affect his magic as a portrayer of that world.

That magic has something to do with the very nature of Cinecittà, where Fellini shot his films and to which *Intervista* can be viewed as an homage as well. What moves us at Cinecittà, why it is so powerfully mysterious to see a tower of arc lights beam into life against the dark, why the immense space of an empty sound stage seems to echo even when it is silent, is that here occurs an argument with mortality. The mere fact that film can fix the moment implies that time is rushing by even when the moment is being fixed. In other words, film, with all its fakeries, understands death. And Fellini, the most honest and lovable faker who ever made a film, understood life. He understood, as he related in his interview with me, that he had to recreate life in a studio instead of using actuality, because he had to put himself in it.

So he did, this most naked of all film geniuses at the same time as he was the world's greatest off-screen actor, convincing us throughout his career of his showman's honesty, his genuineness through artifice, in conjuring the past and the present, the fancied, the contrived, and the true, into a glittering show of his own truth—Fellini's, not the "Fellini-esque," which is already something once removed from the real Italian thing. Let me conclude this section by quoting Guido's line from *8½* that he has nothing to say, but he is going to say it anyway. So too did Fellini, who in the process made it a pleasure, not a lesson, to be present at his creations.

Two of those creations—in which, in the gospel according to Fellini, "the cinema is a woman"—are *La strada* and *The Nights of Cabiria*, each of which I would like to treat at some length here. *La strada* and *The Nights of Cabiria* both point up the distinction, not only between sexual gratification and divine fulfillment, carnal lust and romantic love, but also between what the French auteur Jean Cocteau once called "cinema" and "cinematograph"—a distinction it pays to remember nowadays as the Hollywood "product" more and more crowds out American independents as well as European, Asian, and African imports. Cinema, Cocteau said, conceives of film as an art and is as rare as genuine art (or genuine religiosity, for that matter) always is; while "cinematograph"—literally, a motion-picture camera or projector, or the material of moviemaking as opposed to its spirit—concerns itself with commercial entertainment produced by an industry and anathematizes, art.

Let us begin with *La strada*, which displays the economy of means that Federico Fellini was to employ in the most impressive phase of his career (from *Variety Lights* through *8½*). During this time he was, as I have pointed out, an observer, and observation requires a certain measure of reticence, reserve, or remove. Insofar as he has a style in *I vitelloni* and *The Nights of Cabiria*, say, it is not narrowly technical or formalist but rather broadly constructive. Like his neorealist forbears, Fellini tried to present the world naturally, arranging events as little as possible in order to avoid the creation of mere plots or entertainments. And since his subject in this early period of his career was the incorrigibility of human hopefulness, repetition, not progressive plotting, was crucial to his method. The purpose of such repetition was to illustrate a state of being again and again rather than to move causally toward a dramatic climax, to react to the surface of character from the outside rather than to probe deeply into the psychology of human feeling.

La strada (1954). Directed by Federico Fellini. Shown from left, foreground: Giullietta Masina (as Gelsomina), Richard Basehart (as Il 'Mato'-the 'Fool'), Anthony Quinn (as Zampano). ©Trans Lux Inc. Photographer: A. Piatti. *(Courtesy Trans Lux Inc./Photofest)*

It would not be too much to say, then, that by the time he made *La strada*, Fellini had reached a new stage in the evolution of the cinema where form itself no longer determines anything, where filmic language no longer calls attention to itself but, on the contrary, suggests only as much as any stylistic device that an artist might employ. Put another way, nothing Fellini shows us in this film has any supplementary meaning to the manner in which it is shown; if the camera does not *see* it, it is not in the picture. No lyricism of the image or of montage—the formal composition of the images in relation to one another—takes it upon itself to guide our perceptions, to interpret the action for us. It is in this way that the movies achieved fruition as the art of the real (their fantastic or abstract component having long since been relegated, at least in theory, to a secondary role), where advances would henceforth be tied less to the originality of the means of expression than to the substance of the expression itself. Thus, paradoxically, does a verist film like *La strada* become cinema at its transcendent best, rich in imagination, profound in spirit, and pure in tone. It represents, in a word, the flowering of film possibilities into a new instrument for converting reality into living myth, for enhancing the known.

Here's the "plot" of what I prefer to call a cinematic poem, a song of love. Zampanò, a whoring, drunken strongman whose one accomplishment is to be able to break a chain with his bare chest, pays an old Italian woman a few lire for her daughter Gelsomina's services as a "slavey" and sets off with her in a motorcycle van that is simultaneously strange and commonplace. The girl (or woman: she is ageless, unidentifiable, without history) is deranged but only in the way of one who has broken through the limitations of conventional feeling into a universe of direct perception and spontaneous expression. The strongman himself is a brute, living below the level of conscience or communication. What he wants of Gelsomina is merely to help him in his act; what she wants of Zampanò is to be allowed to remain, in misery and wonder, at his side.

They move through changing landscapes and weathers but seem always to be in one desolate provincial town after another (photographed by Otello Martelli in every shade between the blackness of Zampanò's heart and the white of Gelsomina's goodness, all of these shades seemingly devoid of sunlight). What happens to these two, in accordance with the cinematic style of Fellini that I have noted, is less a narrative than an unfolding; whatever they do is less important than the self-revelation it affords. But there *are* events or consequences. They join a wedding feast at which Gelsomina comforts an idiot child with her astonishing compassion. They meet a gentle clown—better called a "fool," a quasi-Shakespearean one, since he is an *artiste* who plays the violin and performs on the high wire in addition to playing the clown—from whom she learns the meaning of her role, that she has a place in the world and even a destiny, which is to be indispensable to Zampanò. ("If I don't stay with Zampanò," Gelsomina asks, "who will?") They spend a night at a convent where she leaves part of herself behind, anchored in the peace she cannot have with her "master."

Finally, they meet the Fool again, and Zampanò kills him, irritated by his mocking gaiety and baffled by the superiority of his soul, the air of the marvelous that hovers about him. At the death of the Fool, Gelsomina is pierced by a sublime pity and reduced humanly to a little whimper, like a mouse deprived of food: "The Fool is sick, the Fool is sick." Her breakdown is, without question, the most powerful event in *La strada*. From this point on, she is beset by an agony situated in that instant in which the Fool, who had virtually conferred her being on her, ceased to exist. Terrified by the poor girl's suffering—or, better, unable to bear her horror of him—and at the end of his patience, Zampanò abandons Gelsomina asleep in the snow, in her own private Gethsemane.

But just as the death of the Fool had made life unbearable for Gelsomina, so too will Zampanò's abandonment of her and then her death make life unbearable for him. It is only years later that he accidentally learns of this woman-child's passing, after which, following a humiliating beating in a café, Zampanò staggers to the edge of the sea where he at last breaks down, uttering great hoarse cries that are his inchoate sounds of recognition. For him, the road ends here, as he instinctively recognizes that he has repudiated the need for love and that this act has slain his spirit; that, in his animal existence, he has avoided the breath of God and now must lie broken and powerless until it should pass over him again. Little by little, then, this mass of muscles has been reduced to its emotional core, and Zampanò ends up being crushed by the absence of Gelsomina from his life. He is crushed not so much by remorse for what he did, however, or even by his love for her, as by overwhelming, inconsolable, almost suicidal anguish, which can only be the response of his *soul* to being deprived of Gelsomina, who in her innocence, simplicity, and faithfulness could be said to represent nothing less than the communion of saints.

Fellini's point of view is thus the exact opposite of the one that would be taken by a psychological realist. The very being of these characters is precisely in their *not* having any psychology, or at least in possessing such a malformed and primitive one that any description of it would hold little more than pathological interest. But each does have a soul, which reveals itself here beyond psychological or artistic categories.

It reveals itself all the more because one cannot bedeck it, in Zampanò's case, with the trappings of conscience. Where he and the other slow-witted characters in *La strada* are concerned, it is impossible to confuse ultimate spiritual realities with those of intelligent reflection, aesthetic pleasure, or wedded passion. This film is nothing but these figures' experience of their souls and the revelation of that experience before our eyes. A phenomenology of the soul, then, one could call *La strada*, or at the very least (highest?) a "cautionary" phenomenology of the reciprocal nature of salvation, the smallest unit of universal Catholic existence being two loving souls or one human soul in harmony with the divine Christ.

If you do not agree with the above interpretation, you have to conclude, with *La strada*'s secular detractors, that because we see Zampanò's "change" only years after Gelsomina's death and we have not followed him through those years, we have not seen how his change occurred. According to this argument, Gelsomina ends up being the protagonist of *La strada* through the sheer pathos of her condition, whereas she should have been the active agent of Zampanò's internal change, through conflict between him and her leading to a gradual, or dramatized, recognition on his part. Everything depends, in a sense, on how convincing Anthony Quinn (as Zampanò) is in the final revelation of his delayed heartbreak, his mournful solitude. In my view, he is very convincing, giving the greatest performance of his otherwise inflated career. So convincing is Quinn that the tears Zampanò sheds for the first time in his sorry life, on the beach that Gelsomina loved, made me connect their salt with the salt of the eternal sea, which seems, behind him, to be relieving its own anguish at the never-ending sufferings of man and beast.

Giulietta Masina, for her part, is infinitely enchanting in the first starring role given to her by Fellini (her husband, it's worth repeating). A mime in the tradition of Barrault, Marceau, and Chaplin, she uses her miming skills here far more than language—which, after all, in so visual a medium as film can sometimes mediate between us and our affective response to character—to create the childlike character of Gelsomina. A loving, trusting, hopeful, endearing, and enduring person, she has her spirit crushed, finally, not (like adults) by the cumulative weight of experience but by the provisional delinquency of grace. That delinquency kills the Fool before it does her, and he is played by the American actor Richard Basehart with a brilliant virtuosity that he rarely displayed in Hollywood movies such as *The House on Telegraph Hill* (1951) and *Titanic* (1953). To avoid the pitfalls of Hollywood stereotyping, or to work with directors who know something about acting, Basehart escaped to Europe for a time, where he also had a leading role in Fellini's *Il bidone*.

This bitter drama is about three small-time crooks who fleece the poor by disguising themselves as priests, until one of them, severely beaten for trying to swindle his two accomplices, manages to approach salvation because he dies—in a remarkable final scene not unlike *La strada*'s—in a state of moral anguish, all alone on a stony hillside. *Il bidone* was followed by *The Nights of Cabiria*, in which Giulietta Masina again starred as a childlike woman. This time Fellini decided not to attach her to a single, strong male figure like Zampanò; instead he chose only to "react to the surface" of his female character, the prostitute Cabiria, who is placed in successive scenes that illustrate the essential state of her being.

At the start of the film, Cabiria's boyfriend, Giorgio, steals her purse and pushes her into a river. But she is rescued, and the film chronicles her attempts to bounce back from disappointed love. First Cabiria dances at night on the Passeggiata Archeologica, where her fellow prostitutes gather in Rome; her dance ends in a fight, however, when the aging prostitute Matilda taunts her about rejection by Giorgio. Then, to Cabiria's astonishment, since she is hardly glamorous, she gets picked up by the film star Alberto Lazzari but is pushed aside when his girlfriend decides to make up with him in the middle of the night. Cabiria next makes a pilgrimage to the Madonna of Divine Love, where she wants to pray for a miracle for a change in her life for the better, for rebirth. Yet nothing appears to happen.

She is subsequently hypnotized by a magician in a theater into believing that she is eighteen again and in the company of a young man who truly loves her. But Cabiria soon awakens from her trance to sad reality: no lover in her life and an audience of men jeering at her. Still, on the stage of the theater and under the hypnotist's spell, she was photographed (again by Otello Martelli) beneath the glare of a spotlight which, in separating the black out from the white more than is usually the case in a black and-white film, suggests the underlying truth about Cabiria: that she is, and shall remain, less a creature of the "nights," of dark sensuality, than of the "lights," of purity, innocence, even spirituality. Not by accident in Fellini's cinematic oeuvre, it is a magician or artist-figure who is associated here with giving or creating a clear picture of Cabiria's essential nature, even as it was the performing Fool in *La strada* who saw through to the core of Gelsomina's simple, blessed being.

Outside the theater, Cabiria meets Oscar D'Onofrio, who was a member of the audience and who miraculously falls in love with her at once. Cabiria is at first reluctant to accompany Oscar to a café but eventually dates him regularly, falls in love, and accepts his proposal of marriage. She sells her little house, takes all her money out of the bank, and leaves Rome to marry Oscar. They go to an inn in the Alban Mountains, where he plans to push Cabiria off a cliff into a lake and steal her money. At the edge of the cliff Cabiria finally realizes that she has been duped again and, horrified, not only offers Oscar her savings but also asks him to kill her. He runs off shaken, but not before grabbing the money. We last see her wandering dazed along a road, surrounded by young people singing and dancing to the accompaniment of guitars. A girl from this group says, "Buona sera!" to Cabiria, who smiles as the film ends.

Cabiria is, then, incorrigibly hopeful: This is the common denominator in her life, or her life's search for love (as opposed to the mere lust between a prostitute and her customer). She is so incorrigibly hopeful that she seems like a child who has yet to learn from the weight of experience. Indeed, from beginning to end she looks and acts like a child. Like all of Fellini's films, not just the obvious examples such as *81/2* and *Juliet of the Spirits*, *The Nights of Cabiria* has an oneiric quality in the sense that the childlike Cabiria could be dreaming or having a nightmare that she is wandering through an unaccountably cruel world, one to which she is a stranger and to which she is unwilling or unable to sacrifice her hopefulness.

Somewhat as in *La strada*, Giulietta Masina is a woman with a girl's appearance in the film: She is slim-hipped, has a pixie haircut, and wears bobby socks with her penny loafers. Indeed, when she puts on her shabby fur coat for her nights as a prostitute, she looks like a child "playing adult." In a scene omitted from the final version of *The Nights of Cabiria*, moreover, Cabiria says to the Man with the Sack, "Yes, my mother and father both died when I was still a little girl. I came to Rome . . ." (This scene is included on the DVD of the film released by Criterion.) She seems to say here that she came to Rome as a little girl and grew up alone; and it is as if she has remained the little lovelorn girl she was when her parents died.

Fellini is careful never to show Cabiria in bed with any of her customers, for example, even though we know that she has saved money from her work as a prostitute. At one point we see her accept a ride from a truck driver, but it is not clear that she will sleep with him, since she is making her pilgrimage to the Madonna of Divine Love and may want nothing more than transportation. We see her actually reject the advances of a potential customer at another point: The man drives up to the Passeggiata Archeologica, says a few words to Cabiria, gets no response, and drives on. Even as Cabiria seems to be "playing adult" when she dresses up to go out, she thus seems also to be "playing prostitute." That is the effect of not showing her in bed with men and of surrounding her with full-bodied women in high heels and tight-fitting dresses.

Like a child, Cabiria imitates the behavior of adults. When a pimp drops her off at the Via Veneto, she tries to imitate the walk and air of the high-classed streetwalkers of the area. When the film star takes her to a flashy nightclub, she imitates the behavior of the ladies who surround her. And when she finds herself in the procession to the shrine, she looks around and begins imitating the behavior of the other supplicants. Additionally like a child, Cabiria is unable to consume liquor: At a picnic after the pilgrimage, a character says that Cabiria gets drunk after one drink. She even throws tantrums like a child. Twice she goes into a rage at people who mean well: at the men and boys who save her from drowning and at her next-door neighbor, Wanda, who tries to comfort her and learn what is wrong when she returns home muddy and wet.

Of course we understand the source of Cabiria's anger—not only has she been robbed and pushed into a river, but she has also been deserted by the man she loves—yet it seems irrational and inconsiderate. Just as irrational (but *considerate*) is the love that the childlike Cabiria gives as freely as she displays her anger: to Giorgio, to Oscar, to one of her chickens, to the film star's puppy. Cabiria even becomes excited as easily and completely as a child: While Alberto Lazzari is driving her to the nightclub, for instance, she stands up on the front seat and shouts proudly to the prostitutes who line the streets, "Look at me! Look who I'm with!" When they arrive at the club, furthermore, Alberto must coax her out of the car and through the front door as one might coax a shy or frightened child.

Two images especially fix Cabiria in my mind as a needy child-woman, both photographed at Lazzari's garish mansion. The first image is of Cabiria climbing the stairs to Alberto's room in pursuit of the actor, for he has gone ahead of her—just as he did at the nightclub. Cabiria looks like a child climbing stairs that are too large for her, since Fellini shoots the scene from the bottom of the staircase so that the already small Cabiria appears smaller the higher she goes, even as the stairs appear larger. The second image is of Cabiria peeking out through the keyhole of Alberto's spacious bathroom, where she is hiding from his girlfriend. It is as if Cabiria, holding Alberto's puppy, is a child enviously peeking through the keyhole at two adults, a father and a mother figure who are getting ready to go bed. Indeed, Alberto seems like a father to Cabiria: He dwarfs her, as does his home. Like a good father, he urges her to eat supper, and when his girlfriend arrives, he sends Cabiria out of the room with her meal and the dog.

Alberto is one of four parental figures Fellini gives Cabiria in the film. Wanda, the prostitute who lives next door to her, is a mother figure who seeks to comfort the distressed Cabiria and offers common sense where Cabiria can plead only her hope and her dreams. When the latter says of Giorgio, "Why would he shove me in the river for a mere forty thousand lire? I loved him." Wanda replies, "*Love*. . . . You only knew him a month—you know nothing of him." When Cabiria wants to know, almost immediately after the pilgrimage, why her life has not yet changed for the better, Wanda stares at her in disbelief, saying, "What do you mean, *change*?" Wanda is the first to suspect that Oscar is deceiving Cabiria, and, like a loving mother, she cries when Cabiria departs from Rome to marry him, complaining that she has not even met her friend's fiancé. The Madonna of Divine Love is Wanda's spiritual counterpart, just as Giovanni, a lay brother, is Alberto's. Like Alberto, Giovanni disappoints Cabiria, for he is not at church when she calls on him, and even had he been there he would not have been able to hear her confession, since he is not an ordained father. (When Cabiria hears this, she reacts with characteristic hopefulness, saying that she will wait for him anyway.)

Fellini even gives Cabiria surrogate siblings to complement her surrogate parents. Many children populate this film: Three boys selflessly dive into the Tiber in order to save Cabiria from drowning; children contentedly play outside her door on something resembling the "monkey bars" of American playgrounds; boys have started the otherwise harmless fire into which she throws Giorgio's pictures and clothing. Boys and girls run after Cabiria to say good-bye when she is leaving to marry Oscar, while the husband and wife who move into Cabiria's house the moment she vacates it themselves have four or five children. Laughing, frolicking children fill the street as Cabiria and Oscar leave the inn in the Alban Mountains to take their fateful walk. Finally, boys and girls revive Cabiria's spirit at the end of the film with music, song, joy, and kindness.

Fellini once said that, despite this mitigated ending, *The Nights of Cabiria* "is full of tragedy." It is, in the sense that Cabiria is a tragically divided or conflicted character. One childlike quality of Cabiria—her resilience, her inexhaustible energy—enables her to endure many setbacks; yet, another childlike quality—her impulse to love and to trust—is responsible for those very setbacks. There is apparently no way out for her *except* to endure, to suffer in her humanity, and to do so without achieving any tragic recognition: for Cabiria does not change but instead remains hopeful to the end. And that, perhaps, is the real miracle to result from her pilgrimage to the Madonna of Divine Love: not change, not "improvement," but the ability to go on hoping and loving in the face of hopelessness and lovelessness.

If anything has changed in the film, it is the attitude of Fellini's camera and, by extension, our attitude as viewers. Like a shy child, the camera has come upon Cabiria and Giorgio from afar in the opening long shots, has decided to stay with Cabiria, has then followed her through her experience unobtrusively yet doggedly, and in the final shot has come up close to embrace her in love as well as compassion. The camera has been quintessentially childlike in the sense that it has seemed content to observe and record Cabiria's experience rather than analyze, explain, and judge it. Fellini's camera may thus be naïve, but it is not sentimental or melodramatic. No one is blamed for Cabiria's condition; we never learn why she is the way she is, why her whore's heart of gold does not change, or even what her ultimate lot will be. The greatest tribute to this film may be that we do not resent not knowing. We accept Cabiria as she is presented to us, and we care about her. In this way we have been removed from the temporal world of causality, of psychology, and transported to the eternal world of wonder and play. That is, we have been transformed from chronically thinking adults into freely feeling children.

Paradoxically, in reacting only to Cabiria's surface, Fellini has placed her character more firmly at the center of his film than he would have had he probed her character deeply through plot complication or through a dramatic *agon*. He has, in a sense, rescued her from plot. Just as *The Nights of Cabiria* has no structured beginning and middle, no conflict leading to a climax, it does not really have an end or a dénouement: We just leave Cabiria after her betrayal by Oscar, as she walks down the road into the group of strolling boys and girls. Thus, although *8½*, with its self-referential and dream qualities, seems to be the first of his films to locate him among modernists in all the arts, Fellini in fact was already a modernist in the apparently realistic film *The Nights of Cabiria*, where he celebrated not only the incorrigible hopefulness and lovingness of human character—particularly in its childlike aspect—but also its ultimate inscrutability. In Cabiria's case, indeed, God only knows.

In addition to directing *The Nights of Cabiria* and *La strada*, Fellini coscripted these two films (with Tullio Pinelli and Ennio Flaiano). And I connect the quality of both pictures, in no small measure, to the fact that each one was wholly or partly written by its director. This may seem a romantic notion on my part (even after forty years of auteur theory), the chimerical idea in so collaborative a medium as film of the director as higher, shaping, and unifying consciousness, as individual artist-cum-genius apart from the madding, ignoble crowd. But, then again, such a romantic notion is especially apt as applied to two otherwise realistic movies that themselves are implicitly or explicitly about romance—conceived, that is, as an idealized love affair between two human beings (maybe even one) and the mind, or camera-eye, of God.

An Interview with Federico Fellini

The following interview took place in the lobby of the Grand Hotel in Milan, Italy, during the summer of 1986, not long after the release of *Ginger and Fred*.

BERT CARDULLO: Signor Fellini, tell me a little about your background and your first film job.

FEDERICO FELLINI: I reached the cinema through screenplays, and these through my collaboration on humorous publications—*Marc' Aurelio* especially—for which I wrote stories and columns in addition to drawing cartoons. If, one day in 1944, Roberto Rossellini hadn't invited me to collaborate on the screenplay of *Rome, Open City*, I would never even have considered the cinema as a profession. Rossellini helped me go from a foggy, apathetic period in my life to the stage of cinema. It was an important encounter but more in the sense of my future destiny than in the sense of influence. As far as I'm concerned, Rossellini's was an Adamlike paternity; he is a kind of forefather from whom many of my generation descend. Let's just say I was open to this particular endeavor, and he appeared at the right time to guide me into it. But I wasn't thinking of becoming a director at this juncture. I felt I lacked the director's propensity to be tyrannically overpowering, coherent and fussy, hardworking, and—most important—authoritative on every subject: all endowments missing from my temperament. The conviction that I could direct a film came later, when I was directly involved on one and could no longer pull out.

After having written a number of screenplays for Rossellini, Pietro Germi, and Alberto Lattuada, I wrote a story called *Variety Lights*. It contained my recollections of when I toured Italy with a variety troupe. Some of those memories were true, others invented. Two of us directed the

57

film: Lattuada and myself. He said "camera," "action," "cut," "everyone out," "silence," etc. And I stood by his side in a rather comfortable yet irresponsible position. The same year, 1950, I wrote a story called *The White Sheik* together with Tullio Pinelli. Michelangelo Antonioni was supposed to direct the film, but he didn't like the screenplay, so Luigi Rovere—the producer—told me to film it. I can therefore unequivocally state that I never decided to be a director. Rovere's rather reckless faith induced me to become one.

The vocation itself was altogether rather mysterious to me. As I said, my temperament led me elsewhere. Even today, when a film is finished, I find myself wondering how the devil I could have been so active, gotten so many people into motion, made a thousand decisions a day, said "yes" to this and "no" to that, and at the same time not have fallen madly in love with all those beautiful women that actresses are.

BC: Apart from women, how do you find inspiration in our mediocre times? Or perhaps you don't find that we are constantly surrounded by mediocrity.

FF: No, it's a barbaric era all right. People say this is an era of transition, but that's true of every period. Certainly we have no more myths left. The Christian myth doesn't seem to be able to help humanity anymore. So, we're waiting for a new myth to comfort us. But which one? Nonetheless, it's very interesting to live at a time like this. We must accept the time in which we live. We have no choice. Having said that, I feel that my mission in life, my vocation if you will, is to be a witness; and if your life consists of such testimony, you have to accept what you witness. Sure, you can be nostalgic about the past and how great it was, and you can lament the erosion of values, but there's no point in doing that. From a generational point of view, I'm aware that there's a certain regret about things past, but I personally try to live with the confidence that the future will assimilate the past. The past will transform itself into the future, so in a sense it will be relived—not in regret, but as part and parcel of the world to come.

BC: Does this vision of yours have to do with your looking into an interior reality rather than an exterior one? Are the dreams and fantasies of which an interior reality consists the basis of your inspiration?

FF: I don't dwell too much on what it is that inspires me. Instead I have to be in touch with my delusions, my discomforts, and my fears; they provide me the material with which I work. I make a bundle of all these, along with my disasters, my voids, and my chasms, and I try to observe them with sanity, in a conciliatory manner.

BC: What are you afraid of, if I may ask?

FF: I'm afraid of solitude, of the gap between action and observation in which solitude dwells. That's a reflection on my existence, in which I attempt to act without being swept away by the action, so as to be able to bear witness at the same time. I fear losing my spontaneity precisely because of such testimony or witnessing, because of my habit of constantly analyzing and commenting. I also fear old age, madness, decline. I fear not being able to make love ten times a day . . .

BC: Do you make films because solitude ranks high among your fears?

FF: Making films for me is not just a creative outlet but an existential expression. I also write and paint in isolation, in an ascetic manner. Perhaps my character is too hard, too severe. The cinema itself is a miracle, though, because you can live life just as you tell it. It's very stimulating. For my temperament and sensibility, this correlation between daily life and the life I create on screen is fantastic. Creative people live in a very vague territory, where what we call "reality" and "fantasy" are disjointed—where one interferes with the other. They both become one and the same thing. In sum, I enjoy telling stories with an inextricable mixture of sincerity and invention, as well as a desire to astound, to shamelessly confess and absolve myself, to be liked, to interest, to moralize, to be a prophet, witness, clown . . . to make people laugh and to move them. Are any other motives necessary?

BC: Not really! Let's talk now about the description of your early films as socially realistic, while your later ones are described as more hallucinatory.

FF: You could call hallucination a "deeper reality." Critics have a need to categorize and classify. I don't see it that way. I detest the world of labels, the world that confuses the label with the thing labeled. I just do what I have to do. *Realism* is a bad word, in any event. In a sense, everything is realistic. I see no line between the imaginary and the real; I see much reality in the imaginary.

BC: Critics also have termed your characters "grotesque" and "exaggerated." How do you react to such accusations?

FF: To answer this question, I must see my films, which I never do. People say that I'm a bit too much, that I exaggerate. Maybe they're right. But even if it's true, it's not intentional on my part. I'm delighted when I come across an expressive face, however bizarre. I am, after all, a caricaturist, and I have to accept the limitation this imposes on me. A creative person has something childish about him: He both loves to be surprised and wants to do the surprising. So, I choose to show whatever is too big or too small or simply unfamiliar. I try to express the feeling of surprise in the way I myself felt it. The world of Picasso, for example, could be described as strange and monstrous, but not for him. I, too, don't see my characters as strange. I simply try to go beyond appearances, to unveil what lies behind what we call "normality." Maybe I overdo it. People ask me, "Signor Fellini, where do you find such strange characters?" So I respond, "That's what I see in the mirror every day . . . a monstrous face indeed!"

Look, I'm not cruel. It's not true what some critics say, that I hate humanity. For me, curiosity and amusement are proof of my affection for what I depict. When I choose a certain face and have it made up in a certain way, it's not because I want to ridicule, but because I want to convey in an immediate manner something that isn't psychological. My characters never undergo psychological development. My films are a bit more innocent than that, and the characters have to be themselves as soon as they appear. So the need to be expressive is immediate.

BC: You show beauty—of women like Claudia Cardinale and Anita Ekberg—alongside the grotesque: for example, a huge woman like Saraghina in *8 1/2*. Isn't there a dichotomy here after all?

FF: Beauty is not limited to beauty in the classical sense. It can be everywhere. I must admit that I don't recognize the category of the grotesque; to me even the grotesque is beautiful. You mention La Saraghina. In Rimini, near the seminary for priests, there was in fact a big prostitute like that who used to expose herself. When I show something like that, it's usually through the eyes of a boy, and sometimes I exaggerate just to show the astonishment or fear or ecstasy of that boy. Also, if I use a big or fat woman, it's because I'm telling a story about an Italian boy who is hungry for women and wants a lot of woman, so to speak. Just because the Catholic Church has described women as something to put out of your mind, Italian males of a certain generation developed an appetite for *them* and not just for food. So the big women indicate the big appetite of these men—or boys.

BC: How do you feel about the relations between the sexes today, when a certain role reversal seems to be at work?

FF: Man has always been unsure of women. A woman for a man is the part that he doesn't know about himself, so he's always afraid of her. He feels weak and vulnerable with her, because she may cause him to lose his identity. Just by projecting the part of himself that he doesn't know on a woman, he loses a lot of himself. So he knows he can be destroyed, devoured. . . . That's a natural law.

He also probably remembers the very ancient matriarchal society in which man was nothing and women thought they became pregnant just because the wind blew some seed into their vagina, or the seed came from the ocean or from the moon. A thousand years passed before man and woman had a relationship and discovered orgasm. Suddenly someone started thinking, "Wait a minute, why does it take nine months? Which kind of wind is it? What ocean started it all nine months ago?" In those matriarchal societies, if men were to assert themselves, they had to put on false breasts and dress like women, complete with wigs. Men, as men, didn't exist at all—worse than rats. When the queen decided to take a companion, he would last a year, after which he was killed, cut to pieces like an animal, and eaten.

BC: What society was that, Signor Fellini?

FF: Now. It's today. . . . And then, for centuries, man took advantage of women to avenge himself for what he had suffered for thousands of years. Now women want to be considered as persons, not as mere projections, and their attempt to escape the image to which man has confined them frightens man. But finally he understands that he won't be free until women are free as well. I tried to show all that in *City of Women*.

BC: Do you see yourself as a romantic?

FF: I don't think I have a romantic view of the world, because I don't recognize a particular view of the world. I probably have a romantic conception of the artist and art, but of life, no. I like to probe behind appearances and discover what's really there, like a naughty boy. In this I recognize the skeptic, who tries not to put too much faith in façades, who tries to unmask falsehood. I think that's the most important thing: I have no ideology, but if I had to identify myself with one, it would be that the beauty of art is in its unmasking of falsehood; in educating; in planting in people's minds the suspicion that reality is something more complex than it appears to be; in giving people the *pleasure* of suspicion, not just the burden of doubt; in keeping them from feeling too protected by taboos, concepts, ideologies. Life is more complex than all that. If, in my pictures, I were asked to recognize a motif—a thread that runs through them—I'd say that this is the only one. It's an attempt to create emancipation from conventional schemes, liberation from moral rules: that is to say, an attempt to retrieve life's authentic rhythm or mode, its vital cadence, as opposed to all the inauthentic forms life is forced to take. That, I believe, is the central idea to be found in all the films I have made.

BC: Does this mean that you avoid judgment?

FF: That's not really possible. We are slaves of our culture, prisoners of our emotions. We always have a subjective point of view. Subjectivity means that we've had a certain education, that we read certain books, that we have cultivated certain emotions. All these mysterious and contradictory things serve as the basis for our judgment. Even when you can pretend to be just a witness, you can't ignore this subjective element. I try to be open and not to be schematic, but always in terms of what is commensurate with my background.

BC: Is that partly why you don't make films in other countries? Because you're so very Italian?

FF: Yes, in the same way that you're so very American despite your Sicilian last name. . . . When I go to a foreign country, everything is a mystery to me. I see images, colors, lines, but they don't add up to anything. I could make a picture about New York, but in Cinecittà, not in America. I'd have to remember what I saw in New York and what emotions it triggered in me, and then I would try to recreate them here in Italy with the same colors and lights. I was so presumptuous as to say several times to American producers that I wanted to make such a film about America in Italy, where I would be protected by an atmosphere in which I could move without being unsettled or even mortified by laws I don't know and a language I can't speak.

    Your question, by the way, is evidence of a reductive attitude toward the movies. No one ever asks writers why they don't write in other languages. The equivocal birth of the cinema was indeed technical—the camera, the lens, the lights, and then you develop the film—but that's purely a mechanical point of view. If I want to try to express what's going on here during this interview, however, I can't just put a camera in front of us. I would have to recreate the *feeling* of our meeting: what I feel about the fact that you are an Italian-American, about the fact that

Fiammetta is trying to create a bridge between us by helping you with your Italian and me with my English, about the décor of this hotel lobby, the color of the sofa on which we sit. . . . To think that the camera can take all that in by itself is highly reductive, just as it is to think that an Italian like me could make a picture in New York simply by turning on a camera and filming what's in front of me.

People ask me, "Signor Fellini, why do you recreate Venice in a studio instead of using the real one?" And I'm always a bit surprised by such questions. I *have* to recreate Venice, because that's the way I put myself in it.

BC: The décor becomes expressive of your vision, then.

FF: Of course. In America, I'd have to depend on information culled from others—such as the kind of tails a Chicago lawyer wears. Maybe I'm just trying to look for pretexts—the real reason for not filming in other countries being that I'm too old and lazy—but I think it's more sincere to say that I can't create from life that I am seeing more or less for the first time. I need a period of long and immersed reflection. I could do a wholly impressionistic report on a place like New York, seen from a newspaperman's eye as it were, but that would mean absolutely nothing.

BC: Do you feel transformed when you're on the set, or are you always the same?

FF: I'm always the same confused man. There's no difference. When I work, I am perhaps healthier because the pressure to do, to escape, to be alive gives me added neurotic energy. When I'm in between pictures, I'm a bit weaker. But I'm always in the same situation of not knowing what I'm doing.

BC: How does such confusion evolve into a unified, focused vision?

FF: That's a very difficult question to answer. I don't want to appear too mystical or too mysterious, but there's a part of me that sometimes comes out at the last moment. The more confused I am, the more I'm ready for this new tenant that inhabits my imagination to take possession of me. This is what makes everything fall into place. The more I feel lost, the more I believe I can be helped by this unknown source of knowledge or understanding. It's magic. Perhaps I'm being a bit superstitious with this trust of mine in the unknown. Of course, what I really mean by saying that I don't know what I'm doing is that my knowledge comes after I have tried *everything*. For example, I look at a hundred faces to choose one that will just inhabit a dark corner of the screen, and only for a very short period of time. That's the kind of effort I'm talking about.

BC: You're saying, then, that this knowledge of yours goes beyond reason.

FF: That's right. You can get lost by being too rational. But if you work with faith, and you know your limits—at the same time as you are modest, humble, and also arrogant, like a real man—you can arrive at the truth. If you're as true to yourself as you possibly can be, you will be helped, and you'll come closer to artistic truth. Still, I don't claim to know all the secrets.

BC: Does any one of your films represent you more completely than the others? Is any one of them more key than the others—a film to preserve, as they say?

FF: Two of them: *La strada* and *8½*. *La strada* is really the complete catalog of my entire mythical or shadow world, a dangerous representation of my identity undertaken without precaution. The point of departure of that film, apart from the spectacle of nature and the fascination with gypsylike travels, was the story of an enlightenment, a shaking of conscience, through the sacrifice of another human creature. *8½* is meant to be an attempt to reach an agreement with life, an attempt and not a result or conclusion. I think the film may *suggest* a solution: to make friends with yourself completely, without hesitation, without false modesty, without fears but also without hopes.

BC: Critics have often complained that you end your films in a vague, general way: the appeal to hope in *The Nights of Cabiria*, the reminder of the little girl's purity in *La dolce vita*. Your thoughts on this subject?

FF: This is one of the criticisms that I've never understood, for as far as I'm concerned the public writes the ending. The storyteller shouldn't say, "Here the story ends," if he doesn't want his story to be reduced to the level of an anecdote or a joke. If the story has moved you, the ending is up to you—the viewer who has seen it.

BC: How does a project of yours come into being in the first place?

FF: The real ideas come to me when I sign a contract and get an advance that I don't want to give back, when I'm *obliged* to make a picture. I'm kidding, naturally. I don't want to appear brutal, like Groucho Marx, but I'm the kind of creator who needs to have a higher authority—a grand duke, the pope, an emperor, a producer, a bank—to push me. Such a vulgar condition puts me on the right track. It's only then that I start thinking about what I can, and want to, do.

BC: Why do you think you decided to start using color—first for the episode in *Boccaccio '70* and then for *Juliet of the Spirits*? Was there an external factor, such as an offer from a producer, the sheer possibility of doing a film in color, or was this your own aesthetic choice?

FF: The two cases are different. For the episode in *Boccaccio '70*, the choice wasn't mine. It was an episodic or anthology film, and the producers decided that it was to be in color. I didn't object at all. The playful air of the whole undertaking and the brief form of the episode seemed just right for an experiment with color without too great a commitment on my part. I didn't think about the problem very seriously; I didn't go into it deeply. In *Juliet of the Spirits*, on the other hand, color is an essential part of the film; it was born in color in my imagination. I don't think I would have done it in black and white. It is a type of fantasy that is developed through colored illuminations. As you know, color is a part not only of the language of dreams but also of the idea and feeling behind them. Colors in a dream are concepts, not mere approximations or memories.

That said, I certainly prefer a good black-and-white picture to a bad one in color. All the more so because in some cases so-called "natural color" impoverishes the imagination. The more you mimic reality, the more you lose in the imitation. Black and white, in this sense, offers wider margins for the imagination. I know that after having seen a good black-and-white film, many spectators, when asked about its chromatic aspect, will say, "The colors were beautiful," because each viewer lends to the otherwise black-and-white images the colors he has within himself.

BC: You seem to be saying that you prefer black-and-white to color cinematography, period.

FF: Well, making films in color is, I believe, an impossible operation, for cinema is movement, color immobility; to try to blend these two artistic expressions is a desperate ambition, like wanting to breathe under water. Let me explain. In order to truly express the chromatic values of a face, a landscape, some scene or other, it is necessary to light it according to certain criteria that are functions of both personal taste and technical exigency. And all goes well so long as the camera doesn't move. But as soon as the camera moves in on the faces or objects to be lighted, the intensity of the light is heightened or lessened, and all the chromatic values are intensified or lessened as a result. In short: The camera moves, the light changes.

There is also an infinitude of contingencies that condition the color, aside from the grave errors that can occur at the laboratory, where the negative can be totally transformed by its development and printing. These contingencies are the innumerable and continual traps that have to be dealt with every day when you shoot in color. For instance, colors interfere or clash, set up "echoes," are conditioned by one another. Once lighted, color runs over the outline that holds it, emanating a sort of luminous aureola around neighboring objects. Thus there is an incessant game of tennis, let us say, between the various colors. Sometimes it even happens that the result of these changes is agreeable, better than what one had imagined; but this is always a some-what chancy, uncontrollable occurrence.

Finally, the human eye selects and in this way already does an artist's work, because the human eye, the eye of man, sees chromatic reality through the prisms of nostalgia, of memory, of presentiment or imagina-tion. This is not the case with the lens, and it happens that you believe you are bringing out certain values in a face, a set, a costume, while the lens brings out others. In this way, writing with a camera—or *caméra stylo*, as Astruc put it—becomes very difficult. It is as if, while writing, a modi-fying word escapes your pen in capital letters, or, still worse, one adjective shows up instead of another, or some form of punctuation appears that completely changes the sense of a line.

BC: Tell me about something not unrelated to the subject of color: the relationship between your films and television in Italy. I saw *The Nights of Cabiria* on television here a few nights ago, and I'm glad I saw it first in a movie theater some years ago.

FF: *Ginger and Fred*, my latest picture, was made for television, but it was shown in theaters first. Not many such theaters remain in Italy, however. They've just closed 2,117 of them, and there are now many cities, like Perugia—which is the size of Boston—which had three or four theaters but now have none. In Italy, we have over two hundred private television stations. You could watch two hundred pictures on two hundred TV sets at the same time, but that's not all that's wrong.

The movies have suffered not only because of the direct competition of television, but also because television has created a different relationship between audiences and images. For example, they can switch off the image whenever they want. Moreover, you watch TV in a small room, in the light, where you can talk. Thus all the ritualistic attention that movies used to command gets canceled. And the fact that you can change channels by remote control every thirty seconds—or less—has created an impatient audience, even a very arrogant and superficial one. Anything it finds annoying, it eliminates. Add to this the fact that television is available twenty-four hours a day, every day of the year, and that images are deployed electronically—they're doubled and squeezed onto the small screen—and you'll see that the image as we once knew it has been destroyed.

We are no longer used to being seduced by a pure image. We have no interest in following a story from an author's point of view. And since telling stories is what I like to do, I must admit I feel frustrated. The man with the remote control has become director and exhibitor. The audience has gained power at the expense of the movies, such that the cinema has become a tainted old lady teetering on the verge of extinction. I would very much like to please the audience, but in the end, I find, I must be faithful to the picture.

Filmography of Feature Films

Variety Lights, 1950
The White Sheik, 1952
I vitelloni, 1953
"A Marriage Agency," 1953: episode of *Love in the City*
La strada, 1954
Il bidone, 1955
The Nights of Cabiria, 1956
La dolce vita, 1959
"The Temptations of Doctor Antonio," 1962: episode of *Boccaccio '70*
8½, 1963
Juliet of the Spirits, 1965
"Toby Dammit," 1968: episode of *Spirits of the Dead*
Fellini Satyricon, 1969
The Clowns, 1970
Roma, 1972
Amarcord, 1973
Casanova, 1976

Orchestra Rehearsal, 1979
City of Women, 1980
And the Ship Sails On, 1983
Ginger and Fred, 1985
Interview, 1987
The Voice of the Moon, 1990

More from Less

The Movie Aesthetic of Michelangelo Antonioni

HEN, IN MY EARLY TWENTIES, I followed that long, disconso-
late, abandoned island-search in *L'avventura* (1960), that arc
of despair that led to truth—the assurance, that is, in knowing
that one can live without assurances—I knew that it traced what I had
been prepared to feel next; that from then on it would be impossible not
to see existence with the same narrowed, dry-eyed, precipice-crawling
intentness as Michelangelo Antonioni. Now we have all had the experience of watching a film that seems to be changing our perception as it
unfolds, affecting the way we see and not simply offering us exotic or
heightened images of what we have already perceived without the camera's
intervention. And when we leave the movie theater, we discover that the
world, which we thought we knew, has changed to meet the new ways in
which it is being regarded. This reciprocity—a new reality being summoned by a new perceptiveness and in turn compelling that perceptiveness into being—seems to me to be at the heart of the filmmaker's art and
of the filmgoer's experience on the level of creative spectatorship. On any
other level a film, like every object of popular culture, is there to console,
divert, flatter, bludgeon, or confirm—in any case to see to it that we
remain unchanged.

In the preface to a 1963 volume of screenplays for four of his films,
Antonioni himself wrote that "the problem for a director is to catch
reality in an instant before it manifests itself and to propound that movement, that appearance, that action as a new perception." In its rescuing
of the director from the status of a recording agent who decides which
aspects of established reality are to be photographed (or, rather, who

enhances or "dramatizes" those aspects of reality that lie open to the ordinary eye), this seems to me to be as useful a description of the art of filmmaking as we are likely to find, or at least of one aspect of filmmaking. There is another, which is the *inventing* of reality, the making of something that has not existed before.

I would like to think, however, that Antonioni would agree that the two functions are ultimately the same, that the act of discovery of what reality is going to be next, the apprehension of its impending face, is a mysterious cause of the new, a procedure that brings it into being and thus invents reality anew. If this were not true, then the director would merely be prescient and his art only one of prediction. The artist is indeed a kind of prophet, but prophecy is not simply prediction; it is a force, a pressure on things to be other than they would be if left to themselves. And this power, while it may partake of or draw upon fantasy, is not in its most serious uses a faculty of fantasy at all; there is nothing "unreal" or escapist in what it brings to birth.

In the late 1950s and early 1960s, Antonioni began to make a series of films that exemplified far more profoundly than any other works of the time the capacity of the screen to be a source of myth in the sense of crystallizations of centrally contemporary significance, of dreams, and more—picturings of our truest, previously unsuspected selves. These movies, linked to one another much less by subject than by sensibility and attitude, were creations that told us what we were going to be like next, how we were about to act, and the kind of regard we would have for our actions. At the same time—and as a principle of these forecasts—they delineated the world with a scrupulously accurate sobriety, a refusal to enhance or "dramatize" what lay open to the ordinary eye.

I could easily write about any one of these films of Antonioni, or at least any of the four from *L'avventura* in 1960 to *Red Desert* in 1964. This is not because I think them all equally successful or admire them all with the same intensity, but because I cannot help thinking of them as a group, dependent upon one another for a totality of vision—Antonioni's at this time—which is itself my "favorite" or preferred cinematic one. I ought to say this right out: I respond most to austerity and restraint and economy in films. Along with Antonioni, the contemporaries of his I most admire are Robert Bresson, Ingmar Bergman (in his wintry or unlavish moods), Éric Rohmer, Carl Theodor Dreyer, and Yasujiro Ozu.

When I say "austerity" and "restraint" I certainly do not mean narrowness of imagination or skimpiness of theme. I mean a rigorousness of perception and a procedure by indirection, a cinema with silences and absences that can reveal more than thick, dense presences—the kind of hurly-burly activity with which it is all too easy for a filmmaker to clot our eyes. After all, the world is indubitably there in its plethora of detail, and if that is not enough there is always the studio in which to construct spaceships and saloons with swinging doors. But the austerity I am thinking about is not always a matter of a repudiation of physical sumptuousness, and in any case a cinema thick with objects and actions is not necessarily the same as one with visual richness.

A film such as Roberto Rossellini's *Rise to Power of Louis XIV* (1966), for example, triumphs by playing a visual opulence against an austerity of action, and so making the opulence, in its mysterious passivity, its resistance to having anything "dramatic" made out of it, become a sort of artistic action in itself, whereas a work like Fellini's boring *Satyricon* (1969) thrusts forward its gorgeousness, its Arabian-nights exoticism, as a straightforward animated genre painting. Movies are not paintings but interactions of the extremely visual and the interiorly personal, and the austerity or restraint I have been talking about concerns more than anything else the intelligence to resist handing over everything to the purely visual, to action and object for their own sakes.

Rohmer's films further illustrate what I mean. Physically handsome and often splendid, they are controlled by a hard intelligence that works almost metaphysically to limit the things that "happen" and so to make the landscapes and interiors dispose themselves as mute backgrounds for meanings (and not, as in "action" films, the meanings themselves). Against the beautiful lawns and lakefront of *Claire's Knee* (1970), for one, the film's characters do very little but talk, and this encounter of human speech, which is of course human thought made audible, with physical setting is the deepest event of the work. For this reason, when the protagonist does finally brush his hand against the knee of the girl, an action pregnant with significances that have been steadily and quietly gathering, the effect is more shattering than that of all the cavalry charges in the world.

After this digression, which I have to believe is no digression at all but a necessary frame in which to place my discussion, I can go back to Antonioni's films of the late 1950s and early 1960s, from among which I find myself unable to keep from writing about both *L'avventura* and *La notte* (1960). The reason, as I mentioned before, is that I regard this series of films (which includes *L'eclisse*, made in 1962) as an organic whole, any part of which would serve the purpose of communication about what *kind* of experience some presumably knowledgeable filmgoers have found important and satisfying and not about what particular one (akin to my greatest summer vacation or my favorite Italian restaurant) they would like to plump for.

In *L'avventura*, Antonioni introduced to the screen an almost unprecedented quality of randomness or indeterminate narration. The long,

Eclipse (1962), a.k.a. *L'Eclisse*. Directed by Michelangelo Antonioni. Shown from left: Alain Delon (as Piero), Monica Vitti (as Vittoria). *(Courtesy Times Film Corporation/Photofest)*

fruitless search for the girl lost on the island and her subsequently being entirely dropped from the plot were particularly striking instances of an imagination no longer concerned to use the screen for purposes of shapely, narratively consistent, and logically unfolding drama. And it was these gaps and holes, the seemingly aimless movements of the film's action, that were a chief source of the tedium felt by many of the film's first viewers, just as, on the contrary, they were the very basis of its supremely original beauty in the eyes of a minority who could look at it without preconceptions.

La notte takes us to the same place, by a different route. Here Antonioni leads us into the city, into concrete walls and reflections in glass, after the rocks, great spaces, sea, and terraces of *L'avventura*. And here the search (or movement; films *move*, are a tracing of movement, and in Antonioni, as in the best moments of any great director, the movement is everything—action, summation, meaning) comes to the same end or a fractional distance beyond. The acceptance is made of what we are; it is impossible not to accept such a conclusion as this film dies out on its couple shatteringly united in the dust, because everything we are not, but which we have found no other means of shedding, has been stripped away.

La notte, then, is composed according to the same principle of narrative indeterminacy as its predecessor—the same refusal to tell an easily repeatable, anecdotal "story"—and of course it proceeds from the same kind of insight into contemporary moral or psychic dilemmas. The relationship between the insight and its expression is crucial, and I will return to it, but at this point I want to take up the general notion of Antonioni's "meanings." In regard to them, criticism has been all too thorough and self-confident; nearly every commentator seems to have been certain about what Antonioni was up to. Both films, their readings go, are documents of upper-class exhaustion, fables of sophisticated despair. Both testify to present anomie among the privileged, the failure of sexuality to overcome existential ennui, and the spiritual aridity that accompanies all dedicated pursuits of pleasure.

To say these things, though, is to say nothing of real interest, nothing that indicates why Antonioni's films might not be better as novels or why his works of this period are so much greater than, say, Fellini's *La dolce vita* (1959)—another picture on the theme of well-heeled decadence and the moral crisis of the *haute bourgeoisie*, but one marred by its obviousness and the mechanical application of its ideas. The critical failure has always been in not seeing that Antonioni's films transcend their ostensible subject and milieu, as *La dolce vita* does not, that *L'avventura* and *La notte* are creations of universal validity and not simply portraits of a particular class or of a particular species of decadence. They are not really about decadence at all. Like Henry James's novels, these pictures employ privileged characters, men and women with the physical and economic freedom to choose their lives, precisely in order to exhibit the difficulties of such choice, the anguish of such freedom, for *anyone* who has it—even if only in part.

Thematically, Antonioni was treating of human connections no longer sustained by traditional values or by any convictions at all (a humanity with too much choice, as it were) and therefore forced to abide with the most fragile and precarious of justifications. One might say that his films were the first truly existential ones. When I first saw them I was filled with a sense of discovery of a world—a visual one this time, and not a theoretical, abstract one as in Kierkegaard or Sartre—that no longer replied to the questions I had about it and gave me no feeling of nurture, acceptance, or invitation. And that is the way Antonioni's characters move through their environments, in a new and strange alienation, an individual isolation in the midst of constant social interaction: a condition very different from, and far more subtle than, what is suggested by the clichés of modern sophisticated awareness, all our talk (even more feverish in the twenty-first century) about the failure of communication, technological dehumanization, the death of God, the fragmentation or atomization of society, and the like.

This new alienation—this despair or desolation in spite of the superficial appearance of affluence and pleasure, this emotional barrenness that Antonioni himself called (in a public appearance at the 1962 Cannes Festival) "the eclipse of all feelings"—is what we might call Antonioni's "subject" or "theme," but that isn't the same thing as his art, and it is a great mistake to think it is. The basis for my argument that Antonioni's films are not "about" a decadent class—let alone the death throes of capitalism—is that the visual world he composes, the one he discovers beneath appearances and calls into being, is the one we all inhabit, whether or not we have been summoned into any of its particular scenes. This is one reason why *L'avventura* and *La notte* are related in an indestructible unity; in the former, as I have indicated, we move through physical landscapes, bare islands, the sea, or through nature and white-washed ancient towns that seem to be part of nature; in the latter, we move through the city, with its geometry of streets and its assembly of artifacts, the coldest products of modern materialistic "wit" and inventiveness, the new nature. Between them these hemispheres make up the world for us all. But it is Antonioni's "characters" that have been given the task of being its explorers and its exhibited sacrifices.

Coherence, unity, connection between interior self and exterior reality are no longer sustained by this world of commerce and utility, so its inhabitants have to establish for themselves the very ground of their behavior. What is mistaken for boredom in Antonioni's characters, then, is actually a condition of radical disjunction between personality and circumstance. For a vital connection has been broken: The physical world has been dispossessed of the inherited meanings and principles according to which we had previously motivated our lives and structured its psychic as well as moral events. In such a world the idea of a "story," in the sense of a progressive tale leading from a fixed starting point to a dénouement that "settles" something or solves some problem, no longer has any use and is in fact inimical to the way this world is actually experienced.

This is the reason for the broken narratives, the conversations in a void, the events leading nowhere—the search for the lost girl in *L'avventura*, Jeanne Moreau's wandering without destination through the city in *La notte*. For a story implies a degree of confidence in the world, or at least a trustfulness that the environment, no matter how painful or brutal it might be, is knowable, makes sense, hangs together. But of course there is a "story" in Antonioni's films, though not of the traditional kind. Will I be understood if I say that this story is in one sense the tale of the end of the stories with which the screen, along with the novel (which art form film most nearly resembles), has heretofore beguiled us? I mean that our former modes of fiction—the love story, the romantic quest, the action epic—have lost their power of conviction because the world we experience has lost its own such power. The essence of Antonioni's art in these films therefore is to forge, in the face of our lost convictions and acceptances about the world—convictions and acceptances upon which we had based our narrative arts—a new, mercilessly stripped "telling" of our condition of bereftness and chill, one that refuses to find "endings" or resolutions or definitive images that reassure us.

I think this stripped, mercilessly bare quality of Antonioni's films is what was then so new, and what is still so marvelous, about them. The island criss-crossed a hundred times with nothing come upon; the conversations that fall into voids; Jeanne Moreau's head and shoulders traveling, microscopically, along the angle of a building in *La notte*; unfilled or unoccupied distances; a bisected figure gazing from the corner of an immense window in *L'avventura*: all adding up to anomie, anguish, abandonment, diminishment, the anticipated event or sighting that never occurs, just as Godot never comes. For Samuel Beckett and Antonioni are two artists who enforce our relinquishment of the answer, the solution, the arrival, two creators who disillusion us. The search for reality, and not reality as it appears to be, is thus Antonioni's subject; his discovery is that the real world is lying, is insubstantial, and even treacherous, a thoroughgoing accomplice of our lovelessness.

Lovelessness, and the tiny, sorrowing, infinitely vulnerable gestures we try to make to restore the possibility of love—these, too, are Antonioni's subjects; they, too, make up the new reality he has discovered. Both *L'avventura* and *La notte* end in scenes of almost unbearably painful acceptance; of our having to be what we are, of there being no fiction that will exonerate or console us, no *ending*. Monica Vitti places her hand on Gabriele Ferzetti's head in the most delicate, dry-eyed, yet anguished acceptance of what they are: frail, faithless, destined to defeat. The victory is in the recognition of this. And the couple of *La notte*, writhing carnally in the dust on the rich man's lawn, struggle ferociously toward truth or rather toward truthfulness. They do not love; they may love again; they have at least begun by acknowledging their suffering and despair.

Clearly, *L'avventura* and *La notte* are movies without a traditional subject. (We can only think they are "about" the despair of the idle rich or our ill-fated quest for pleasure if we are intent on making old anecdotes out of new essences.) Yet they are about nothing we could have known with-out them, nothing to which we had already attached meanings or sur-veyed in other ways. They are, without being abstract, about nothing *in particular*, being instead, like most paintings of their period, self-contained and absolute, an action and not the description of an action. To para-phrase Beckett on the fiction of James Joyce, *L'avventura* and *La notte* are films *of* something, not "about" something.

They are part of that next step in our feelings that true art is con-tinually eliciting and recording. We had been taking that step for a long time, most clearly in painting but also in music, in certain areas of fiction, in antitheater or metatheater (of the kind, still scarce, which through new parodic languages, breaks with everything moribund or dead in our the-ater). It might be described as accession through reduction, the coming into truer forms through the cutting away of created encumbrances: all the replicas we have made of ourselves; all the misleading, because logical or only psychological, narratives; the whole apparatus of reflected wis-dom, inherited sensations, received ideas, reiterated clichés. For, as the leading woman says in *L'avventura*: "Things are not like that . . . every-thing has become so terribly simple."

Abstraction, reduction, irony, and parody are all forms of aggression against the traditional subject, against what art is supposed to treat. They are, much more than direct violence, our most effective means of liber-ating our experience, releasing those unnamed emotions and perceptions that have been blockaded by everything we have been taught to see and hear and feel. What continues to excite me about these movies by Antonioni is the sense they communicate, to one degree or another, of extending the areas of freedom—troubled freedom because a price is paid when you are always half engaged in repudiating your erstwhile captors—that we have gained from the other arts.

I would like to go back now to what I said earlier about film's resemblance to the novel. It ought not to be necessary also to say that this resemblance is of an intellectual and aesthetic kind and not a physical, merely formal, one. Movies are obviously not filmed literary statements but creations obeying their own principles and accomplishing their own special, visual effectiveness. In this way, Antonioni's movies, like other great works of film art, can be seen as sharing in the flexibility and potential subtlety of imaginative prose, which stems from the very ab-stractness of words, their not being "real" objects—just as film, being made of reflections cast on a screen, is not "real" either.

Every remark I have made about Antonioni's world of alienation and disjunction is thus exemplified not merely by what his characters do and say but by the images they compose and that are composed as the context for their cinematic existence. I think now of the revelers eddying like dry leaves across the rich man's lawn in *L'avventura*; the rain on the car window making a screen between the woman and her potential lover in *La notte*; the final, fifty-eight-shot montage in *L'eclisse* from which not only the young couple but all human contact has been banished; the camera tracking slowly around the woman's room in *Red Desert*, painstakingly exhibiting every domestic object in its absolute separateness from, and indifference to, her feelings; and last, the magnificent seven-minute take at the end of *The Passenger* (1975) that proceeds, in a 360-degree pan, out of the reporter Locke's hotel room, through a wrought-iron grill on to a dusty Spanish plaza, then finally returns to the room where Locke now lies dead. All these images are of a world newly forced to yield up its true face, to *look like* what we have secretly felt it to be.

"The fundamental problem of the cinema is how to express thought," the great critic and fountainhead of the French New Wave, Alexandre Astruc, wrote sixty years ago in *L'Écran Français* (30 March 1948). *L'avventura* and *La notte* (along with *L'eclisse* and two or three other Antonioni films) are movies in which thought—indissolubly fused with image, lying behind it, selecting it, and justifying it—produces an art worthy of ranking with any other. Indeed, I do not think it too much to say that the movies, having come into their maturity at this time—the middle of the twentieth century—have been giving us, ever since, more (or more useful) freedom than any other form. In Antonioni's own day, that freedom ranged from the narrowest and most preliminary liberation as bestowed by British movies such as *Room at the Top* (1959), *Saturday Night and Sunday Morning* (1960), and *A Taste of Honey* (1961), with their mostly traditional procedures but temperamental and thematic rebelliousness, to the far more solid and revolutionary, because more purely cinematic, achievements of *L'avventura* and *La notte*.

In between were the films of the Frenchmen Jean-Luc Godard and François Truffaut, with their neoexistential adventures proceeding by nonmotivated or arbitrary acts, the camera jiggling or running along at eye level and sometimes freezing fast in not entirely successful visual implementation. There was Alain Resnais, who seemed to be doing with time what Antonioni was doing with space, if such a distinction is admissible in a medium that is preeminently the fuser of the temporal and the spatial. (The reality of his *Last Year at Marienbad* [1961] is that of time, of memory and anticipation, in which past, present, and future are mixed, the images from each realm advancing and retreating, fading, reemerging, repeating, coalescing, and finally coming to exist simultaneously— the way the mind actually but unavowedly contains them.) And then there was Bergman, with his new, not wholly convincing legends and his preachy

Director Michelangelo Antonioni, 1975, with footage from *The Passenger*.
(Courtesy MGM/Photofest)

discontent, but also his powerful and clean images—or isolations—of
(im)mortality in a context of abrasive psychology, harsh topography, and
inclement weather. Let us not forget Federico Fellini, either, whose *La
dolce vita* may have been vastly overrated but some of whose earlier films—
particularly *I vitelloni* (1953) and *La strada* (1954)—were full of lucid,
plangent vision, and whose later *8½* (1963) combined the plangent with
something close to the hallucinogenic.

In the entire range of Antonioni's calculated "boredom" and refusal
of clear resolution, then—as of Godard's antinovelistic, anti-illusionary,
anticulinary devices; Resnais's solicitation of time as something unprogres-
sive and nonconsecutive; and Bresson's extreme leanness of image and
austerity of incident—we see being fought this tendency of narrative to
turn into an extended anecdote that serves either to legitimate or mytholo-
gize actuality and thus to turn it into nothing more than an illustration of
what we have already undergone, surmised, or wished for. That Antonioni,

like other filmmakers who try to present not new stories but new relationships between consciousness and reality, was expected to do otherwise was the basis not only of complaint against ostensible failures of his like *L'avventura* and *L'eclisse* but also of extreme outcry (particularly in American film circles) against the apparently more "mod," more mainstream *Blow-Up* (1966)—even among many of Antonioni's erstwhile supporters.

But in *Blow-Up* Antonioni was not attempting a portrait of London, swinging or otherwise, so the accusation at the time, "That's not what it's like," was especially obtuse. If anything, Antonioni's stranger's eye on London provided him with the perspective of strategic naïveté, the freedom from any complacent conviction of knowledge, the antisophistication that he needed to be able to set about his real business. (And Antonioni, like any artist, was in need of unsophistication on the level of the human and the social, for one creates in order to find out, not to exemplify what one already knows.) This was precisely to deal with the relationship between what we think the world is like—our ideas derived mainly from what others have thought it is like and, especially today, from *publicized* ideas about it—and what the imagination together with all other perceptive powers is compelled to decide.

Blow-Up is really "about" something society, as society, cannot know in regard to itself: the fact of life caught between complacent knowledge and radical doubt, passion and enervation, reality and illusion. Its subject is not London or sexual mores or ennui among the chic, but the way in which the imagination attends to such things. The film's central sequence—the fashion photographer Thomas's "discovery" of a murder concealed in the fine grain of one of his photographs—conveys the theme concisely. It is only by blowing up tiny sections of the picture that this new reality, of death, can be revealed; that is, only by adapting an alternative perspective can we get a different sense out of what we perceive. All of Antonioni's movies are similarly new forms of perception about, and artifacts of, our continuing dilemmas and contradictions and perplexities, not representations of them. That is why I still remember my first experience of such a picture, have gone back to it here, and will continue to revisit it, like my experiences of other Antonioni films—in movie theaters as well as in the movie theater, or mind screen, of my imagination.

Postscript

In 1985 Michelangelo Antonioni had a stroke that paralyzed his right side and his power of speech. Nonetheless, in 1995 he made *Beyond the Clouds*, a four-part work, one part of which had substance, and all of which was couched in the cinematic style I describe above. Reports and photos told us how he managed to command the shooting despite his handicaps. Then Antonioni presented another short film, *The Dangerous Thread of Things*, which is also the title of three brief prose pieces from his book called *That Bowling Alley on the Tiber*. The pieces were adapted for the screen by Tonino Guerra, Antonioni's collaborator since *L'avventura*, and the resulting filmic piece is one of a trio of shorts titled *Eros*. Unfortunately, *The Dangerous Thread of Things*—made in 2004 when Antonioni was ninety-two—has no substance and is only faintly reminiscent of this past master's style. (The other two short films in *Eros* are *The Hand*, by Wong Kar-Wai, and *Equilibrium*, by Steven Soderbergh, and *Eros* is better for what they contribute than for Antonioni's work.)

Here is a summary of the action in *The Dangerous Thread of Things*. A young husband and wife who live on the Tuscan coast are no longer close in feeling. When she sunbathes topless, he disregards her—somewhat deliberately. Later they drive off and stop at a waterfall where two naked girls are bathing. Next they go to a restaurant where the husband notices an attractive girl, who lives in an ancient tower near his house, riding by on her horse. The next day he visits the tower, meets the girl, and makes love with her. Months pass. Then one day, while the husband is away in Paris, the wife takes a walk on the beach, takes off her clothes, dances in the sea, and lies down. The girl from the tower happens to come along, strips, dances in the sea, and, nude, meets the nude wife.

This is a scenario out of which symbolic meaning might be inferred or on which it could be imposed. Throughout the film we long for the chance to do either, but Antonioni does not provide it. For a viewer like me, who otherwise could not be more sympathetic, the picture is merely studied and affected, without resonance, noteworthy only for the fact that, like some other aging male directors, Antonioni fills the screen with female nudity.

The disparity between this piece and his epoch-making films treated in this chapter, together with Antonioni's present physical condition, provokes a suspicion. His passion for his work—he has often said that, for him, to live is to film—is perhaps being cosseted by some who want another piece by Antonioni for his name's sake alone. What makes this new picture even more discomfiting is that there are two Antonioni features, *The Oberwald Mystery* (1980) and *Identification of a Woman* (1982), which have never been released in the United States. Neither is a major work in his career, but either of them is a feast compared with this latest scrap and would have been more welcome, all the more so because a sort of theme song in *Eros* is morbidly called "Michelangelo Antonioni," as if in telling homage to an old master who has already passed (which he did in 2007, after this postscript was written).

An Interview with
Michelangelo Antonioni

The following interview took place in June 1978 at the Plaza Hotel in New York City, shortly before Antonioni was to return to Italy to begin shooting *The Oberwald Mystery*.

BERT CARDULLO: How do you like New York, Signor Antonioni?

MICHELANGELO ANTONIONI: Well, I have been here a number of times, but still, I have a sense of unreality whenver I am in this city. It's as though I'm living in a film. I have never made a movie in New York, but I am ready to do so the day the screen becomes vertical.

BC: I know that you are going to return to Italy soon to begin shooting *Il mistero di Oberwald* (*The Oberwald Mystery*), so, aside from a few general questions, I'd like to concentrate today both on this upcoming work and on the three feature films you made prior to it, all of them outside your own native country: *The Passenger*, *Zabriskie Point*, and *Blow-Up*. The last film you made in Italy was *Red Desert*, right?

MA: Yes, that is correct. And after three films abroad, I have to say, I feel rootless. I don't think it is useful to stay out of your own country for so long. I need to shoot a film in Italy, to which I now feel I can go back and not repeat myself. I need to hear Italian. I'm fed up with hearing only English. Most people are blind in their own country; they can't see at all. What does a Roman know of Rome? Only his own itinerary. But I am trained to *look*, to use my cultural baggage and education in a creative way—not to speak English.

BC: Your English isn't so bad.

81

MA: You miss my point. As Brecht used to say about his English, "I say what I can say, not what I want to say." I have to complicate my thoughts in a foreign language; I have to change my nature and think in American or British terms. It must be something similar for an actor who has to play many parts and who therefore has to change many times.

In any event, whatever language I am using, I am not a man of words. A film director is in some way a man of action even if this action is intellectual. Words are symbols, whereas images are what they are. And I may be someone who is successful—I don't know, perhaps—with something to show, not something to say. I can't find the right words; I'm not a writer, and I'm not a speaker, either.

BC: Do you do a lot of research before you start shooting a picture?

MA: Yes. If I didn't do so much research for my films, my work would then be a lie. I must always start from more or less scientifically proven data. The biggest danger and temptation of cinema is the boundless possibility it gives movie directors to lie.

BC: When did you first put your eye behind a camera?

MA: "When" is not so important, but what happened at that moment was. The first time I got behind a camera was in a lunatic asylum. I had decided with a group of friends to do a documentary film on mad people. We positioned the camera, got the lamps ready, and disposed the patients around the room. The insane obeyed us with complete abandon, trying very hard not to make mistakes. I was very moved by their behavior, and things were going fine. Finally, I was able to give the order to turn on the lights. And in one second, the room was flooded with light . . .

I have never seen again, on any actor's face, such an expression of fear, such total panic. For a very brief moment, the patients remained motionless, as if petrified. That lasted literally only a few seconds, followed by a scene really hard to describe. The men and women started having convulsions, then they screamed and rolled on the floor. In one instant, the room turned into a hellish pit. All the mad people were trying to escape from light as if they had been attacked by some prehistoric monster.

We all stood there, completely stunned. The cameraman didn't even think to stop the camera. Finally, the doctor shouted, "Stop. Cut off the lights!" Then, when the room was dark and silent again, we saw piles of corpses, slightly shaking as if they were going through their final death throes. I have never forgotten that scene, and it is one of the reasons I keep making films.

BC: Research aside, how mentally prepared are you when you arrive on a set to shoot?

MA: Just as an actor, in my view, must arrive on the set in a state of mental virginity, so, too, must I. I force myself not to overintellectualize, and I force myself never to think the night before of the scene I'll be shooting the next morning. I have a lot of confusion in my head, a real mess—lots of thoughts, lots of ideas, one of which cancels out the other. That's why I can't think about what I'm doing. I just do it.

Once on the set, I always spend a half hour alone to let the mood of the set, as well as its lighting, prevail. Then the actors arrive. I look at them. How are they? How do they seem to feel? I ask for rehearsals— a couple, no more—and then shooting starts. It's while I'm shooting that everything, so to speak, becomes real. After a shot is finished, I frequently continue to shoot the actors, who don't know that I am doing this. The aftereffects of an emotional scene, it had occurred to me, might have meaning, too, both for the actor and for the psychological progression of his character. Once shooting really stops, sometimes it takes me fifteen minutes of complete silence and solitude to prepare for the next scene. What I still cannot do, however, is concentrate when I feel the eyes of a complete stranger on me, because a stranger always interests me. I want to ask him questions.

BC: Could you say something about your work with actors, about how you work with them?

MA: An actor does not have to understand; he has to *be*. Somebody will object that in order to be, you have to understand. I don't think so. If that were so, the most intelligent actor would also be the best. In reality it is quite otherwise, indeed the complete contrary. It was so from Duse to Garbo. Intelligence is a brake on an actor, and to use it is equivalent to putting on the brakes. For me the secret is this: to work, not with psychology, but with imagination. It is no use trying to turn it on automatically. Our imagination has no switches which fingers can flick when we wish.

In the cinema, an actor must make the effort to follow what the director tells him as a dog does his master. If you change your direction and take a different street from usual, your dog will raise his head and look at you in surprise, but at a signal he will come along behind you. The method that I prefer to use is to provoke certain results through a "secret process": to stimulate the actor by playing on those chords of his being which he himself doesn't, perhaps, know. One must excite his instincts, *not* his brain. One mustn't justify but rather illuminate.

BC: Giovanni Fusco, who composed the music for *L'avventura* and *Red Desert*, among other films of yours, has complained of the difficulty of working with you. He once said, "The first rule for any musician who intends to collaborate with Antonioni is to forget that he is a musician." What, then, is your view on the use of music in films, since directors sometimes use it to buttress a weak or at least less than scintillating performance?

MA: Even though I have studied music ever since I was a boy, every time I have music in films it means a terrible sacrifice for me. In my opinion, the image is not enriched but rather is interrupted, even, I'd dare to say, vulgarized. The image loses its purity. If I could, if a producer would let me, I'd assemble a soundtrack with only natural noises, in which noise itself would be the music. And I'd get a conductor to orchestrate the sounds for me.

BC: But in *Blow-Up*, for the first time, music played a significant role in the story. And the same was true of *Zabriskie Point*.

MA: The rock music you're referring to was natural at the time. It was a kind of new language for young people. But even in these instances I was hesitant, suspicious, because rock music in the end—and especially in America—has less to do with rebellion or even revolution than big business.

BC: Where do you get your ideas for films?

MA: How can I say it? It's one of my failings that everything I read or see gives me an idea for a film. Fortunately, I can't do them all. If I could, maybe they would all be very bad. One thing I can say: Until I edit a film of mine, I have no idea myself what it will be about. And perhaps not even then. Perhaps it will only be the reflection of a mood; perhaps the film will have no plot at all in the conventional sense. I depart from my shooting script constantly, so it's pointless beforehand to release a synopsis of the film's action or to discuss its meaning. In any case, my scripts are not formal screenplays but rather dialogue for the actors and a series of notes to the director—myself. When shooting begins, there is invariably a great degree of change. I may film scenes I had no intention of filming, for example, since things suggest themselves on location, and you improvise. Only in the cutting room, when I take the film and start to put it together—only then do I begin to get an idea of what it is all about.

Usually I write the original stories of my films myself, but I never start out with an idea that afterwards turns into a story. Most of the stories which go through my hands in search of form are simply germs which have been breathed in as from the air. If, when the film is finished, it turns out to be saying something, it has happened *a posteriori*, and that is natural enough. I am a human being, and I am not lacking in perceptions about the people and affairs of this world. If I make the film in all sincerity, then these perceptions will inevitably reveal themselves. However, it is the story which fascinates me most; the images are the medium through which a story can be understood. To be a lover of form for me means being a lover of substance.

BC: Are you ever satisfied with any of your films?

MA: Sometimes I think *L'eclisse* is my best work. Other times I like *L'avventura* better. The other day I screened *La notte* again and thought it was pretty good. But I don't think *Blow-Up* is one of my best pictures, and I don't know why. I guess I am never really satisfied; I amuse myself by experimenting. Even though my experience is deeper now, and technically I am more mature—everything I have to say comes out fluently— I'm not happy after I complete a film. I'm not even happy while I'm shooting it. Again, I don't know why. Still, I don't look back, or at least I try not to. These are the best years because they are the only years. You can't afford to look back; you have to make the best of the present, whatever it may send your way—and however, finally, you may respond.

BC: You clearly respond to urban landscapes in your cinema.

MA: True, but in *Zabriskie Point*, for example, there were two locations: Los Angeles and the desert, the desert and the city. In the United States people can go into the desert. In Southern California, it is only an hour or two away by car. Yet it is so different. And it is nothing, an enormous area of nothing. We do not have spaces like that in Europe. Perhaps the existence of such great spaces so close to the city says something to me about America. You see, this is how I work: putting things together and seeing what the result is. I try to compress my feelings about a subject.

I have to say, though, that I love cities above all. I have never felt salvation in nature. An urban landscape with its masses of concrete and steel, and even of flowers and grass, which repeat themselves indefinitely— the repetition makes me dizzy; and it is exactly this repetition that can make reality so fleeting at times, and the thinking, feeling, aware man consequently so insecure. And such a cityscape—I like the word—takes away all the meaning of nature, which becomes like a word you repeat too often. The static immobility of nature is what really scares me. Take a tree: Nothing weighs heavier on me than an old tree. Look at it: It goes on aging for centuries without having ever really lived, without ever changing. The Empire State Building doesn't change, either, but the people around it are changing all the time. An urban landscape, you see, is in a state of perpetual transformation. And when I am far away from the city, I feel I have left the world and detached myself from the struggle of life. What progress there is goes on in the cities, and I want to be present.

BC: Your films often deal with lonely or isolated characters in such a landscape.

MA: Yes, and I think that the theme of most of my films is loneliness. Often my characters are isolated, as you say; they are individuals looking for social institutions that will support them, for personal relationships that will absorb them. But most often they find little to sustain them. They are looking for a home, and "looking for a home," in a wider sense, could be said to be the subject of all my films. That said, I never think in terms of a conflict between the solitary individual and the masses. I'm not a sociologist, and I never propound political theses. If I place a character against a landscape, however, there is naturally a relationship, and I would prefer that my meaning derive implicity from such a visual juxtaposition.

BC: You say that you never propound political theses in your films, and I agree with you. But you yourself obviously have political views, right?

MA: Yes and no. For example, I have a view of technology, and *Red Desert* was among the first films, if not the very first one, to deal directly with the destructive relationship between people and industrial technology in their environment. And other films of mine have dealt, if only indirectly, with the issue of technology and communication. In my view, technology doesn't help communication. It hinders it. The fact that you are forced to be a specialist to be successful: That in itself works against communication, because everyone is a specialist and knows little else. I don't see how you can communicate in a world of technological specialities. Technology forces people to adapt to it, rather than adapting itself to people.

But none of this means that I'm a Communist, which is how some critics describe me. It's just not so at all. My only political wish is to see the Italian bourgeoisie crushed. It is the curse of Italy, the worst such class in the entire world, the most hypocritical, the laziest, and the most cowardly. I hate it. And I speak with some authority: The experience that has been most important in making me the director I have become is that of my own middle-class background. It is that world which has contributed most to my predilection for certain themes, certain conflicts, certain emotional or psychological problems; and in that very general sense, my pictures are autobiographical. With an obstinacy that can only be called "pathetic," we persist in our allegiance to an aging morality, to outworn myths, to ancient conventions, and the bourgeoisie is the reason why.

Once there was what I would call the "Ptolemaic fullness" of the individual in a God-centered world; then, after Copernicus, Renaissance man found himself thrown into an unfamiliar universe, even if at first its unfamiliarity was not acknowledged. We are still there, with all our fears and hesitations, loaded down with baggage and pushed by forces that condition our situation without helping it, that get in our way without offering a solution—all courtesy of the puniness of the middle class.

Let me end here by putting the matter of my, or my films', politics another way: I would say that my films are political, but they are not about politics. They are political in their approach; that is, they are made from a definite point of view. And they certainly may be political in the effect they have on people.

BC: Of the great film directors now at work, you are arguably the most contemporary. In expressing your chief thematic preoccupation—modern man's often crushing feeling of alienation—you have evoked a profound sense of recognition in a number of your films, most notably *L'avventura*, *Blow-Up*, and *The Passenger*. Moreover, as you youself have noted, you communicate as much as possible through images rather than through words—stark images of desolation and despair that, paradoxically, could scarcely be more dazzlingly beautiful. You have described your art as "narrating with images," in contrast to traditional literary cinema's focus on language, as being concerned with nonverbal communication and with abstracted emotions. And some commentators have even called your films "interior realism," because, as you well know, you are concerned more with the inner lives of your characters than with worldly or physical action.

Yet, as you also know, many critics and viewers find your work pretentious, boring, and needlessly perplexing. They say that your films are intentionally ambiguous, so much so that the motivations of your characters become obscure and even inexplicable. For instance, David Locke's casual abandonment in *The Passenger* of his own identity in order to take on the identity of a man whom he knows virtually nothing about, but whom he chances remarkably to resemble. What is your response to this negative perception of your films?

MA: My films are mirrors of life, and life itself is ambiguous. Indeed, if life were not ambiguous, if everything in life were unmysterious and fully explained, we would all be miserable to the point of wanting to die. In any event, I find that Americans—who make up the preponderance of the critical spectators you are talking about—take films too literally. They are forever trying to puzzle out "the story" and to find hidden meanings where there are perhaps none. For them, a film must be entirely rational, without unexplained mysteries. But Europeans, on the other hand, look upon my films as I intend them to be looked upon, as works of visual art, to be reacted to as one reacts to a painting, subjectively rather than objectively. For Europeans, "the story" is of secondary importance, and they are not bothered by what you have described as "ambiguity."

BC: Let me follow up with an additional criticism made of your films: that they are so slow-paced and, for the most part, without dramatic incident—filled with long stillnesses and rambling, seemingly pointless conversations. Any comment?

MA: Again, my films mirror life, and life is lived mainly from day to day without unusual incident, without melodrama, without moments of bombast and high emotion. More than anything, I hate melodrama, as in the films of a director like Luchino Visconti. Melodrama is the easiest thing in the world to do—the scene of the drunken whore or the brutal, shouting father—and it is the cheapest thing to do, too. And so not worth doing. Far more difficult, more complicated, and thus more artistically challenging is to make a film that reflects the true rhythms of life. Of course, cinema cannot create an exact portrait of reality. The best it can hope to do is create a personal reality. I began, you know, as one of the first exponents of neorealism, but by concentrating on the internals of character and psychology I do not think that I deserted the movement. Instead, I pointed the way to extending its boundaries. Unlike early neorealist filmmakers, I am not trying to show reality. I am attempting to re-create realism. In fact, while I mean in no way to suggest that we are comparable artists, you must think when looking at my films of Proust's novel *A Remembrance of Things Past*—I like the literal translation of the French title better, *In Search of Lost Time*—rather than of other films. That is, my films are indeed "slow-paced" and "without dramatic incident," but in the same way as Proust's stellar fiction is.

BC: You mentioned Visconti in your last response, and I think it would be helpful to contrast your work with his and also with Fellini's.

MA: Let me do so by speaking of three films: *L'avventura*, Visconti's *Rocco and His Brothers*, and Fellini's *La dolce vita*. All three films deal with a certain condition of society today. But while in *La dolce vita* and *Rocco* the analysis is directed towards the actions of the characters, in *L'avventura* the emphasis is on the inner world of the individual, particularly in relation to that individual's feelings. There is also a fundamental difference of style among these films. While Visconti tends to dramatize his material to a maximum degree, and Fellini carries his dramatic tension to the extreme in visual terms, my intention is the opposite: I try to remove the external drama from my characters and create a situation in which the conflict remains inside. Both *La dolce vita* and *Rocco* are "outer" dramas in this sense, while *L'avventura* is an interior narrative.

BC: Over the years, you have been very outspoken on the subject of love. I remember that, when *Blow-Up* was released, you had a few things to say about the subject.

MA: Yes, the very quality of the emotion has changed. Indeed, we live in a world where nothing is stable anymore. Even physics has become metaphysical. The young people among whom *Blow-Up* is situated live in a world that has finally broken down all barriers between one individual and another. Especially now, you can talk with anyone about anything. If you like to smoke marijuana, you can say so without fear. If a girl likes sex, she is not afraid to admit it. *Blow-Up*'s generation and the generations to follow have sought a certain aimless freedom from restrictions of all kinds. And, to be sure, the pursuit of such freedom can give man his most exciting moments. But once it is achieved, once all discipline is discarded, then you have decadence—and decadence without any sign of change in sight.

Sexual freedom also means freedom from feelings, and that means I don't know whether young people can ever love again the way my generation loved. They must suffer, I guess, but I'm sure they suffer for reasons very different from those of people my age—and never romantic ones. They have taken leave of all norms, all traditions, and there is a price to pay for that. Eroticism, you see, is the most obvious symptom of an emotional sickness. There would not be this eroticism if Eros were still in good health. And by good health, I mean perfectly in harmony with the measure and condition of man.

Let me give an example of the weakness or paleness of Eros, or love, from the time of *Blow-Up*, which is when I began to notice the decadence of this emotion. When the Soviet Cosmonaut Titov came back from his flight among the stars, he was asked by the press whether from the heights he had reached he'd once thought about his wife. "No," said Titov quietly, before returning to live with her.

BC: Some critics faulted you less for your depiction of the quality or nature of love in *Blow-Up* than for your embroidering the set design, if you will.

MA: Yes, when I was making *Blow-Up*, there was a lot of discussion about the fact that I had a road and a building painted. Antonioni paints the grass, people said. To some degree, all directors paint and arrange or change things on a location, and it amused me that so much was made of it in my case. I did it in *Red Desert*, too, and in *Zabriskie Point* I did some set painting again: an airport runway, some hangars, and some other things. And I put up some billboards on the front lawns of the houses across the street from the airport. When I do something like this, it is not so much to make the scene more attractive visually—it is to compress. I can only show so much. In *Blow-Up* there were only so many scenes, and yet there were many things I wanted to show. So by painting a house or a road, I was able to compress, to show more in fewer shots.

BC: *Blow-Up*, one could say, was about the feel of London in the 1960s, just as your earlier trilogy—consisting of *L'avventura*, *La notte*, and *L'eclisse*—had examined the state of Italian society in the late 1950s. Similarly, was *Zabriskie Point* about the condition of American society around 1969 or 1970?

MA: How could it not have been, when America—the location of this film—was constantly changing or transforming at the time, even physically, and therefore demanded that such change be reflected on the screen?

BC: Is there a certain visual quality that represents America in your eyes, and were you trying to express that in *Zabriskie Point*?

MA: No. Not in the way I had in the past, as with *Red Desert* and *L'eclisse*. The only place where I tried to have the landscape play an equal role to that of the characters was in Death Valley, especially around Zabriskie Point. In that portion of the film I needed to surround the characters with a lunar-type landscape, to suggest solitude. Otherwise, I was not using American architecture symbolically in this film.

BC: What do you think of revolutionary or at least experimental theater of the kind once represented in America by the Living Theater and the Open Theater? You were obviously once interested in it, since you chose Sam Shepard to help with the script of *Zabriskie Point*.

MA: I liked the experiment of the Living Theater, but I was never able to see all of their work. I feel much closer to the work of the Open Theater. It and Joe Chaikin are part of the cast of *Zabriskie Point*, you will recall. They didn't use the word; they used the *sound* of the word. Of course, I don't agree with those old-fashioned critics who say that theater is the word, that it is essentially or primarily verbal. That's ridiculous. And one of the ways in which the Open Theater, and the Living Theater, deemphasized the word was by always attempting to involve the audience in the *experience* of the action and not the *idea* of the drama. They even sold tickets to their rehearsals, less to see the "show" than to experience the rehearsal process.

BC. You made *Zabriskie Point* for MGM but it is obviously an Antonioni film, not a Hollywood product.

MA: Yes, I made *Zabriskie Point* in the United States, but, as you suggest, my way of working was, and remains, diametrically opposed to the way things are done in that enormous bureaucratic machine known as Hollywood. Of course, I'm not talking just about opposite working methods, but about an opposite approach to life itself, a refusal to accept embalmed ideas and clichés, affectation and imitation.

It was in 1967 that I started work on *Zabriskie Point*, when I went across the United States and saw a good many things. Then I went back to Rome and looked over my notes and gradually decided to do a film about two young Americans. In August, just before we were going to begin shooting, I went to Chicago for the Democratic national convention. What I saw there—the behavior of the police, the spirit of the young people—impressed me as deeply as anything else I had seen in America. To some degree, *Zabriskie Point* was influenced by what happened in the streets of Chicago. Not directly, you understand; the film is not about Chicago, or the politics of the convention—inside or outside. But my ideas about young Americans were shaped by what happened in Chicago, and I hope that somehow those ideas were expressed in the film.

BC: Filmmakers and other creative people often go through life as you did in Chicago: looking, recording, and interpreting, rather than participating.

MA: That's true, and the film I made after *Zabriskie Point*—*The Passenger*—deals in part with this very theme. In it a journalist stops being an onlooker and becomes a doer, even though he isn't sure what he is doing. I myself was a kind of onlooker when I accepted the assignment of directing *The Passenger*. It is the first time that I agreed to make a film from someone else's script entirely—Mark Peploe's in this case—so I got involved with this project in a cool, detached way. I had to use my brain at first, not my instinct, though eventually my instinct took over, and I had to change the script somewhat according to my own nature.

BC: Jack Nicholson played David Locke in *The Passenger*, and, as you well know—and I guess you knew at the time—this is not the kind of role he normally performs.

MA: No, you are right, but the thing I discovered in Jack was that he was very different from what I had expected. In some way he was humble with me—and he's not in life particularly. He is very intelligent. He immediately finds a way to deal with someone.

He had to do everything in a most natural way in *The Passenger*. I didn't give him any opportunities to do something his way. This journalist, Locke, was not an extraordinary man. This was a most difficult character to play, for Jack somehow had to find a way not to do anything. He usually acts more, and here everything was almost static.

BC: So, to continue the metaphor of the onlooker versus the insider or initiator, Nicholson had to play Locke from the outside in, instead of the way an American actor—particularly one of Nicholson's magnetism—usually plays a character: from the inside out.

MA: Yes, I think that is a fair assessment. You know at the time of *The Passenger*'s release, a lot of people thought that, though breathtaking to look at, the film didn't seem, upon reflection, to make sense. What, they wondered, had been the meaning of Locke's change of identity, of his travels, and of his ultimate death? But the theme of this film is not so hard to determine: I was trying to investigate the myth of objectivity, the idea that looking at something from the outside is better than looking at it from the inside. As an onlooker, or someone maintaining that pose in his life as in his work, David Locke was frustrated: His marriage was a failure; he had failed in his relationship with his adopted child; and he wasn't as committed to his job as he would have liked to be. Hence he sought to make a change—and a drastic one at that.

BC: Is the camera itself an outsider at the end, traveling in circles?

MA: You could put it that way. I didn't want to show the actual killing of Locke, which is how it's usually done in suspense melodramas. I didn't want to film the death of a man, Locke, who, having assumed the identity of a dead man, was in a sense already dead himself—doubly so, as a matter of fact. So I used the Westcam—a camera mounted in a ball and stabilized with gyroscopes, which can shoot 360-degree pans when further stabilized from a crane—to shoot a seven-minute take that proceeds out of Locke's room, through a wrought-iron grill onto a dusty Spanish plaza, and then finally returns to the room where Locke now lies dead. The "objective" camera had its back turned, you could say, while inside his hot, airless hotel room Locke was murdered for being someone he wasn't or for not being who he really was—a subjective, ambiguous moment like life itself.

BC: Your upcoming picture will offer you several firsts with which to end the 1970s, or begin the 1980s, won't it?

MA: Yes, in addition to my working in Italy for the first time since 1963, *The Oberwald Mystery* will also be the first time I have worked with Monica Vitti since I made *Red Desert* in the same year. Above all, it will be the first time I have worked with television cameras and with magnetic tape that will later have to be transferred to film.

BC: This is your first film adapted from a play as well, right?

MA: Yes, I adapted the screenplay from Cocteau's *Two-Headed Eagle*, which was a romantic vehicle for Edwige Feuillère and Jean Marais, first on stage and then on the screen. But I have to say that this is one of the worst things Cocteau ever did for the screen.

BC: Why Cocteau's play in particular?

MA: I thought of *The Two-Headed Eagle*, not because it was a work that appealed to me particularly but because it seemed as good a vehicle as any for trying out television cameras, which for years I had wanted to do. In addition, the play offered me a chance for intellectual noncommitment. It is a novelettish story, this tale of an anarchist who infiltrates the queen's castle and ends by killing her for love rather than ideology. Of course I don't care a damn about this queen and the anarchist. Somebody will perhaps enjoy reading some contemporary significance into it, connections with the terrorist Red Brigades and all that. However, I won't try to camp it up, which is something that doesn't come naturally to me. I'll try to be neutral. If the film becomes camp it will be because the subject matter is what it is. One cannot achieve miracles with the camera if you are bound to a text like this. I don't think anybody's capable of miracles these days, not even the Almighty.

BC: How will Miss Vitti adapt to a romantic tale like this?

MA: The part is very declamatory, very theatrical. And Monica comes from the theater, you know. I myself am not used to big set-speeches in my films, but with this play it's difficult to avoid them.

BC: So, in the end, the television cameras are what interested you most in this project? How different do you think shooting will be from what you are used to?

MA: Well, of course I will have to take into account the fact that the format for the two screens is different. Close-ups on television's square screen require different compositions from the cinema screen. Consequently, I will often compose the image in two different ways for the same scene. An example is a scene where the anarchist whips a tablecloth off a table, and all the objects fall to the floor. For the cinema, I would compose the frame with the female figure in the background, the man in the center, and the objects in the foreground. For television, I will lose either the female figure or half the objects on the floor I want in the shot, so I'll have to start the shot on the objects and pan up to take in the characters. You are limited by space, by the presence of other cameras, and by the wall behind you. Where the operation becomes interesting is in the use of color. Certainly it can change everything for you, even the faces of the actors. The subtle use of different shades of light and dark is possible, but it's a complicated technical process on TV. What is fascinating about it is that you can make corrections afterwards, even violent ones.

BC: Are there technical problems in transferring the magnetic tape to film?

MA: Yes, it isn't at all easy. In Italy it's impossible. I've decided to have it done in California. I'm not completely satisfied with what they can do there, but I'll go over myself and personally supervise the printing.

BC: It'll be seen first on television?

MA: Yes, it was made for Rete 2, the second channel, for which the Taviani brothers' *Padre Padrone* was also made. I should add that I don't pretend that I will resolve all the problems of the relationship between cinema and television. Don't expect anything particularly revolutionary in terms of technique. Probably the differences between the cinema and television, except in the case of obvious effects, will not be discernible.

You will find close-ups according to TV and close-ups according to the cinema. The novelty consists only in the fact that I will film both versions with electronic means yet shoot each one in a different way. With a script like this with so much dialogue, you are limited anyway in creative visual terms. It will remain a theatrical *pièce* even if my coadaptor Tonino Guerra and I try to make it as cinematic as possible.

BC: What would you have done, may I ask, had you not become a film director?

MA: If I had not become a director, I should have been an architect, I suspect, or maybe a painter. *Seeing* for a filmmaker is a necessity, even as it is for a painter. But while for the painter it is a matter of uncovering a static reality, or at most a rhythm that can be held in a single image, for a director the problem is to catch a reality which is never static, which is always moving towards or away from a moment of crystallization, and to present this movement, this arriving or moving on, as a new perception. Film is not sound—words, noises, music. Nor is it a picture—landscape, attitudes, gestures. Rather, it is an indivisible whole that extends over a temporal duration of its own, which determines its very being. The people around us, the places we visit, the events we witness—cinema is the spatial and temporal relations these all have with each other, the tension that is formed between them, and the meaning they possess for us today. And our effort as directors must be that of bringing all this data from our personal experience into accord with that of a more general experience, in the same way as individual time accords mysteriously with that of the cosmos. This is, I think, a special way of being in contact with reality. And it is also a special reality: that of film. To lose this contact, in the sense of losing this *way* of being in contact, can mean aesthetic—not to speak of human—sterility.

BC: Despite what you said earlier, since you write or cowrite the scripts of all your films, wouldn't you call yourself a writer as well as a director?

MA: No, I would not. To repeat myself, I feel that I am a person who has things he wants to show rather than things he wants to say. There are times when the two concepts coincide, and that is when we arrive at a work of art.

Making a film is not like writing a novel. Flaubert said that living was not his profession: His profession was writing. To make a film, however, *is* to live, or it is for me. My personal life is not interrupted during the shooting of a film. If anything, it becomes more intense. This sincerity in art, its being in one sense or another autobiographical, this pouring, as we say, of all our wine into one barrel, is surely nothing more than a way of taking part in life, of adding something that is good—in intent anyway—to our personal patrimony.

BC: In a world without film, what would you have made?

MA: Film.

Filmography of Feature Films

Story of a Love Affair, 1950
The Lady without Camelias, 1953
The Vanquished, 1953
"Suicide Attempt," 1953: episode of *Love in the City*
The Girlfriends, 1955
Il Grido, 1957
L'avventura, 1960
La notte, 1961
L'eclisse, 1962
Red Desert, 1964
"Preface: The Screen Test," 1965: episode of *The Three Faces*
Blow-Up, 1966
Zabriskie Point, 1970
The Passenger, 1975
The Oberwald Mystery, 1980
Identification of a Woman, 1982
Beyond the Clouds, 1995: codirected by Wim Wenders
"The Dangerous Thread of Things," 2004: episode of *Eros*

PART II

Franco-Finnish Relations

"Everyone Has His Reasons"

The Words and Films of Jean Renoir

JEAN RENOIR (1894–1979) COMPLETED his thirty-ninth motion picture, *The Little Theater of Jean Renoir*, in 1970. His first film, *The Water Girl*, was made in 1924 during the silent era. What comes between is perhaps the most impressive body of filmmaking ever directed by one person. But, before any consideration of the length or quality of Renoir's career, one must first consider the length of his life—of *his* life, not just anyone who happens to survive for eighty-four years—because it gave him a unique place that would affect his art.

Jean Renoir connected *La belle époque*—the period of his equally famous father, the painter Auguste—to the last quarter of the twentieth century. And this made him an exponent of a view of art that does not promise to be generated again, and that the director amply elucidated in any number of interviews he gave from 1939 to 1975: art as community, from which one can make every bitter expedition into blackness, as Renoir certainly did, but whose communal nature supports the expedition and strengthens its unsentimental insistence. Renoir, then, was the film world's first, and perhaps last, great embracer: a loving man who saw clearly what it was that he was loving.

No one knows better than Renoir did, for example, that films cost money and that it would be foolish to think that movies are produced for purely artistic reasons. The cinema, after all, is a business that has to sell, so considerations other than the aesthetic must come into play. Yet with outsized geniality Renoir found a way to coopt this condition, as he would tell Charles Thomas Samuels in *Encountering Directors* in 1972:

> Noncommercial films are rarely good. When you make a film just for yourself, the chances are high that it won't be a good one. . . .

99

Jean Renoir, circa 1960s. *(Courtesy of Photofest)*

> My ambition was to belong even more than I did to the world of commercial films. I believe in professionalism. I may sometimes have been stopped from making a film by a producer, but once shooting started, I was always free.

His only objection to producers, as he told me, is that they want to make what they call "good films," while he wants to "bring in a little piece of humanity."

Any director who could reach such a formulation in the face of experience (for instance, he could not raise the money for *Grand Illusion* [1937] until Jean Gabin agreed to be in it) has arranged a pleasant state of mind for himself—in fact, one through which that "little piece of humanity" is more likely to be permitted. Whatever the blandishments Renoir had to practice on others and himself, the results of his tactics lie before us: a body of films that range widely in subject (more widely than is generally assumed) and in quality (more widely than is generally assumed) but are in the main informed with a spirit broad and high, generous and compassionate, always humanistically concerned. Of course he repeats himself in interviews, and some pronouncements that he delivers from a throne to which others had elevated him are not free of airy affectation. Still, the current of Renoir's talk is so full, knowing, and free-flowing that perhaps his many interviews explain why his autobiography, *My Life and My Films* (1974), is meager: He had already said most of it before.

How, indeed, Renoir loved to talk! And that talk brings us riches of more than one kind. As when he speaks—to Jacques Rivette and François Truffaut in *Cahiers du cinéma* in 1954—about how he depends on collaboration as part of creation, how he folds it into his work:

> It's difficult to be sincere when you're all alone. Some people manage to do it, and they are gifted writers. I'm much less gifted, and I can only really find my own expression when I'm in contact with others. (my trans.)

This is a compact description of the perfect filmmaking temperament—one that, in Renoir's case, usually led to his collaboration on screenplays, for which he usually originated the ideas himself. Such a remark, like many others he made during his career, typifies an artist's purposely transparent practicality as proof of his profound suitability for his art, in which, like a judo expert, he would frequently be called upon to turn the pressures of brute filmmaking against themselves.

Here are other samples of this director's aesthetic wisdom, on subjects that recur throughout his recorded or transcribed conversations. On the technical case versus difficulty of filmmaking, he had this to say to Rui Nogueira and François Truchaud in *Sight and Sound* in 1968:

> When I started to make films we really had to know what a camera is; we had constantly to know what was going on. The technical dangers are bigger today because technique is perfect, and perfection is terribly dangerous in this world. . . . With the perfection of technique, all the solutions are brought to you, anything you want. . . . The danger is that of finding yourself confronted with answers which are not your own, answers you didn't have to work, to use your imagination, to find. Now that technique is perfect, you must become a great technician and then forget about technique. But first you must become a great technician.

Renoir spoke further on the deification—and subversion—of technique in a 1958 interview with André Bazin in *France-Observateur*:

In the cinema at present the camera has become a sort of god. You have a camera, fixed on its tripod or crane, which is just like a heathen altar; around it are the high priests—the director, cameraman, assistants—who bring victims before the camera, like burnt offerings, then cast them into the flames. And the camera is there, immobile—or almost so—and when it does move, it follows patterns ordained by the high priests, not by the victims.

Now . . . the camera finally has only one right—that of recording what happens. That's all. I don't want the movements of the actors to be determined by the camera, but the movements of the camera to be determined by the actor. . . . It is the cameraman's duty to make it possible for us to see the spectacle, rather than the duty of the spectacle to take place for the benefit of the camera. (my trans.)

Renoir acted in some of his "spectacles" and, truth be told, one negative feature common to all his pictures (aside from straggling or muddling storylines that lose themselves in a wealth of incident, as in the case of the adaptation of Gorky's play *The Lower Depths* [1936]) is the maddeningly erratic level of their acting. The director gave a possible reason for this unevenness of performance in a 1970 interview with James Blue at the American Film Institute:

I am very bad at casting. I am very bad, and sometimes to be bad helps me. In the way that I am attracted by a certain innocence. I am afraid of clichés, tricks. I am afraid of repeating situations we already saw on the screen. People with not too much skill sometimes help me to keep a kind of—I use a very ambitious word, excuse me—to keep a kind of innocence.

Flawed or not, the actor's expression distinguishes the style of a Renoir film. Structured improvisation, allowing the performers *to be themselves as others*, determines how the other elements of the picture will be created. For this is a man who believed that one discovers the content of a film only in the process of making it and who insisted that his completed pictures have often turned out to be something quite different from what he had originally intended, so much so that it is difficult to associate with Jean Renoir a particular narrative style or tone. Unlike Marcel Carné, who threw over anything he touched a fog of atmospheric fatalism (*Bizarre Bizarre* [1937] honorably excepted), unlike René Clair, whose *Italian Straw Hat* (1927) is discernible in *The Grand Maneuver* (1955), and whose *Le Million* (1931) occasionally breaks through the more ponderous *Beauties of the Night* (1952), Renoir speaks in many voices.

And the fact that his "voice," whatever it may be, is finally translated, interpreted, or expressed by the actor is made clear in the following analysis of realism, which the director supplied during his extended conversation with Charles Thomas Samuels:

> The word "neorealism" implies a certain style that may not have anything to do with reality. Consider an eighteenth-century play in the style of *commedia dell'arte* and then a modern play or picture about the railroad. In the latter, the actors will wear real grease on their faces, and their hands will be dirty; but if they are hams, they will be hams. If the actor who plays the eighteenth-century shepherd is good and has been helped by a good director, however, he will be convincing and real, even though he is not a shepherd and isn't even authentically dressed like one.

That theater actor, in an eighteenth-century play, would be helped not only by a good director (Renoir preferred the term *meneur du jeu*, which might be translated as "master of revels" and has fewer connotations of rigid control). This performer would also be helped by the theater itself, as Renoir explained to Louis Marcorelles in *Sight and Sound* in 1962:

> In the theatre there is greater freedom because there is discipline. The awful thing about the cinema is the possibility of moving about exactly as one wants. You say, "Well, I must explain this emotion, and I'll do it by going into flashback and showing you what happened to this man when he was two years old." It's very convenient, of course, but it's also enfeebling. If you have to make the emotion understood simply through his behavior, then the discipline brings a kind of freedom with it. There's really no freedom without discipline, because without it one falls back on the disciplines one constructs for oneself, and they are really formidable. It's much better if the restraints are imposed from the outside.

On a related subject, the one for which he is aesthetically most noted, the use of theatrical ideas of space in motion pictures—of nearly abolishing the border between the screen and the stage through full shots, deep focus, long takes, and camera movement within a scene in place of cutting—Renoir makes clear in his many interviews that the day sound was ushered into the cinema, film artists were forced to accept certain rules of the theater. *Certain* is the operative term here, however, not *all*, for, as Renoir pointed out to Charles Thomas Samuels, there is something

in particular that renders spoken dialogue in a film "cinematic" rather
than "theatrical":

> The accompaniment of a close-up. People underestimate the im-
> portance of close-ups in film. It brings the actor closer to the au-
> dience, and it makes each spectator feel that the performance is
> directed at him alone. It makes you forget the crowd, as you do not
> forget it in a theater.

That "crowd" nonetheless consists of any number of ideal viewers,
would-be filmmakers, as it were, who make their own movies—in their
minds—even as they watch other people's. Thus, Renoir explained in
1960 to Joan and Robert Franklin of the Columbia University Oral History Project,

> A picture must not be the work only of an author or of actors and
> technicians; it must be also the work of the audience. The audience
> makes the picture, as well as the authors; and it seems to be strange,
> because you could ask me how the audience can make a picture
> which is already shot, done, printed. Well, a picture is different with
> every type of audience, and if you have a good audience, the picture
> is better. It is a mystery, but we are surrounded by mysteries. . . .
> I have nothing against that. I believe in it.

Still, this audience, according to Renoir in his 1954 conversation
with Jacques Rivette and François Truffaut, has lost the use of its senses
in the almost sixty years since the invention of cinema. "This is due,"
he declared,

> to what we call progress. Note that it's normal for them to have lost
> the use of their senses: We turn a button and we have light, we push
> another button, and we have a flame on a gas range. Our contact with
> nature takes place through so many intermediaries that we have al-
> most completely forgotten how to feel natural things directly. We can
> therefore say that people don't see very much now. (my trans.)

Renoir here is discussing visual perception in terms of color versus black-
and-white film, and he argues for a color cinematography that "sees things
clearly" where the spectator cannot.

He even seems to argue for a cinematography that sees things for
the very first time, as in this passage from a 1960 interview with Gideon
Bachmann in *Contact*:

You know my old theory of nature—that it follows the artist. I believe that nature is something vague, almost non-existent. I am not sure that the sky is blue and the trees are green. Probably the sky and the trees have no color, just a kind of indefinite gray, and I believe that God gave man the ability to finish the job. In other words, if man truly wants to exist, he must collaborate with God in the shaping of nature.

Such comments as these, it should be clear by now, are a long way from the pretentious or banal mutterings of most film-journal interviews, let alone the silence of many filmmakers, who as a group are not particularly disposed to speak for the record about their work, preferring instead to let the movies themselves communicate method, philosophy, and intention to the audience.

Jean Renoir was one of the exceptions to the above rule. He had what seemed to be total recall of the conditions of production for all his films, and he could be quite specific about his aims and strategies. His interviews as a whole disclose a candid, cultivated, and unselfish man, genuinely and also slyly self-critical, imaginative yet sometimes merely fanciful, at all times a source of beaming warmth. Soon the suspicion grows that Renoir saw his interviews as components of his career. He was not greatly guileful, but neither was he too naïve to know the sort of persona he had, and he knew that to make that persona as present as possible would only make his films more resonant. As André S. Labarthe wrote in the *Cahiers du cinéma* (in English) of January 1967, "Renoir doesn't *converse* at all. He doesn't try to convince his interlocutor, but rather, he tries to *overwhelm* him—not only with an argument, but also, even largely, with his personality."

Renoir's interviews in the end span several decades, during which one can sense his ideas evolving and ripening. He had a love for paradox as well as a strong Cartesian streak. Hence the text is full of his playing with ideas, developing them, putting them into conjunction and counterpoint, even ordering his replies in such a way that, frequently, they provoke as well as inform. From time to time, in fact, Renoir will reply to an interviewer with a response not to the question that was asked but rather to the question that *should* have been asked. All this he does, to be sure, with grace, good will, wit, immense style, and intrinsic passion.

Renoir kept up this process for so long that, by now, those who knew him feel that the man reflected the films and vice versa. This is not true of other interviews with first-rank directors—Alfred Hitchcock interviewed by Truffaut (one of Renoir's own interlocutors), for example, or Ingmar Bergman (a first-rank theater director as well) interviewed by

Björkman, Manns, and Sima. Hitchcock's interview provides fascinating information about the making of his movies, but no one except a specialist need read it in order to enjoy those pictures. Bergman's intellectually superior interviews can be read with profit by any cultivated person who never saw, or never cares to see, his films. But the conversations with Renoir seem almost synergistic with his work. Obviously, they need not be read in order to enjoy the films; obviously, too, once read, they seem essential.

This is dangerous. A persona has been adduced from Renoir's films; then its reenforcement by interviews makes the persona so seductive that it can blur judgment of the films themselves. I have no intent in the emperor's-new-clothes vein with these remarks: Jean Renoir is inarguably one of the great figures in film history. Still, not all his movies are of equal interest (despite some books about his work that maintain the opposite). But seeing many of them again, as I have done, abundantly confirms his directorial distinction and personal flavor. That incorrigible charmer, Renoir himself, will, rightly, have the last word on his life and work: because of the length and variety of his career, because of the huge influence he has had on other filmmakers, and because his persona, preserved in his interviews and inferable anyway from his films, is like a guardian angel against even sympathetic criticism.

The man or the persona and his longevity-cum-loquaciousness aside for the moment, Renoir's career, it must be remarked, encompasses a history of change in film style. His most celebrated stylistic hallmark, as I noted earlier, was the ingestion into cinematic syntax of theatrical "place," composition, and—as possible—duration: the combination, that is, of the flow of cinema with the relationships within a frame that are standard practice in the theater. The basis of this style is deep-focus shooting combined with the "sequence shot"—that is, the shot that contains a sequence of action. In the deep-focus approach, the reliance is on the content of any one shot, rather than on a succession of shots as in montage. The shot is held, and people may come in or leave; the camera itself may move (as Renoir's often adroitly does): It is the absence of cutting that makes the difference, the exploitation of different planes of depth within one shot to make the film progress, rather than the addition of new views.

Renoir did not invent this idea—you can see the conscious, deliberate use of it in Edwin S. Porter's *Great Train Robbery* (1903) in the scene where the posse captures the bandits—but he used it as a principle, a reaction against the principle of montage that had been dominant since D. W. Griffith (who was quickly followed in this approach by Eisenstein and Pudovkin). To many, the idea of composition in depth was a philosophical position. André Bazin, who *mutatis mutandis* was Aristotle to

Renoir's Sophocles, said that such a cinematic style was capable of expressing everything without fragmenting the world, of revealing the hidden meaning in people, places, and things without disturbing the unity natural to them. (Montage, by contrast, relies on joining bits and pieces of film together in rhythmic and pictorial relationships so that an effect is created out of the very way the pieces are joined, an effect additional to the effects of the separate bits unto themselves.)

Renoir's own rationale for his camera style was his belief in the primacy of the actor as focus of cinematic interest and source of inspiration. My view is that Renoir was at least partially motivated by sheer confidence, in himself and in film. He felt that the (still-young) film medium no longer needed to prove its selfhood by relying so heavily on a technique that no other art could employ. The cinema could now be sure enough of itself to translate into its own language a lexicon from another art, the theater. Indeed, Renoir went on to include literal theatrical imagery in his films, from *La chienne* (adapted from the play by André Mouézy-Eon) in 1931 to his last one, which was actually titled *The Little Theater of Jean Renoir*. And, in the 1950s, he directed three plays, Shakespeare's *Julius Caesar*, a comedy of his own, and Odets's *Big Knife*. (The world première of his play *Carola*, directed by Renoir himself, took place in 1960 at the University of California, Berkeley.)

It is mainly because of his theater-in-film style (though there are other reasons) that Renoir had such an enormous influence on subsequent filmmakers: the Italian neorealists (perhaps above all Luchino Visconti, who had worked as Renoir's assistant on *Toni* [1935] and several other pictures), Orson Welles, Satyajit Ray, and François Truffaut, to name a few outstanding examples. One of the endless individual moments that could be cited is from Jean-Luc Godard's *Breathless* (1960). In one sequence Jean-Paul Belmondo is in a taxi with Jean Seberg. He gets out and walks up the street away from us to speak with someone; the camera waits in the cab with Seberg, watching. When Belmondo has finished his conversation, he returns. The camera, for its part, has not moved, and the sequence has been contained in one shot: There has been no cutting. The deep-focus composition of lengthy duration has thus changed the "shape" and "time" of the screen for a few moments. Such visual variety is not nothing, nor is temporal variation. And more important, through its arrangement, the shot itself has implicated Seberg, in the foreground, with Belmondo's activities in the background.

An example from Renoir's own cinema is *Grand Illusion*, an anatomy, on the eve of World War II, of the upheaval of 1914–1918. Maréchal, a mechanic who might never have been an officer in an earlier, unmechanized war, and Rosenthal, a prosperous Vienna-born Jew whose parents emigrated to France, are in the farmyard belonging to Elsa, the young German widow who has sheltered them. Maréchal, who has become Elsa's lover, says he does not have the courage to tell her that they must leave now that Rosenthal has recovered from his injury. So the latter agrees to do it, goes into the house, and delivers the message. Elsa nods and disappears. Then Rosenthal opens a curtained window, and we see Maréchal, still where he was, out in the yard leaning on a wagon. The opening of the window, suddenly deepening the screen, the addition of that plane to the composition, creates a tension between Maréchal outside and what has just happened in the room—a device often used in the theater by lifting a drop or lighting up a dark area.

Now I shall turn to some generalized consideration of Renoir's films, in which, along with the theater, nature (often in the form of water, "nature's bloodstream") is a primary motif. At what I consider his height— *Grand Illusion*, which acolytes rank lower apparently because it is widely admired, and *The Rules of the Game* (1939), in which Renoir himself plays a leading role as Octave—he added first-magnitude stars to the cinema sky: unshakable, time-proof masterpieces on the collective subjects of class, war, friendship, and societal structure. Other films of his have beauties that only he could have given them: for instances, *Boudu Saved from Drowning* (1932), *The Crime of Monsieur Lange* (1935), *The River* (1950), and *The Human Beast* (1938).

But *Boudu* (adapted from the play by René Fauchois), about a modern Pan invited into civilization, is vulnerable to attacks of facile French camaraderie. *M. Lange* blends stock gay-Paris romantic quaintness with Popular Front characterizations (Renoir was involved in French Communist Party activities during the mid-1930s), and its lovely cursive camerawork does not greatly sublimate the picture's content. *The Human Beast*, from Zola, masterfully evokes railway workers' lives and (like several other films by this director) dispels the idea that Renoir's work is all sunny and affirmative; nonetheless, the inherited affliction of the engineer is treated more like an old-fashioned gypsy curse than Zola's symbol of generations of oppression, and what was intended as tragedy becomes stunted into melodrama. *The River*, made in India—after its maker's wartime Hollywood sojourn—from a Rumer Godden novel, has more lyrical camerawork (in color, for the first time in Renoir's career), but today it looks like the granddaddy of *Masterpiece Theater* in its Occidental meditation on an Orient centered around an endlessly changing yet endlessly constant Ganges.

I cite the above instances of "lesser Renoir" because it may not be remembered that before World War II, and even for some time after it, Jean Renoir was by no means ranked as the supreme French film director.

The Rules of the Game (1939), a.k.a. *La Règle du jeu*. Directed by Jean Renoir. Shown from left: Jean Renoir (as Octave), Roland Toutain (as André Jurieux), Nora Grégor (as Christine de la Cheyniest). © Cine Classics Inc. *(Courtesy of Classics Inc./Photofest)*

Marcel Carné, René Clair, Jacques Feyder, and Julien Duvivier were all considered at least his equals or even his superiors. His work, by comparison with theirs, was felt to lack polish and dramatic shape; both technically and morally, Renoir's movies seemed rough, often tentative or self-questioning. It was only around the early 1950s, with the advent of the *Cahiers du cinéma* school of auteurist criticism, that his stock began to rise even as that of the other 1930s directors (with the sole exception of Jean Vigo) fell. Speaking for his fellow *Cahiers* critics and New Wave directors, Truffaut hailed Renoir as "the father of us all." And his prewar films were received, upon rerelease, with an enthusiasm they had rarely received the first time around. (This was particularly true of *The Rules of the Game*, which initially had been attacked as frivolous, clumsy, and downright incomprehensible.)

During the heyday of *Cahiers du cinéma* and the *politique des auteurs*—the so-called auteur theory—the young French cinema was rejecting the established criteria of cinematic merit, which had much to do with literary orthodoxy and which celebrated such cinematically barren but financially successful films as Marcel Pagnol's popular prewar trilogy

Marius, Fanny, César (all three adapted from Pagnol's own plays). The *Cahiers* critics favored a cinema of authorial primacy for the writer-director that ignored the pedigree of literary antecedents preferred by their elders. And the critical impulse that brought auteurism into vogue prepared the way for the intensely personal cinema of the *nouvelle vague*, the New Wave of critics turned filmmakers who shocked the bourgeoisie at the same time as they energized French moviemaking.

That the Cahierists, who hoisted the "auteurial" flag and gave the world the New Wave, venerated Renoir above all other French filmmakers is not a surprise. Renoir took chances, made films on risk or instinct, insulted political sensibilities, challenged the Hollywood studio system during his self-imposed wartime exile, and actually managed to make some interesting movies in the United States despite the best efforts of American producers not to understand him. Few today would dispute Renoir's status as one of the greatest of all filmmakers, and most would accept that the films made between 1932 and 1939 (from *Boudu*, that is, to *The Rules of the Game*) consist of his best work and some of the best work ever committed to the screen.

Where disagreement sets in is with the subsequent pictures, from 1940 onward. There are those who feel that with his departure for America Renoir's career went into a decline from which, despite some fine moments, it never really recovered. For many critics, however, the late films are no less great than the earlier ones, merely different: masterworks of pantheistic humanism produced by a supreme moviemaker mellowing into tranquil, autumnal richness. The love of life, the sense of nature, the texture and density of the earlier pictures remain, but the concern with transient social objectives is transmuted into an all-embracing affirmation, a belief in art as an expression of the ultimate harmony of existence.

The argument over Renoir's *oeuvre* frequently takes on a political dimension. Many of those disappointed by the later films ascribe his decline (as they see it) to an abdication from political commitment; conversely, their opponents have tried to play down or explain away the polemical content of the prewar pictures, suggesting that *The Crime of Monsieur Lange* smells altogether too strongly of the poetic realism of Jacques Prévert, or that Renoir, tolerant and obliging as ever, made *The People of France* (1936) mainly to gratify his friends. Ultimately, though, debate over Renoir's "true" political views may be beside the point. If the aspirations of the Popular Front lend an added bite and immediacy to Renoir's films of the period, they hardly account for the consistent richness and vitality of his total output, even less for its curiously pervasive melancholy. Even overtly optimistic pictures such as *M. Lange* and *French*

Cancan (1955) are tinged with poignancy, while sadness suffuses the comedy in *The Rules of the Game* as well as *The Elusive Corporal* (1962).

It is this complex of conflicting emotions—of ambiguities, tensions, and uncertainties—underlying all his work that makes the earlier pictures so rewarding on each reviewing and that redeems the later ones from triteness. Indeed, one could argue that, had Renoir felt more secure in his political beliefs, his films would have been the worse for it. From the innate contradictions within his psyche, he created movies that, despite (or even because of) their weaknesses, seem to breathe life. Not that Renoir himself ever made such a claim. As he says more than once in his interviews, it is presumptuous of any director to suggest that he is presenting real life on the screen, for reality is always bigger, more amusing, and more audacious than any artistic invention. Nonetheless, few other directors have succeeded in conveying so intensely a sense of messy, turbulent, unstructured reality in the cinema.

Perhaps this is because of still another paradox or tension in Renoir's aesthetic self, for he was the prime exponent on film of unanism, the poetic movement in early twentieth-century France that reacted against art for art's sake and sought its sources in the lived life around it, yet without returning to pseudoscientific naturalism and without any attempt at overt "social significance." Six hundred years of Renaissance humanism, predictably ripening to decline, found a film elegist, then, in this Frenchman born and nourished at its center, the son of a painter who had given *La belle époque* some of its sensual loveliness. Yet Renoir himself did not paint with large canvases. His pictures have a modesty or lack of pretension, not to speak of their fluctuating subject matter, which is disarming and occasionally conceals the true depth of his work.

From the extraordinary diversity of his material, in fact, one might jump to the conclusion that Renoir worked, John Hustonlike, as an adaptor, occasionally revealing by chance glimpses of himself but choosing his subjects without system from whatever happened to be offered at the time. But such a hastily formed judgment does great injustice to his stature as an artist in his own right. For, while frequently drawing upon other people's work for the bases of his films, Renoir always interpreted their art through his own feeling. As he told Gideon Bachmann, "Shakespeare took his themes in some cases from the cheapest Italian fiction—stories that were quite banal, nothing really. But he made them great because of his own constant communion with the world of which he was a part."

Just so, *A Day in the Country* (1936) is purged of its cynicism: Renoir makes it more humane than de Maupassant's story, finding consolation and tenderness instead of bitterness and frustration in the film's epilogue. And *The Golden Coach* (1953), sentimental and flimsy in its original form (a play by Prosper Merimée), is given a new, richer meaning by Renoir, in which playacting (on stage or off) is presented as a means of reconciling art and life, reality and aspiration. Through such acceptance and even admiration of what is and not what ought to be, in his consistent understanding of the importance of the continuity of life and tradition, in his steadfast refusal to compromise humility with sentimentality, Jean Renoir became one of the few persons of the cinema to attain the status of artist. His imagination was his intelligence: subtle, immensely complex, prophetic, transparently stylish, astonishingly lucid, and always eager to engage, to converse.

The worldview of this artist, as well as the ethos behind his art, can best be summed up in this complex yet transparent remark by Octave from that filmic combination of comedy, tragedy, realism, impressionism, melodrama, and farce known as *The Rules of the Game* (itself derived from Musset's *Follies of Marianne*, inspired by Marivaux's *Game of Love and Chance*, and prefaced by a quotation from Beaumarchais's *Marriage of Figaro*): "You know, in this world there's one thing that is terrible, and that is that everyone has his reasons."

An Interview with
Jean Renoir

The following interview took place in June 1975 in Renoir's home in Beverly Hills, California, where he lived most of the time during the latter part of his life.

BERT CARDULLO: I'd like to start off in general terms, discussing the way that you worked on your films, your ideas about acting, screenwriting, technical improvements in film art, and so on. Then we can move to particular instances of your work, like *The Rules of the Game* and *Grand Illusion*, if that is acceptable to you, M. Renoir.

JEAN RENOIR: That's fine, my boy, but first let me say that I don't like the word *art*. It actually frightens me. Because the more work I do, the more I'm influenced by the literary forms and language of the eighteenth century; and until the romantic period, moreover, art simply meant *doing*, the way in which you do something. There was the *science* of medicine, and that meant a man had read all the books on medicine and that he was theoretically familiar with all medical problems. And there was the *art* of medicine, which involved caring for sick people—that is, the *practice* of this science. I find that this idea of practice applied to art ennobles the word. Whereas today, the word *art* is often given a rather vague meaning: something that relates to dreams, to sublime and incomplete creation, all of it tied up in a certain attitude toward life, in a certain tone that people use in saying, "Oh, he's an artist!"

One becomes an artist only *after* the fact, and, even then, sometimes one doesn't even notice that this has occurred. The awareness of a mission's importance comes only after the mission has been accomplished. I believe, in any case, that the importance—or the unimportance—of *everything* we do is noticeable only after the thing is done. I don't believe in

113

plans, what you Americans call "blueprints," in films any more than I do in life; I don't believe in scripts. They must, of course, be carefully written, but there must be enough room for change so that the inspiration of the moment isn't killed, which, in my opinion, is the only inspiration that contributes anything.

BC: So are you saying that during your career you preferred filming an original, "unfinished" screenplay, as it were, as opposed to a script based on a completed work of fiction?

JR: Yes and no. You know, I'm obsessed with filming stories that just come to mind, stories that are based on observations I've made about things around me, on adventures I've lived or my friends have lived, and the truth is I'm not sure whether this isn't a mistake, because it demands a huge amount of work. It also requires a lot of time. And I often finish by producing very little. When you have a novel like *The Human Beast*, by contrast, the adaptation is much easier. After all, the greatest writers did it in this way: Shakespeare, all the great writers. The French neoclassical authors copied the Latin classics, which copied the Greek classics. It helps a great deal when you don't have to worry about inventing a story, only about the dramatic construction of an existing story. You can create a much more rigorous structure in this way. With original stories, given one's inescapable self-doubt, you're forced to leave in some ambiguity so that you can constantly readjust or tamper with the narrative. *The Rules of the Game*, for example, was a constant balancing act. I pushed on one side and then the other, and then set it all upright. "It's going to fall on its face, it's going to fall down," I kept saying. You feel as though you're walking a tightrope, with just a big stick and your own weight. But it's exciting, I must say.

BC: How does this way of writing translate into a way of working on the set?

JR: I work, or worked, the same way on all my films. I arrive on the set in the morning. I read the dialogue first. If I can have a few actors with me, that's good—that is, I don't often have them, because, after all, they have to get made up, get ready, get dressed. Generally I do it alone with some assistants, the script girl, or the cameraman. I imagine the scenes and partially form them in my mind. But I don't plan any angles. In my opinion, the angles have to be decided once the actors have rehearsed. Nevertheless, it's only at this moment of conception, if you will, that I get a general idea of the scene, which becomes a kind of line to follow and to stay close to, so that the actors can be entirely free.

I think that the difference between this method and sticking to the script is similar to the difference between Indian music and Western music since Bach and Vivaldi—that is, since the invention of the tempered scale. In Indian music, there is a general theme, which is four thousand years old, and you must follow it. And then there is a general note given by a string instrument that in this case has only one string. Before beginning, everyone comes to an agreement about how to proceed, and then the note is repeated constantly, so as to bring the other instruments back to tonal unity. In other words, there is a theme and a tone, and aside from that, everyone is free. I think it's a marvelous system, and I try to do a bit of that in motion pictures. It's like something Picasso said, "When I paint, I simply start and I don't even know what I'm going to do." That's very important. And I think that's the number one rule in art, whatever art it may be. You must allow the elements of the art to conquer you. Afterward you may manage to conquer the art, but first it has to conquer you. To wit: You have to be passive before you can be active. You have to start off assuming or knowing that you know nothing and want to discover everything.

BC: What role did Karl Koch, a sometime collaborator of yours, play in this process?

JR: Well, among other things, he had been a collaborator of Bertolt Brecht's. And Brecht always had a very strong influence on his collaborators. He was the enemy of vague or inconsequential dreaming, and therefore he tried to give everyone around him a great feeling for logic. That was his major influence: in the area of logic. Those who worked with him always became the enemies of useless dreams. And Koch brought this kind of rigorous logic to our discussions of scripts and scenes, a logic that for Brecht often led to conclusions that seem baroque but aren't. The problem is that the public doesn't always see the logic. The public believes that truth is not like that. It is preoccupied with the hunt for clichés.

Koch and I were good friends, let me say. He had worked with me on *Grand Illusion*, and he worked with me again on *The Rules of the Game*. His role varied according to the situation. For *La Marseillaise*, for instance, I asked him to stay with me and to help me avoid banalities, because sometimes you let yourself get drawn into things that seem easy, and often you don't even realize it yourself. He was a man with a very disciplined mind, and if filmmaking were politics, we would say that in the miniature government of the film crew, he played the role of advisor.

Koch helped me enormously in our own cliché-hunting, helped me to destroy them wherever we found them. So he was my advisor, but when I made films, everyone was my advisor. There is no such thing as bad advice.

BC: Did Koch bring Brecht's politics with him?

JR: Not really. In any event, films don't influence politics. They influence customs or habits of mind. Motion pictures can determine the way people think but cannot be at the root of a political action. For example, people were nice enough to think that *Grand Illusion* had a great influence and told me so. I answered, "It's not true. *Grand Illusion* had no influence, because the film is against war, and the war broke out shortly afterward!"

But films influence moral thought and even behavior, yes. For example, today the world is condemned for being violent. Films cannot help but add to the violence, or they cannot help but add to the peace. It depends on the film. Obviously, the literature from the Cathars or Cathari helped give a certain gentleness to the end of the Middle Ages, which was an extremely gentle period. People weren't cruel at the end of the Middle Ages; people became cruel when they knew too much. The *Renaissance* was cruel.

BC: Do auteurs know too much, to use your term, and to return our subject to the filmmaking process?

JR: Well, they do, and they don't. Moreover, the problem of the auteur— as screenwriter and director, and sometimes editor and cinematographer all in one!—is not a problem; it's a fact. The world evolves, and what we pretentiously call "art" evolves as well: I myself would rather have lived in a period when the creator didn't count. For primitive art is great art: the art of Greek statuary, hundreds of years before Christ, when each statue was anonymous; the art of the cathedrals. We don't know who sculpted the statue of St. Peter or the Angel Gabriel. Nevertheless, the personality of each creator shines through. We feel the hand of the creator in every stroke, yet we don't know his name. There is a creator, and there isn't. I obviously like this kind of primitive art immensely, but the existence of such an art requires conditions that we can't satisfy right now. It requires, first of all, that religion and life be closely intertwined. All primitive peoples live by religion: Eating is a ritual; making love is a ritual; hunting is a ritual; and all these connections between religion and life give the expression of life—which is art—a religious meaning that can be absolutely magnificent. Hence our passion for African sculptures, the sculptures of New Guinea, for primitive Egyptian art, indeed for all primitive art.

By the time we get to the auteur, we have become much more demanding: We require that he gather all the elements that in the past were gathered by an entire tribe or even by an entire nation. It is for this reason that there are very few good auteurs. And if we look at it from a practical point of view, how can we then have many good films? The adversaries of the idea of the auteur in film are right. We want to have many good films, and we want to give each movie theater in the world one film a week, but it's obviously almost impossible to find that many people who are both writers and directors. I also look at the matter from another point of view: the temporal perspective. The thousands of films that come out in the theaters every week don't interest me at all. What interests me is the occasional *Citizen Kane*, the occasional *Gold Rush*. It's at such a moment that I know the auteur is necessary. I know that Chaplin's masterpieces were made possible only because he conceived them, wrote them, acted in them, edited them, did the music, did everything. I have one man's expression before my eyes. It happens that that's the way it is—the author's expression in the twentieth century is like that. And it may be a reaction against the masses. We live in a time when we have ten thousand cars motoring along on a road, a little red light flashes on, and everyone stops, all ten thousand in their aptly named automobiles. What is the reaction to this? It's a wild, exaggerated trend for the auteur. I neither approve nor disapprove of it; I observe the phenomenon, that's all.

BC: What do you think of the idea of the actor as auteur?

JR: First of all, I would use the term *character* as auteur. No characters, no films. There is a great danger in acting, in the profession of an actor or an actress—we are not talking about movie stars here—which is the pleasure of acting out the moment. One must be very wary of that. You must act out the moment, but only after having acted out the character as a whole; one must begin with the character. If you act out the moment alone, you will come to the conclusion that a girl playing the role of a mother who has lost her child must cry, and this may be a great mistake. If you act out the character, her reaction at that moment may be laughter, and this laughter will be honest. The truth is that one must do what Stanislavsky did and let the character, as well as the actor, live. That's why films shot on location are generally better, because the actors leave their spouses, their children, their eldest who was left back in high school, the swimming pool, domestic worries. In short, they're at a hotel, they're cut off from life, and they're surrounded by other actors; they're surrounded by the *film*, so it's easier to become the characters that they're supposed to represent, and they can allow themselves to go so far as to laugh at tragic moments and to cry at comic ones.

When I shoot a scene, I always try to escape the moment. Many directors believe in the moment. Maybe they're right, but I don't agree with them. I know that in general the stage direction consists of saying, "Okay, now your child is dead, and you're torn apart, so cry!" That may be the truth, but it's not my truth. I'm convinced that there are a thousand truths, billions of truths, as many truths as there are inhabitants of the earth. And mine is to believe in the individual, in general, not in the moment.

I think of only one thing, then: how to express the personality of the actor within the framework of a defined role. But often the actor and I break away from this framework. It's like the *commedia dell'arte*, but with one great difference: The *commedia dell'arte* was geared to an audience that was completely different from the film audience, the twentieth-century audience. Another thing: The *commedia* troupes changed cities; they didn't stay long in any one place; and there weren't millions of viewers seeing the same play, or at least they were spread out over many different locations. Whatever the case, it was possible to reuse the same material; and that's a good thing because, in my opinion, if you can free yourself from the subject matter—from the various "moments"—you stand a chance of doing better work. I think subject matter is necessary, of course. I believe in great subjects, but I also think it's a terrible weight to have to drag around. In short, I believe that the director's first task is to rid himself of the subject. In the *commedia dell'arte*, they had an enormous advantage, which is that they had already worked on their subjects five hundred times, so they knew them by heart. The subject matter no longer counted, and the character's appearance and movement no longer counted, either, since Harlequin's costume and blocking were always Harlequin's costume and blocking. Once his appearance and movement, as well as the subject, were out of the way, the actor could concentrate on the essentials—that is, on the character, the dramatic situations, and the way to deal with them. As I have already made clear, this is exactly what all the classic authors did, including Shakespeare. Shakespeare very rarely invented his own subjects; even *The Tempest* is said to have been taken from Montaigne.

I must admit something here: I'm absolutely in favor of plagiarism. I believe that if we want to bring about a great period, a new renaissance in arts and letters, the government should encourage plagiarism. When someone is convicted of being a true plagiarist, we should give him the Legion of Honor right away. I'm not kidding, because the great authors did nothing but plagiarize, and it served them well. Shakespeare spent his time rewriting stories by little-known Italian authors and by others. Corneille took *Le Cid* from Guillén de Castro and made it French, and

Molière ransacked the Greeks and the Latins, and they both did a good thing. The habit of using a story already invented by someone else frees you from the unimportant aspect. What's important is the way you tell the story. If the story has already been invented by someone else, you're free to give all your attention to what is truly important, which is to say the details, the development of the characters and the situations.

BC: To continue along these lines, shouldn't the viewer be added to the list of people who are active in the birth of a film, along with the actors, the auteur, and anyone whom the auteur may have plagiarized?!

JR: Yes, obviously. It's impossible to have a work of art without the spectator's participation, without his collaboration. A film must be completed by the audience. That's why absolute precision is dangerous. On the other hand, however, intentional imprecision or incompleteness is dangerous as well. I think that one of the ingredients for success is to have a lot to say, to have *too* much to say, so that you do say it, but you don't say it all. There are certain parts that you cannot manage to formulate, that you forget, or for which you simply can't find the words, the terms, the camera movements, the lighting, or the right expressions for your actors. The audience compensates for all that. What's interesting is that each person in the audience, each viewer, compensates in his own manner. The truth is that a film is as many films as it has viewers. If there are a thousand viewers, you have a thousand films, if it's a good film. If it isn't a good film, it's precise or exact, and as a result it's the same film for each viewer.

BC: We could therefore define the success of a work by the many interpretations it allows for.

JR: I think so, yes. You see, the big mistake in commercial filmmaking right now is the search for perfection. Often people say to me, "Oh! Producers are disgraceful people, disgusting people: They think only of money, they think only of how much they'll make, they think only of what's financially successful." It isn't true! I claim that producers are the most disinterested people in the world, that they are people who really love film. My only criticism of them is that they want to make good films, which in my opinion is completely ridiculous. It's not a matter of making good films, it's a matter of bringing out a little piece of humanity. It's a matter of opening a little door onto what we think we have discovered about the human mind or about a situation, a situation that leads us inevitably to characters. It's a matter of getting to know people, and that's all. When producers seek technical perfection, as they often do, with the earnest desire of producing a work of art, I think they are making a huge mistake. What happens is that these absolutely perfect products, these products to which nothing can be added, wind up being boring, and audiences wind up getting tired of films because they've been shown too much—too much perfection.

The audience's collaboration is even a necessity now, because there are many people whose lives are not much fun. These are people who live in big cement apartment buildings, and every morning they go to an office or to a factory, and they do the same thing, make the same motions, all day long. They drive their cars on highways where they stop and start, stop and start: They stop for the red, and they start at the green. It's rather disappointing, isn't it? Other periods had their disadvantages as well, of course. I'm talking about the disadvantages of our times without suggesting that they are better or worse. And our period does have its disadvantages. One of those disadvantages is solitude. Everything leads to solitude, and, in addition, people want solitude: They think solitude is good. Someone who tells you they bought a house in the country says, "I have a marvelous house. Just imagine, there isn't a soul around me for miles, not even a mouse, only fields, nothing." They don't realize that human beings are the interesting part of life. What's interesting is meeting people, not meeting trees. Trees are magnificent if they exist in relation to a human being, but I couldn't care less about trees by themselves. They just don't interest me. They excite me as soon as they bring me closer to the people who planted them, to the people who created the civilization around them, or when they bring me closer to the people in my neighborhood, to emotions I've felt, when they bring memories to mind; but trees by themselves don't do anything for me.

So one of the ways of fighting against modern solitude is through art. Art is a little bridge that you erect. The director of a film, if he has a bit of talent, sometimes succeeds in creating a little bridge between the screen and the audience, and then we're all together, and we can create together: We build the film together. The audience makes this contribution, and this contribution is very important.

BC: Could we go back for a moment to the idea that the search for technical perfection in filmmaking is misguided? This seems like a paradox, and I'd like you to say a bit more about it if you would.

JR: Of course. First of all, technical perfection can create only boredom, because it is merely the reproduction of nature. Imagine a time when film will be able to create the perfect impression of being in a forest. We'll have trees with thick bark, ever larger screens, screens surrounding the viewer. We will truly be in the middle of the forest, where we will be able to touch the bark of the trees, to smell the smell of the forest; there will be machines automatically dispensing perfumes that imitate the smell of moss, for example. You know what'll happen then? We'll get on our motorscooters, and we'll go to a real forest instead of to the movies. Why bother going to a movie theater when you can have the real thing? Consummate imitation can only end an art.

BC: Which is to say that, once we push this way of thinking too far, we will finally come to regret, so to speak, that film has a finer and finer grain.

JR: Absolutely. And I'm very sorry about it. Let's look, for example, at the photography of primitive films—the arrival of a train, the first American Western—and let's look at the photography of Max Linder's films. In general, it's superb. But perfection is an insane joke. I can cite more proof of this right away: Chaplin's films were considered by all technical specialists at the time to have been poorly photographed, poorly lit, poorly designed, with poorly conceived scripts, and so forth. In my opinion, however, his films are still masterpieces. I believe that none of us is ready to come close to Chaplin, yet all the lovers of perfection criticized him. I'm sorry, but I regret the technical improvements in filmmaking.

Listen, when I was young, I fought to introduce panchromatic film to studio photography. I was even the first one to have used it. I made all my equipment myself in the attic at the Vieux-Colombier. I made a small studio in which to shoot *The Little Match Girl* on panchromatic film. Orthochromatic film was used at that time, and the lighting in studios was made for orthochromatic film; that is, there were arcs and tubes of mercury. I said to myself: Why don't we use panchromatic film, since it produces more nuances, it renders grays, it translates intermediary colors? It avoids the contrasts that can seem ugly—the orthochromatic contrasts that make everything go right from black to white. I asked myself why we shouldn't use panchromatic film in the studios. The reason was that we didn't have the light spectrum needed; the lights we used didn't emit the ultraviolet rays required for panchromatic film. So I studied the question a bit, very generally, because I don't have a scientific mind; and in the end I found someone from Philips, the makers of lighting and electrical systems, who advised me to try to boost the bulbs slightly—ordinary bulbs—which is what I did. So I and some friends made reflectors with zinc that we had cut, and then we made rheostats with pieces of metal that we had twisted, and we put the contacts at different points on some springs, and finally we shot *The*

Little Match Girl. The photography wasn't so bad; in fact, it was very good. We developed it ourselves, in our kitchen.

We did all that. We did amateur work that was exciting, but I realize today that I was acting against my deepest convictions. I believed in progress, but now I don't believe in it anymore. As I have already noted, currently the photography of many films is quite beautiful, very polished, and imitates nature very well, but it is completely pedestrian and therefore perfectly boring. It is very often the case, then, that the most perfect films today are also the most boring films photographically. How can that be? How can we explain this, if not by this general rule that I am trying to express, which is that progress works against art, against artistic expression? Without admitting this truth, how can we explain why primitive films are so exciting?

BC: And, in the end, what technical progress are we really talking about, since reels of film eventually deteriorate, and, despite the enormous and devoted efforts of various archives, prints do disappear?

JR: Yes, it's very upsetting. You become aware—I noticed it each time I saw screenings of my earlier pictures—how fragile the craft of moviemaking really is. When I began in film, I considered that one of the ways in which films were better than the theater was that they were tangible and lasted, as a painting or a statue lasts, whether good or bad. I'm not talking about quality, only about duration. But in the end, this isn't true: They don't last. So now I'm sure of it: Film is also an ephemeral craft. For example, some years back I was able to reconstruct *Grand Illusion* to what it was when I shot it, with the help of a few duplicates found here and there. We produced a very good copy, the whole film in fact, but it took an enormous amount of work, and, in any case, the complete negative itself has disappeared—as will this copy eventually, if it hasn't already done so.

Yes, the truth is that a film is a very temporary thing. Seeing my old films again led me to revise this idea about the permanence of my profession, of my art, to reconsider its comparison to the plastic arts. The cinema isn't as temporary as journalism, but it's less lasting and less solid than, say, a book.

BC: A painting fades, too. The colors change with time, and a painter has to anticipate that.

JR: Yes, but he does anticipate it, whereas the filmmaker doesn't. I guess that what we should ask ourselves, then, is whether all human production, all artistic work, isn't in fact temporary, even a painting, even a statue, even a piece of architecture, even the Parthenon. No matter how solid the Parthenon is, relatively little is left of it, and we have no idea of what it was like when it was first constructed. And even what is left is going to disappear. We may manage, by putting cement into the columns, to hold it up for one hundred more years, two hundred more years, say five hundred years—even one thousand years. But in the end, the day will come when the Parthenon no longer exists. I wonder whether it wouldn't be a more honest approach to what we call an "artwork" to bear in mind that this work of art is temporary and will disappear and that the truth is, all things being relative, there isn't much difference in the end between a work of architecture built in solid marble and a newspaper article printed on paper that we throw out the next day. I'm even at the point of wondering whether the only excuse for a work of art isn't the good it can do mankind. I don't mean by this good the exposition of theories—my fear of messages is well known—but rather a small contribution to man's culture: the betterment of man morally, or, most of all, philosophically and spiritually.

BC: Still, when the Parthenon is completely destroyed, the memory of it will remain. The idea of the Parthenon will survive, like that of Phidias, for example, none of whose sculptures has endured.

JR: Absolutely. That's why I ask myself if the idea that remains of a work isn't more important than the work itself, and if, in turn, the importance of this idea isn't based on the good that the idea was able to do for people. This good is absolutely undefinable in strict terms, and I would not attempt to classify it. I refuse to say, "This is good, and this is bad." But there is a good, and there is a bad just the same, no doubt about it. There is, in any case, a philosophical plane where the good and the bad get played out. Ever since the world has been the world, there has been an attempt to escape from matter and to approach the spiritual, and I believe that every work of art that brings us one tiny step closer to this spirituality is worthwhile.

BC: Given that films are not eternal, that reels of film deteriorate, where does the importance of this art lie, since one hundred years from now there may be no more films?

JR: I believe I just answered your question. Would you ask me where Homer's importance lies, because, between you and me, no one has read Homer? Suppose there were six thousand of us here, and we asked the question, "Has anyone here read Homer?" If the people are truthful, they'll say no. Homer is very important, nonetheless. Something strange happens with a work of art: It outlives its existence. I don't know why, but it's a fact; there's an indirect influence. Think about it, and let's be honest: Take any great work of art; take the best painting in the Louvre. How many French people have seen it? A tiny proportion, maybe one in a thousand, I don't know, yet its influence is obvious, and it is the influence of French works of art on French civilization. I believe, in the end, that a work of art works mysteriously. I believe a great deal in radar in life, in human radar. There is a kind of radar that causes the work of art to influence people, but not directly or obviously.

BC: Could we continue to discuss the relationship between film and the other arts, particularly painting?

JR: Certainly—it's an important subject, after all. I think there is a relationship among all the arts. After all, it's a question of expressing oneself. The big difference between film and an art like painting is that many people express themselves on one film. The actor has to express himself, the director has to express himself, the technician has to express *himself*. There is also another big difference, which is that the means given to film directors are complex, whereas the means given to painters are extremely simple. The truth is you can paint with a piece of charcoal on a white wall, or at least draw, whereas to make a film you need a camera, film stock, sound, so many things. This is not to film's advantage, because I think that technical resources are against what we generally call "art"— something that I suggested earlier in our conversation. The more technical resources you have, the more difficult it is to express yourself. You wind up drowning in wealth, so to speak.

I believe it is a great advantage for a painter to be able to paint anywhere; he doesn't need much equipment. Second, when one's technical concerns are limited to the essentials, these essentials become much more profound and become more special as well. I believe that a good painter is harder to find than a good filmmaker, because a good painter, since he doesn't have very advanced technology, since he is limited in his means, has to be more clever. You know the expression, "Don't spread yourself too thin." I think that this is extremely important in art. The painter has the advantage of digging into the same little hole every time, and as a result he can go very, very deep. He can even go so far as to find the relationship between eternity and the instant, between the world and the spirit, the body and the mind. Painting can go very far. I believe that painters are the great philosophers of our time. I would even go as far as to say that the motion picture is way behind painting. What's done in painting is done in the motion picture fifty years later. Fifty years!

BC: Are you saying, then, that because painters have fewer technical resources at their disposal, it is easier for them to avoid merely copying nature—that they have to recreate or reconstruct it from the start?

JR: That's exactly what I am saying. *Nana* was the first film in which I discovered that one doesn't copy nature but must reconstruct it, that every film, every work that aims to be artistic, must be a *creation*, whether good or bad. I discovered that it was better to invent something, to create something bad, than merely to copy nature, no matter how well one might do so. By nature, I don't mean just the trees and the fields. I mean human beings and everything else. I mean the world.

Connected with this, one thing that has been a convenient source of inspiration for the French over the past one hundred and fifty years is what we have agreed to call "realism." But this realism is not realism at all. It is simply another way of translating nature. I am absolutely convinced, for example, that the way in which a writer like Zola or Maupassant translated what he saw around him was just as digested, just as composed, as it was for a writer like Marivaux. Then, too, nature changes, because nature in a civilized country is created by people. So a country's appearance changes considerably over time. That's why what remains of an artist isn't his copy of nature, because this nature changes. It's temporary. What is eternal is his way of *absorbing* nature.

To bring our discussion back to painting, I like to claim that all great art is abstract, that Cézanne, Renoir, and Raphaël are abstract painters, so they can't be judged by the resemblance of their paintings to their models. The great artists themselves were absolutely convinced that they were objective and were mere copiers of nature, but they were so powerful that, in spite of themselves, they created their own portraits and not just that of a tree.

BC: Whereas painters who want to be abstract from the start may violate the spirit of art?

JR: Yes, they often end up with something a bit dry and end up not showing themselves at all, because in trying to show themselves, they start by hiding from themselves; they start by creating an *idea* about themselves. An exact portrait can be done only unconsciously. It's like photography. If someone says to you, "I'm going to take your picture," you immediately freeze up. You make a funny face, and so the photograph looks nothing like you. But if you don't know that you're being photographed, the photo is often good and looks very much like you.

BC: The reverse is also true, isn't it? That in order to make reality seem fairylike, certain filmmakers go to a great deal of trouble to present it in a truly strange light.

JR: Yes, but if we leave reality as it is, it's already fairylike.

BC: This is certainly true of such prewar films of yours as *Toni*, *The Lower Depths*, *The Crime of Monsieur Lange*, and *La nuit du carrefour*.

JR: Such a quality comes solely from my desire to try to observe reality. I love reality, and I'm happy to love it because it brings me infinite joy. But it happens that many people hate it, and most human beings, whether or not they make films, whether they're workers, store owners, or drama-tists, create a kind of veil between reality and themselves. And in order to create this veil more easily, they use elements provided by society: the people around them, conversations in the street, newspapers, theatrical productions. This veil is extremely monotonous, because it becomes the same for everyone. And so when someone pierces through it and shows the reality behind it, people say, "Oh, no! That's not true! That's not the way it is!" But it *is* the truth.

After all, the reality is in being enchanted. It demands great pa-tience, work, and faith to find it. I'm convinced, in any case, that it isn't a question of talent or gifts, just of good faith. If you want to find reality, you'll find it. You just have to eliminate whatever seems to you to have been created by the habits of your times; you have to eliminate these habits first but to take back later the ones that seem to conform with reality. The reality of daily events, as well as romantic adventures, is absolutely twisted, deformed, as if they were seen in a funhouse mirror. And I think that the reality of romantic adventures is the one that is the most deformed. It's insane how lovers who fight suddenly see facts and the world through a distorted lens and lose all sense of reality. This is the romantic tradition. We have to deal with a hundred and fifty years of romantic tradition concerning love, what we call the "emotions," and the way to approach women. Despite its lace covering, the reality of love seems much truer to me in Marivaux and up until the end of the eigh-teenth century, even in the politically revolutionary works.

Anyway, because romantic adventures are often used as a basis for narrative art, and because these romantic adventures are very distorted, we wind up with a literature and a cinema that are themselves rather distorted.

BC: It's a question, then, of trying to see things as they are.

JR: Yes, and it's also the idea that there are no gradations in the events that affect us. Every event is important. Or no event is important. There are no gradations, no different classes, because first and foremost we are all one.

By contrast, newspapers and advertising today give weight to events according to the number of people who are affected. They say such an event is important because there were six thousand victims. Fine. But if there is only one victim, and if I'm that victim, then the accident, with its one victim, is as important to me as the disaster with six thousand victims is to each of the six thousand victims. The quantity, in my opinion, is not very important, and I don't believe in rankings, either. Einstein's death, if you like, was no more important than the death of a Mexican worker digging holes in Los Angeles, because for the family of this Mexican worker, for everyone surrounding him, his death is just as important. And even for the world's equilibrium—how do we know, maybe he'll leave a gap as important as Einstein's. We don't know. How can we judge that?

This obsession with ranking things, with numbering things—he's number one, he's number five—I don't think it's true. Each person is number one for certain people, in a certain place, in certain circumstances, and then he becomes number five or number one hundred thousand in other circumstances. There are no gradations, really, or there are so many that they make no difference in the end.

But there are certain people who claim to pay no heed to different gradations, in order to be democratic. In my opinion, that's also false. These people say, "Oh! Excuse me! The worker is just as important as Einstein!" It seems to me that there is a demagogic side to this kind of judgment that makes it false, because equality is paradoxically absolute *and* relative, for the worker may suddenly be more important than Einstein under certain circumstances, but Einstein will be more important in other circumstances. The one thing we don't know is the comparative importance of these circumstances. The worker's situation may be more important than Einstein's—and there again, I don't believe that, because in saying that it's more important, I'm still establishing gradations. Let's just say, as important . . . or as unimportant.

We forget one thing, which is that relativity doesn't exist only in time and in space. Everything, absolutely everything, is relative. We're surrounded by relative truths; there are only relative truths; everything depends on the circumstances, on the moment. I don't give a story about a baker any more importance than one about people who don't want to go to war. It's always a matter of seizing a certain aspect of life seen at two moments, probably different yet related aspects, without establishing a hierarchy between the two.

BC: Seizing life, for you, also means seizing the voices, the noises, of the moment, doesn't it?

JR: Yes, I don't like postsynchronizing dialogue, because I still belong to the old school that believes in life's surprises, in the documentary, which argues that it would be wrong to neglect the sigh heaved unconsciously by a young girl in a certain situation and which can never be reproduced. Or if it is reproduced, it becomes part of what we were talking about earlier: a blueprint, a plan.

I think that film, and all art in fact, is made up largely of lucky accidents, and obviously there are people who are lucky and who happen to have these fortunate accidents more than others do. But if these chance occurrences are planned and determined by the director, they're not as good, in my opinion. A director is a fisherman. He doesn't make the fish, but he knows how to catch them.

Now, you do have to follow a precise plan for postsynching. The expressions, the vocal intonations, which one tries to bring back during postsynching, are planned, are part of a framework—a limited framework that cannot be changed. Note that I believe in frameworks but only if you can then forget about them. For instance, in ancient architecture. Let's use the example of Greek temples, which are so beautiful. Greek temples were very convenient for the artists who worked on the architecture and sculptures for them. That's because they didn't have to draw up a blueprint, for the blueprint was the same, throughout the world. They had a blueprint that was so unchanging that they wound up forgetting it; it was as if it no longer existed. The blueprint was changed only for practical reasons: Because of a boulder, for instance, in the middle of a plot of land, the architect was forced to add a curve in a particular wall in order to go around it, but those were real reasons, not just the genius of an architect who decided to add a curve because it would be nice. In other words, I'm enormously wary of my own ideas when I make plans, and I'm wary of other men's ideas as well. I feel that what we find around us—and especially what others, what the richness of other people's personalities, can bring to us—is more important than one's personal pride as a director.

BC: So what you are saying is that the theme was there, in the framework, if you will. Only the variations remained to be found.

JR: Right! And it was the same with literature. *The Song of Roland* was probably told a million times by different troubadours. They worked within a framework—the "*Song of Roland* framework," let us call it—but they were absolutely free within it. And they were writers. The big mistake today, as I pointed out a little while ago, is to think that being a writer means inventing a story. I don't believe that. I think that being a writer is in the way you *tell* the story.

We have something like the equivalent today of *The Song of Roland*. It's the conventionality of certain American genres like the Western. Westerns are good because they always have the same script. This fact has helped the quality of Westerns enormously. Refined people often claim the right to scorn them because these movies always tell the same story. In my opinion, that's an aid, an advantage, a quality.

I am not a genre filmmaker, but I could say something similar about myself: I feel that sometimes voluntarily, often involuntarily, I've been following the same line ever since I began making films. I've basically shot one film, I've continued to shoot one film, ever since I began, and it's always the same film. I add things, I see things that I haven't said before and that I have to say, but the truth is, it's the same conversation that I began years ago with the audience—a rather limited audience, by the way, since the number of people interested in this kind of cinematic art is severely restricted.

BC: Could we talk about a film of yours that, initially, itself had an extremely limited audience?

JR: You mean *The Rules of the Game*. Yes, let's talk about it, because of all the films I've done, it is, as you know, the one that was the biggest failure. When it came out, *The Rules of the Game* was a perfect flop! I've had quite a few flops in my life, but I don't think I've ever had one like this! It was a complete and total disaster. I made this controversial film in 1938–1939. I had no intention of startling conventional people with it. I simply wanted to make a film; I even wanted to make a good film but one that, at the same time, would criticize a society that I considered to be rotten and that I continue to consider to be absolutely rotten, because this society is still the same.

That said, in making *The Rules of the Game*, I wanted to make a likable film, so I used as my source a writer who is a lovable creature, someone whom you can't help loving. I used Musset. *Les caprices de Marianne* was my source, but a very distant source, indeed! The resemblance is very slight, but there is something in my film's plot that reminds us of *Les caprices de Marianne*. And then, you know, you always need a point of departure, so let's just say that *Les caprices de Marianne* was my point of departure.

What happened in my conception of *The Rules of the Game* is what happened with all my films, with everything I've written, with all that I've tried to do. Throughout my career, I've been obsessed initially by a certain general idea. It's always very strong, but in the beginning I can never find the right way to present it. I don't know how to express this idea. It's just there. It's very powerful, it obsesses me, but I have no idea how to express it, how to give it form; and then, very often, when I'm lucky, I find in addition a little idea, an idea that relates solely to the plot, a purely vaudevillian touch. For example, here, I had the idea of trying to imitate the action of one of Musset's comedies. That's the exterior. Sometimes this secondary idea can be used as a vehicle for my general idea, and then everything works out well and I'm happy. That's what happened with *The Rules of the Game*.

The Rules of the Game also represented my desire to return to the classical spirit, my desire to escape from *The Human Beast*, from naturalism, even to escape from Flaubert. It represented my desire to get back to Marivaux, Beaumarchais, and Molière, as well as Musset. This is quite an ambition, I know, but allow me to point out to you that if you're going to have mentors, the bigger they are, the better. It doesn't mean that you compare yourself with them; it simply means that you try to use them as your models.

So *The Rules of the Game* was an attempt at a classical work. I accompanied it with classical music, and I had it acted in somewhat of a *commedia dell'arte* fashion, with a bit of pantomime style. I used extremely simple characters, but ones who, simply stated, took their ideas or developed their thoughts to the limit. They are candid characters. I hope that my portrayal of this society leads us to love it, delinquent though it may be, because this society has at least one advantage: It wears no masks.

When *The Rules of the Game* was shown in July 1939 at the Colisée, many people wanted to destroy the seats. I went to these screenings, and I can tell you that such an event breaks your heart. It's all very well to say you don't care, but it isn't true. You do care. It's very upsetting to hear people whistle at you and insult you. I received plenty of insults because of *The Rules of the Game*.

All that's over now. What I wanted to tell you is that because of the whistling that broke my heart, I decided to cut the picture, and that is why the full and complete version of *The Rules of the Game* no longer exists. There is one that is almost complete, and I hope it's the one you have seen. It was reconstructed by some film laboratory technicians, who were able to find the negative, develop it, and remake a complete copy. In short, they were able to reconstruct the film. There is only one scene missing in this reconstruction, a scene that isn't very important. It's one with me and Roland Toutain that deals with the maids' sexual interest. You see, it isn't very important!

BC: One of the things that is important, though, is connected with character. That is, one of the questions one asks oneself after seeing *The Rules of the Game*, and it may be one of the things that disturbed viewers in the beginning, is, "Who is the main character?" Is it Dalio, is it Nora Grégor, or is it Roland Toutain? How about Octave? I don't think there is one.

JR: I agree with you, there is none. And while I was shooting, from time to time I said to myself, "It's this character," or "It's that character." The truth is, I didn't know. And it's one of the rare cases in the making of films, in my filmmaking, that the concept I had in the beginning—that is, that it was going to be a film about a group of people, a film representing a society, and not a personal case—this concept was still present in the end. I may have forgotten it sometimes during the shooting, but it was the same at the beginning and at the finish, when I found myself with all the footage for the editing. In the end, I was united with my original concept. Again, I wanted to show a social group; but I was even more ambitious, for I wanted to show almost an entire class.

You know, when you're faced with a good subject, and *The Rules of the Game* has a good subject, it devours you. You can't do what you want. You're drawn in; in spite of yourself, you shoot many things you hadn't foreseen, because that's the way it is, because they belong to the subject. I like to let myself be absorbed, but in this case, in *The Rules of the Game*, I allowed myself to be completely absorbed by the subject, and also, of course, by everything that reinforced that subject—like the actors, who were extraordinary and who were completely immersed in the inn where we went together. We lived there, far from Paris. It's very important to be far from Paris for a story like that. We were really cut off from the world, and this whole ambience—the actors and the landscape and also the subject, as I said—wound up devouring me and happily made me do lots of things that I hadn't planned on doing.

BC: And one has the same impression with the scenes as with the characters in *The Rules of the Game*. I don't think you can say, "This is the key scene." There's a center somewhere, but one can't really say, "This is *the* scene."

JR: If there is one, I don't know which one it is. I don't know, and seeing that I made the film, I don't think that those who didn't make the film know, either.

BC: *Grand Illusion* doesn't have this "problem." Did it have any others related to interpretation?

JR: There is one aspect of the film that I have never read any comment about. Let me explain: I wanted in *Grand Illusion* to show French officers as I had known them when I was in the army before and during 1914. Military style has changed since then much more than we think. The way a soldier or an officer presents himself today is completely different from the way this same soldier or this same officer would have presented himself sixty years ago, even thirty years ago. And the change has not occurred in the direction people think. People think that behavior was much more rigorous, much stiffer before, but it was the complete opposite. There was a kind of ease that seems to have disappeared. The expression in the military code on which military instructors put the most emphasis was the phrase "without affectation or stiffness." Now it seems to me that today, military men in France carry themselves with a bit of affectation and a great deal of stiffness, which are not consistent with the French spirit. The French spirit is an easygoing spirit, a relaxed one. It's an aristocratic spirit, whereas this new, stiff manner of carrying oneself is, in my opinion, more plebeian than aristocratic.

BC: Let's talk about *Toni* for a minute, for it is a picture that seems to contradict what you said earlier in reference to *Nana*: that realism is less a matter of copying nature than of reconstructing it.

JR: Yes, you have a point there. *Toni* is a film that corresponds to one of my "realism-crises," one of those times when you tell yourself that the only way to make a film is by recording with photographic precision everything you see, including the skin texture of the people you put before the camera. To satisfy this craving for realism, I chose a true story, a news item. A very good friend of mine was a police commissioner in Martigues, and he told me *Toni*'s story. It's a terribly sad, extremely gripping, completely true story, and a story that, in addition, took place in the foreign workers' section of Martigues, which itself is very interesting. And the portrayal of this section allowed me to dwell on a theory that has always been dear to me, which is that the people of this earth are not divided into nations but instead are divided into work categories. What we do is our true nation. My friend and I went to visit all the places where *Toni* had lived, where he had loved. The police commissioner reenacted his investigation for me, and, little by little, the story built itself up in my mind. He established a short summary of the facts for me, and, with this summary as a base, I wrote *Toni*.

    Toni is therefore a story that, to a certain extent, represents what we now call "neorealism." I left for Martigues, I brought along a camera, and I lived with the people of Martigues. I entrusted my nephew Claude with this camera, by the way. It was one of his first major films. We shot it with local people, while breathing the local air, while eating the local food, and while living the life of these workers. And that's the whole extent of it.

BC: Let me address one more apparent inconsistency in your remarks. When I asked you before what you thought of the idea of the actor as auteur, you responded that you would use the term *character* as auteur. But what about the instance of Michel Simon and *Boudu Saved from Drowning*? Isn't Simon the actor-as-author in this picture?

JR: He is both: actor-and-character as auteur, and that's what happens when an actor's gifts match up to such an extent with a character's traits. *Boudu* is Michel Simon, who is one of the greatest actors in the history of theater and film. *Boudu* is an homage to Michel Simon. It's Michel Simon, by the way, who suggested that I do *Boudu*. When we had finished *La chienne*, we tried to find another subject to work on together. We had many ideas but couldn't really come up with anything. Then finally he said to me, "We should do *Boudu*." At first I didn't understand. I read the play, which I admired a great deal, as it's a beautiful play. But I couldn't see how we could make it into a film. One day it came to me, it hit me. I saw Michel Simon dressed as a hobo. I had already filmed Michel Simon as a hobo, in fact. It was at the end of *La chienne*. So when I went to see the end of *La chienne*, *Boudu* hit me. I said to myself, "That's it, now we can shoot *Boudu*. We've already shot it."

For *Boudu*, technically speaking, I wanted to take advantage of the fact that Michel Simon was so real, that he was a hobo among hoboes, he was all the hoboes in the world; and it was interesting to see whether all the hoboes in the world could be absorbed by the Parisian crowd. For this kind of shot, I obtained a very long lens, the kind of lens that is used in Africa to film lions from afar. But instead of filming a lion, I filmed Michel Simon. I stationed my camera in a second-floor window so that I would be above the roofs of the cars going by, and Michel Simon-Boudu walked on the piers, through the streets of Paris, among people who didn't notice him. And I shot many scenes just like that.

Boudu is a film that I see quite often, not because I take pleasure in contemplating my former work, but simply because of Michel Simon. When I see *Boudu*, I forget that I made the film; I forget what happened, and I see only one thing: a great actor, in character, on the screen.

BC: Didn't *A Day in the Country* similarly grow out of your desire to do a film with Sylvia Bataille?

JR: Yes, but that was a bit different; and, in any event, *A Day in the Country* is not Bataille in the same way that *Boudu* is Simon. Here is the real origin of *A Day in the Country*: For a long time I had wanted to do a short film that would be done as carefully as a feature-length work. Normally, shorts are done in a few days, are botched up, and are sometimes shot with actors who aren't very good—as well as with inferior technical means. It seemed to me that if we filmed a short carefully, it could be part of a film composed of several shorts. My idea was to make a film lasting about forty minutes, and with three forty-minute films, you would have a picture as long as a feature-length film and one that might be more varied. Some people like that sort of thing, because today—at that time it wasn't done, but it has become popular since—there are many films with such vignettes. So it was basically a matter of a first step in the direction of a film of vignettes, what we now call an "anthology" or "omnibus" film.

I decided on Maupassant for one very simple reason: I love him, and it seems to me that there's a bit of everything in a little story like *A Day in the Country*. It sums up a part of the world, and, of course, there are few love stories as touching as the one in *A Day in the Country*. This "inclusiveness" or "universality," let us call it, is common for Maupassant; it's common for many great authors, of course.

Another thing was that this extremely short story didn't limit me. It's not like a play that forces you to use certain dialogue. *A Day in the Country* didn't force anything on me. It only offered me an ideal framework in which to embroider. And I truly believe in this idea of a framework within which one can embroider. It's a question, once again, of happy plagiarism.

A Day in the Country takes place on the banks of the Seine. But I couldn't shoot on the banks of the Seine, because the Seine of 1935—the year in which I shot *A Day in the Country*—was no longer the Seine of eighty years earlier; it was no longer the boating Seine my father knew. The Seine in 1935 was a Seine with factories, steamboats, and lots of noise. So I shot on the banks of the Loing. I was lucky enough to have a friend, Anne-Marie Verrier, whose husband was the ranger in the forest of Fountainebleau, and they were living in this absolutely marvelous, absolutely delicious little house in the forest, right on the banks of the Loing, near a bridge. We were a bunch of friends, and we moved into Anne-Marie Verrier's place, where we shot *A Day in the Country*. It all seemed to us like a kind of happy vacation on the banks of a very pretty river.

By the time of *A Day in the Country*, I have to admit, I was already beginning to share René Clair's opinion—he's the first one to have expressed such a view—that there should be a "cinematic period," just as there was a *commedia dell'arte* period, and that this period should be the second half of the nineteenth century. This is an idea that I approve of one hundred percent: Get rid of contemporary realism entirely, and do all our films with costumes from a period that would be known as the film period, 1851 through 1899 to be exact. It's the opposite of *cinéma vérité*—which is all that I have to say.

Filmography of Feature Films

The Water Girl, 1924
Nana, 1926
Charleston, 1927
Marquitta, 1927
The Little Match Girl, 1928
Tire au flanc, 1928
Le tournoi, 1928
Le bled, 1929
On purge bébé, 1931
La chienne, 1931
La nuit du carrefour, 1932
Boudu Saved from Drowning, 1932
Chotard & Co., 1933
Madame Bovary, 1933
Toni, 1935
The Crime of Monsieur Lange, 1935
Life Belongs to Us, a.k.a. The People of France, 1936
A Day in the Country, 1936; final cut, 1946
The Lower Depths, 1936
Grand Illusion, 1937
La Marseillaise, 1938
The Human Beast, 1938
The Rules of the Game, 1939
Swamp Water, 1941
This Land Is Mine, 1943
Salute to France, 1944
The Southerner, 1945
Diary of a Chambermaid, 1946
The Woman on the Beach, 1947
The River, 1950
The Golden Coach, 1953
French Cancan, 1955
Elena and Her Men, 1956

Le testament du Docteur Cordelier, 1959; made originally for television
Picnic on the Grass, 1959
The Elusive Corporal, 1962
The Little Theater of Jean Renoir, 1970

Dostoyevskyan Surge, Bressonian Spirit

Une femme douce and the Cinematic World of Robert Bresson

W HEN HE COMPLETED *L'ARGENT* (*MONEY*) in 1983, Robert Bresson (1901–1999) was probably the oldest active director in the world. But his evolution had been in striking contrast to that of his contemporaries. Even if we do not take into account those film-makers whose declines had been conspicuous, most of the senior states-men of the cinema showed in their later phases a serenity of style, an autumnal detachment from reality that compares with that of elder artists in other genres such as the drama, the novel, and poetry. Not so with Bresson. *L'argent*, his thirteenth and final film (freely adapted from the 1905 novella *The Counterfeit Note*, by Tolstoy), was made in essentially the same strict, tense, controlled style—here used in the depiction of extraor-dinary violence—that he used in *Les anges du péché* (*Angels of the Streets*) in 1943.

Hence Buffon was mistaken: Style is not the man himself, it's the universe as seen by the man. (Many a disorderly person has been an artist with an orderly style.) But neither is style a separable system into which an artist feeds material. Van Gogh did not look at the night sky and decide that it would be pretty to paint the constellations as whirls. And Joyce did not decide it would be clever to describe that same sky as "the heaventree of stars hung with humid nightblue fruit." Neither artist had, in a sense, much choice. His style, of course, was refined through a lifetime, and first drafts were not often final drafts, but the temper and vision of that style were given from the start.

Robert Bresson. *(Courtesy of Photofest)*

Thus it is impossible to imagine Bresson *deciding* to make *L'argent* as he did. On the basis of his career, we can assume that, at some time after he had read Tolstoy's story, his mind and imagination shaped the structure and look of his film in ways that his mind and imagination had long been doing. It is a kind of fatalism, I believe. Not all fine artists work in the same way all their lives: The Japanese director Yasujiro Ozu is one who did not. But some, like Bresson, do.

Consequently you know, if you know Bresson's *oeuvre*, that *L'argent* was made with nonactors. He rarely used professionals, and he called his untrained nonprofessionals "models," whom he instructed to speak their lines and move their bodies without conscious interpretation or motivation, in a determined attempt on this director's part to keep them from psychologizing their characters. Bresson hated acting and often said so. He chose people instead who had what he considered the right personal qualities for their roles, and he said that he never used people twice because the second time they would try to give him what he wanted in place of what they were. It is as if he were guided by Kleist's line, from his essay "On the Marionette Theater" (1810), that "Grace appears most purely in that human form which either has no consciousness or has an infinite consciousness: that is, in the puppet or in the god." Since Bresson couldn't employ gods, he got as close as possible to puppets—with nonactors. They enact the story of *L'argent*, as of Bresson's other films, much as medieval townsfolk might have enacted a mystery or morality play, with little skill and much conviction.

Apart from the acting or nonacting—you also know, if you know Bresson's films, that if the subject was contemporary, the sounds of metropolitan life were probably heard under the credits. You know that the story was told with almost Trappist austerity and emotional economy, in such an elliptical, fragmentary, even lacunary way that only in its interstices can be found its poetry—indeed, much of its meaning. You also know that Bresson's camera fixed on places a moment before characters entered and remained a moment after they left, not only to include environment as a character but also to signify that humans are transient in the world; and you are aware that, in any one of his films, a chain of consequences would probably begin with an event seemingly unrelated to the conclusion.

In our time, when we are saturated more than ever with images of the most superficially realistic kind, particularly on television, Bresson thus tried to wash our eyes and lead us to see differently—to bathe our vision, as it were, in an alternative reality. Moreover, his distrust of words— Bresson's laconic dialogue is almost as characteristic of his work as the neutral tone of its delivery—often made him choose characters (like Mouchette in the 1967 film of the same name, or like the truckdriver of *L'argent*) who have little or no ability to speak and who therefore suffer their oppression in silence. And often we see as little of them as we hear of their dialogue, for Bresson liked to focus his camera on a door through which a person passed or on a "headless" body approaching a door, turning the knob, and passing through. (His rare moving shots were usually reserved for that kind of traversal.)

When it is not doorknobs in *L'argent*, it is cell doors—in prisons that are so clean and well-run, so intensely physical as well as aural, so much a part of society's organization, that they freeze the marrow. (The suggestion, of course, is that man himself, inside or outside prison, is trapped behind four walls. Possibly prisons figure so often in Bresson's films—in additon to *L'argent*, they can be found in *A Man Escaped* [1956], *Pickpocket* [1959], *The Trial of Joan of Arc* [1962], and as early as *Les anges du péché* [1943]—and are the most emblematic of his décors, because he himself spent eighteen months in a German POW camp during World War II.) Bresson thus put places, things, and people on virtually the same plane of importance. Other directors do this, too—Antonioni, for instance.

But with Antonioni, it is to show that the physical world is inescapable, almost a person itself; Bresson, by contrast, wanted to show that the world and the things in it are as much a part of God's mind as the people in the world.

Let me address the world of *L'argent* for a moment, because its pattern is simple yet common in the work of Bresson: A pebble is moved, and the eventual result is an avalanche. A teenaged Parisian from a wealthy home asks his father for extra money, besides his weekly allowance, to repay a debt. The money is refused. The teenager then consults a friend of his age and station, who has counterfeit banknotes (no explanation of the source) and knows where to pass them (no explanation of the knowledge). The youths pass off a false note to a woman in a camera shop. When her husband discovers the fraud, he passes off the note to the driver of an oil-delivery truck. The truckdriver is subsequently framed as a passer of counterfeit money, and the ensuing scandal causes him to lose his job. In order to continue supporting his family, he tries driving a getaway car for some criminals, but their heist does not go so well, and he is sent to prison for three years. While incarcerated, his child dies of diphtheria, and his wife leaves him. Crazed upon release from jail, the former husband and father turns to theft, violent crime, and eventually cold-blooded murder before turning himself in to the police—for good, as it were.

This seemingly random and ultimately sensationalistic story holds because, as in all of Bresson, the focus is not on the story; it is on matters of which we get only some visible-audible evidence. That is to say, to the devoutly Catholic Bresson, evil is as much a part of life as good, and what happens here en route to God's judgment is not to be taken as proof or disproof of God's being. Though the sentimentalist in Tolstoy (on display in *The Counterfeit Note*) would disagree, God does not prove, does not want to prove, his existence by making the good prosper and the wicked suffer, by aiding the morally weak or rescuing the ethically misled. (The most religious person in the film becomes a murder victim.) This world is, after all, only this world, says *L'argent*; God alone knows everything, the suffering of the faithful and also the suffering of the sinner.

Bresson's worldview is well conveyed here by his two cinematographers, Emmanuel Machuel and Pasqualino de Santis (who has worked for Bresson before). All the colors look pre-Raphaelite, conveying the innocent idea of blue or red or any other color. And this fits Bresson's "innocent" method: Violence runs through *L'argent* but is never seen. When the truckdriver commits a double murder, for instance, all we see of it is the tap water that runs red in the basin for a few moments as he washes his hands. When he commits ax killings, the only stroke we see occurs when he hits a lamp. This "innocence" extends to the last sequence of the film. The driver, who has killed off a family in an isolated country house, goes to an inn, where he sits and has a cognac. It is then that he turns himself in by calmly walking over to some policemen standing at the bar and confessing his crimes. In the next shot we are with the crowd outside the inn door. As they watch, the police come out, taking the driver away. We never see him again; instead, the camera places us with the innocent bystanders, who continue to watch the door, watching for more police, more prisoners. But there will be no more, and the film ends on the image of the crowd—waiting and watching.

The other remarkable aspect of Bresson's *oeuvre*, aside from the consistency of his style, can be deduced from the content of *L'argent* as summarized above: To wit, forty years after his real beginning in 1943 with *Les anges du péché*, his films still had the power to create scandal. (The director disowned his first feature, a comedy titled *Les affaires publiques* [1934], which appears to be lost.) This power was particularly welcome in the early 1980s, when world cinema showed few signs of rejuvenation and did not seem willing to experiment. Even as *Pickpocket* (1959) was rejected by many at the time of its release (but hailed by New Wave filmmakers such as François Truffaut, Jean-Luc Godard, and Louis Malle, then making their first films, as a landmark in modern cinema), *L'argent* was booed by the audience at Cannes in 1983 despite the fact that it won the Grand Prize for creative cinema (together with Andrei Tarkovsky's *Nostalgia*). The director himself faced a violent reaction when he received the award from Orson Welles—himself no stranger to rejection and scandal. The irony in this instance was that Bresson, the avowed Catholic and a political conservative, was attacked by all the right-wing newspapers in France that in the past had defended his films. At the core of this attack, one can detect an exasperation with, even a hostility toward, an artist whose lack of commercial success had nonetheless never made him sacrifice one iota of his integrity and who always maintained his rigorous artistic standards.

It is sometimes forgotten that part of Bresson's integrity—his moral or ethical rigor, if you will—was his insistence on treating his share of socially as well as linguistically marginalized characters, in such films as *Pickpocket*, *Au hasard, Balthazar* (1966), and *Mouchette*. Yet no one would ever have called him a "working-class naturalist" like Luc and Jean-Pierre Dardenne, whose pictures, even though they sometimes have an implicit Christian component (especially *Rosetta* [1999] and *The Son* [2002]), are closer in subject to the social-problem play tradition of the European naturalistic theater. Bresson, by contrast, was a transcendental stylist concerned to unite the spiritualism of religious cinema with realism's redemption of the physical world in its organic wholeness if not otherness, its inviolable mystery, and its eternal primacy or self-evidence.

I would now like to reconsider here, in detail, what I believe to be Bresson's most underrated film: *Une femme douce* (1969), or *A Gentle Creature*, his first work in color, his ninth film, after the 1876 novella by Dostoyevsky (sometimes called *A Gentle Spirit*), and his fourth picture derived from or suggested by a Dostoyevskyan source. (*Pickpocket* was based on *Crime and Punishment*, *Au hasard, Balthazar* was inspired by *The Idiot*, and *Four Nights of a Dreamer* [1971] was adapted from the story "White Nights.") Bresson regarded Dostoyevsky as the world's greatest novelist, doubtless for his spiritual strain—an almost existential one, in contrast with the sentimental religiosity of Tolstoy—because Bresson avoids the Russian's preoccupation with truth and his probing of human psychology. Put another way, this most Catholic of filmmakers (French or otherwise) always forbids the surface as well as the depths of naturalism from distracting us from the mystical moments in his films, which cannot be explicated or revealed in any positivistic manner.

Those moments, to be sure, involve cinematic characters, but Bresson makes us focus, not on the story in the human beings on screen, but on the human beings in the story and their sometimes complete lack of connection to or understanding of what happens to them. Bresson almost disconnects character from story in this way. His is an extreme reaction to decades of "dramatic" pictures, where character is action and action, character; "action" movies, in which the characters are designed to fit the exciting plot; and films "of character," where the plot is designed to present interesting characters—those with a "story," that is. To the oversimplifications of character of the cinema before him, Bresson responds by not simplifying anything, by explaining almost nothing. To the self-obsession of the Hollywood star system, the "dream factory," Bresson responds in the extreme by calling for complete self-denial on the part of his actors. (Hence his designation of them as "models.")

Let us begin simply with the plot of *Une femme douce*, so that we can instructively compare what Bresson and Dostoyevsky do with more or less the same series of events. A contemporary young woman, unnamed, of uncertain background and insufficient means, for no apparent reason marries a pawnbroker, also unnamed, whom she meets in his shop. She tells this man that she does not love him, and she makes it very clear that she disdains his, and all, money; if she is marrying to escape her origins, it remains unclear exactly what those origins were and why she is choosing to escape them in this particular way. The woman (as she is called in the credits, like "the man") and her husband go through periods of much unhappiness—we even see her with another man at one point, but we cannot be sure that she has been unfaithful—and some calm. Then she nearly shoots her spouse to death in his sleep. Later she becomes quite ill, and, once she recovers, matters appear to be righting themselves between her and her husband. Nonetheless, she proceeds to jump to her death from the balcony of their Paris apartment.

The plot of Dostoyevsky's novella *A Gentle Spirit* is substantially similar to this one, allowing for differences in time (mid-to-late nineteenth century) and place (the harsh Russian countryside), with one major exception: The young wife in Dostoyevsky's narrative is initially very loving toward her older husband, with the result that the main turns of the above plot are easily explained. The husband in the novella—the narrator both of the novella and of Bresson's film—distrusts, out of his own perverse obsession with verifiable as opposed to intuited truth (his Dostoyevskyan surge, if you will), his wife's love for him, so he decides to test it. He is cold toward her and holds over her head the fact that he has rescued her from her poor beginnings. For these reasons, she eventually comes to hate her husband and almost to commit adultery. Finally, she is even ready to shoot him. With his wife's gun at his temple, the man awakens but does not move. Yet she cannot fire. A religious woman, she feels great remorse and atones for her "sin" by leaping to her death while clutching a Christian icon. The wife in fact is lying on her bier at the beginning of the novella with her husband at her side, reviewing his marriage in an attempt to understand why she committed suicide. What he comes to understand is that his own contrariness is the cause of all his unhappiness and that all men live in unbreachable solitude.

Any such explanations of what happens in *Une femme douce*, however, pale beside the facts—and the facts are almost all Bresson gives us (here as elsewhere in his *oeuvre*) and all that we should consider if we are to be able to interpret his film justly. One fact that critics have inexplicably ignored, and that I take to be the foundation of any sound interpretation of *Une femme douce*, is the young woman's declaration in the beginning that she does not love the man she intends to marry. Put another way, it is not at all clear *why* she marries him (*her* Dostoyevskyan surge, in opposition to the husband's in Dostoyevsky's novella), and certainly the sum of the evidence points to the conclusion that they are so different from each other as to be nearly exact opposites. (No, the "opposites attract" theory of romance does not work here, for nothing the young woman does indicates that she is even attracted to the pawnbroker, let alone in love with him.) The pawnbroker, for his part, although he may wish to marry this woman, does not make known why, after so many years of bachelorhood, he suddenly wants to wed someone about whom he knows so little. (Bresson makes him forty or so and gives him a live-in maid-cum-assistant whom, significantly, he does not dismiss after his marriage.) Certainly he gets little or no response from his fiancée, however much he may think he loves her, and they could hardly be said to carry on anything resembling a courtship.

In a word, these two are simply not meant for each other, and I am maintaining that Bresson makes sure we know this right from the start. Bresson's subject is thus not the rise and fall of a modern marriage, say, on account of financial problems or sexual infidelity (as it is Germaine Dulac's subject in *La souriante Madame Beudet* [1922], a kind of early feminist film that deals with the problem of a husband's economic domination of his wife, and to which, in letter but not in spirit, *Une femme douce* bears some resemblance). The couple in *Une femme douce* do not even fall out in direct conflict with each other over a genuine issue that is raised in the film: the spiritually transcendent way of life over the materially driven one. These two are fallen out, as it were, when they first meet.

What Bresson does in *Une femme douce*, then, is the reverse of what Dostoyevsky does in *A Gentle Spirit*. The latter has the husband test the love of his wife and conclude that all human beings live in "unbreachable solitude." Bresson has the husband and wife living in unbreachable solitude from the start and tests the duty, if not the love, toward them of the maid Anna, the character whom Bresson adds and purposefully names so that she will stand in for us, the audience. (Although Bresson could just as easily have had the husband narrate the story of his marriage alone and unseen, in intermittent voiceover, he has us watch the husband tell it to Anna in the same room where his wife's corpse lies on their marital bed; like the wife's body lying in the street after she jumps to her death, which we see at the *start* of the film, this is another telling image—the dead woman juxtaposed against the (re)union of man and maid—of the end-of-the marriage-in-its-beginning.) Whereas Dostoyevsky had used the spiritual to express the nihilistic, Bresson thus uses the nihilistic to express the spiritual.

Let me go into some detail as to how he does this, chiefly by concentrating on the contrast between the figures of the man and the woman. Since most of what we learn about her is designed solely to establish how different from the pawnbroker she is, she does not add up to a unified character of depth and originality, or "color," with whom we can readily identify. She walks into the pawnbroker's shop, and immediately the otherwise beautiful Dominique Sanda, in her first screen role (and giving more of a "performance" here than Bresson usually allowed his "models"), is unsympathetic: Her clothing is drab, her hair is disheveled, she makes very little eye-contact with anyone, and her walk has about it at the same time a timidity and an urgency that make it unnerving.

The pawnbroker, by contrast, is meticulous in appearance, sparing in gesture, and steady in his walk; he looks directly at all whom he encounters (whereas his customers avert their gaze) but with eyes that one cannot look into and a face that, eerily, is neither handsome nor plain. This is clearly a man (as "modeled" by Guy Frangin) who "understands" the world and how to get along in it, as opposed to being "had" by it: Money is everything to him, and what cannot be seen, touched, and stored is not worth talking about (which is one of the reasons, as he himself says, that he is unable to pray). He accumulates item after item in his pawnshop, yet we never see him sell anything: He likes his money, but apparently he likes his "things," too. His wife, however, gives away his money for worthless objects when she is working in the pawnshop, before she was married, she pawned her own last possessions in order to get a few more books to read. Her husband, for his part, has shelves of books—not one of which we ever see him take down to read.

He likes them for their "thingness," yet he will not read those books so as to rise above the world of things. The woman longs to do so but realizes that, as a human being, she can only achieve her goal to a limited extent. She indirectly reveals this knowledge when, early in *Une femme douce*, she declares, "We're all—men and animals—composed of the same matter, the same raw materials." Later we have this truism visually confirmed when the young woman and her husband visit a museum of natural history, where she goes on to ask, "Do birds learn to sing from their parents, or is the ability to sing present in them at birth?" The wife yearns beyond a universe in which all is such nature, nurture, *matter*, and where human being themselves frequently seem to behave in a preconditioned manner: preconditioned to beautify the self, to marry, to reproduce, to gather wealth and possessions, to enter society, and so on.

Throughout the film the suggestion is that, himself obsessed with possessing matter (including his wife, or her body), the husband responds to situations in a preconditioned or "correct" manner, whereas his wife responds in the most unforeseen, and sometimes bizarre, of ways. Indeed, almost all her behavior is choreographed according to this ideal of the unexpected or the gratuitous. When she and her husband enter their bedroom on their wedding night, for example, the young woman quickly turns on the television set but does not watch it. The man does, but what he sees could be the image of his own dead-end behavior pattern: cars racing in a circle. (He drives an automobile; she does not.) Later the husband will watch horses racing around a track on the same television and then World War II fighter planes flying round in endless circles as they try to out-maneuver one another in dogfights.

Meanwhile, incongruously, the wife nearly runs about the room in preparation for bed, wrapped in a towel that dislodges itself by accident as opposed to being dislodged in an act of sexual enticement. At one point she carelessly tosses her nightgown onto the bed, in much the same way that she will leave underclothes strewn about it during the day and scatters her books everywhere, showing no respect for the material, for objects or possessions. At another point, this young woman takes a bath but does not drain the dirty water and even leaves the faucet running, which her husband then turns off. Moreover, she spurns money yet likes to eat fancy pastries; she enjoys jazz but plays Bach and Purcell. The wife wants a bouquet so much she goes as far as to pick sunflowers alongside a road, then quickly tosses them away when she sees that, nearby, some couples are gathering their own bouquets of sunflowers.

This woman is different even in dying. (Her suicide ends as well as begins the film.) We do not get her point of view of the street before she leaps from the balcony, nor do we await her fall from below, from the position where she will soon find herself. As the wife jumps in daylight, we "innocently" see a potted plant fall off the small table from which she leaped, we watch the table topple over, and we are given a slow-motion shot of this woman's shawl floating discursively to the ground after her—as if it were both her surviving soul or spirit and a final reminder of the unpredictability of her human nature—to be followed by a series of shadows and feet that flutter toward her dead body. (She placed a white shawl around her shoulders before jumping, even as she fingered the Christ figure retained from the gold crucifix she had pawned at her future husband's shop.) Off camera during her fall, the young woman lands in the street, cars screech to a halt, and we await her husband's discovery of her death.

If, even in suicide, the wife's behavior has not been categorizable, has once again been somewhere "in between"—we can never predict quite where; we do not know quite why—then Bresson's camera itself is always literally somewhere in between, except when it is teasing us with a subjective camera-placement or point-of-view shot (as when the man and woman, together with us, attend both the French movie *Benjamin* [1968]—a costume drama trading on the wiles of love—and a production of *Hamlet*, the kinds of narratives or dramas, unlike *Une femme douce*, we are accustomed to seeing and hearing, in which we are more or less easily able to identify with the characters, their worlds, their experiences.) There are many shots of doors, of empty stairways, of the objects filling the pawnbroker's shop and his apartment. The camera is also "in between" in its representation of people: We get hands and arms cut off bodies, bodies cut off from heads, just torsos, just feet. As usual in his work, Bresson thus makes matter of the human body, even as he films the material world, the literal distance between the husband and the wife, as much to bring this matter to (spiritual) life as to emphasize the fact that these two people live in unbreachable solitude, on either side of a great chasm. The last shot of *Une femme douce* is of the lid to the woman's coffin being screwed tight, as the material world—the actual coffin lid, the world of things that she has at last transcended—continues to separate her, in death, from her husband, just as it did in life.

If these two characters are so permanently "separated" or irreconcilably different, one might ask, why did they choose to get married? I do not know; I do not think that they know (if they do, they do not tell us); and Bresson does not care, because, as I have more than suggested, this couple's "psychology" is not the focus of *Une femme douce*. Perhaps the man and the woman get together out of their own perversity, but the film does not contain this idea; it just does not contradict it. Just as it does not contradict the possibility that the young woman marries the pawnbroker only because it is the unexpected thing to do. For Bresson, then, their marriage is not a relationship to be explored but instead a device to be used.

To wit: Marriage is universally perceived to be the most intimate state in which two people can live, and Bresson counterpoints this perception of ours with the almost total lack of intimacy that exists between the husband and the wife in his film. In other words, the director does not allow us to identify with the marriage of the pawnbroker and the young woman, to see ourselves in them, because he does not indicate that they marry for the reasons *we* usually associate with marrying: love, money, convenience, convention, children. They wed; they are unhappy; they reach a fragile understanding; then she kills herself. The husband, in his narration—it is not narration in the proper sense, but more on this later—attempts to discover why his wife committed suicide, but he cannot find an answer. He does not know why she killed herself, nor do we, and neither does Bresson.

My point is not that every human action in *Une femme douce* is without explanation, without cause or motive—for instance, the wife's near murder of her husband after he discovers her with another man *can* be accounted for—but that these individual explanations become beside the point when one considers that there is no explanation in the film as to why the pawnbroker and the young woman got married in the first place. What becomes important, therefore, is not so much their relationship with each other as our relationship with each of them and Anna's with the pawnbroker. This is why the camera shifts periodically from *its* illustration of past events to the husband pacing back and forth in the bedroom in the present, telling *his* story of the marriage: not only to point up that *neither* narrative account provides the "answers" but also to emphasize that this man, as character or person apart from his story, is the proper focus of our concerns, as is his wife, literally apart from her story in death, lying in the road at the beginning of the film even as she lies there at its conclusion.

Clearly, then, Bresson wants more from us than our "understanding" of the husband and wife's relationship, our feeling sorry for them for their frailties and obsessions, because ultimately this is only feeling sorry for ourselves; or it is making these characters do the work of our living, which is too easy. The remarkable aspect of this film is that we do much of the feeling and querying for the actors, not in identification with them as they do it, but *in their place*: We feel and query for them as we imagine they would. And this has the effect of making us think absolutely about their situation, instead of about theirs plus our own. Bresson, in this way, wants us to feel for and care about characters whom we do not "recognize," who reveal as little that is "like us" as possible, namely, the heights and depths of strong emotion: love, hate, anger, regret, happiness, sadness.

To this end, Bresson forces his actors to deny themselves in their portrayal of their characters. He denies *himself* in his shooting of these characters: For the most part, the camera is held steady in the middle distance; there is no panning or tracking; and there are no high- and low-angle shots—objectivity or distance that Bresson can afford because of the very lack of appeal of his main characters. The director asks us in turn to deny ourselves in our perception of these characters and their actions. He demands that we pay attention to the husband and wife for themselves, no matter how uninviting or inexpressive they may appear, no matter how their story resembles little more than a skimpy newspaper report.

The fact that, as in the case of *Une femme douce*, Bresson almost always made his films from preexisting texts should be a signal that he was not interested in the creation of original character for its own sake, or even in the recreation of traditionally arresting and appealing character (which is one reason we never learn the name of the husband or wife). The fact that he frequently began his films by telling us what would happen at the end should be a signal, as well: that he was not primarily concerned to tell stories for the suspense they could create. Related to this, the effect of having the husband narrate parts of the story to Anna, the enactment of which parts we then see in flashback, is less to show us discrepancies in the husband's version as compared with "what really happened" than to obliterate the newness or freshness of story, the interest in it per se—precisely through the filming of both the husband's narration and its subsequent repetition in action instead of words.

Bresson asks us, not to fully fathom this "double-narrative," to decipher the how and why of the whole story, but simply to believe that it occurred and to take witness if not pity. His is a nearly perverse demand, which is to say a kind of religious one. If we can comply and perform the requisite act of faith, of utter selflessness, together with a leap of the imagination, *Une femme douce* becomes for us something resembling a religious or spiritual experience—an experience, moreover, that teaches us that we must acknowledge the existence of the inexplicable in, as well as beyond, art. For it is art's job not to make people and the world more intelligible than they are, but instead to represent their mystery or ineffableness, their integrity or irreducibility, if you will, their connection to something irretrievably their own or some other's, like God himself. All may not be grace for the young woman at the end of *Une femme douce*, then, as it was for the curé of Ambricourt at the conclusion of Bresson's *Diary of a Country Priest* (1951, from the 1936 novel by Georges Bernanos), who utters these words of spiritual certitude ("All is grace") as he is dying. But all is not nothingness, either.

Anna the maid seems to have learned the lesson of inexplicability or irreducibility from life rather than art, for she knows as little as we do about the motives for, and causes of, the husband's and the wife's behavior, yet she utters not one querying or querulous word to either of them in the course of the picture. Indeed, Anna utters only a few lines through all of *Une femme douce*. Yes, she is the couple's maid, but her silence and impassivity (especially as she is played by Jane Lobré) here appear to go beyond the call of a servant's duty. Before the end of the film, Anna leaves the room in which she has quietly listened to the husband's narrative of his and his wife's relationship, but she will not leave him. She will remain with him during and after the funeral of the young woman because, as the husband himself admits, *he will need her.*

Journal d'un curé de campagne (1951), a.k.a. *Diary of a Country Priest.* Directed by Robert Bresson. Shown on right: Claude Laydu. © Union Générale Cinématographique. *(Courtesy Union Générale Cinématographique/Photofest)*

Bresson, by implication, asks the same of us: that, figuratively speaking, we do not desert this man in his time of need, that we recognize his humanity despite the fact we cannot comprehend his or his marriage's deepest secrets. If there is anyone in *Une femme douce* with whom we should "identify," then, it is Anna. And if it can be said that we identify with the husband and wife at all, it is in the sense, as I have implied, that they seem as puzzled by what is happening to them as we are. This is not only character almost disconnected from story, it is character nearly disconnected from *self*. Thus are we disconnected from *our* selves, our certain egos, and made to look, not for the moral or balance in the story, the symmetry of feeling and form, of ideas and execution, but simply and inescapably for the only remaining tie that binds us to the characters depicted on screen: the human one, or the only one that cannot be explained away.

As one can doubtless deduce from my concentration above on *Une femme douce*'s method, as well as on *L'argent*'s after it, Bresson's films are even more distinguished for their method or their style than for their individual subject matter. That is because Bresson's subjects pale beside his treatment of them, so much so that it is almost as if the director were making the same movie time after time. How ironic, or perhaps appropriate, that he filmed the ninth in color (though elegantly understated or "innocent" color it is, as photographed by Ghislain Cloquet) because, as he later wrote in *Notes on Cinematography* (1975), he felt color was more true to life. Like André Bazin's true filmmaker, Bresson thus attained his power through his method, which, to rephrase something I said at the start of this chapter, is less a thing literally to be described or expressed (as in such terms as *color, deep focus, handheld camerawork,* and *long takes*) than an inner orientation enabling an outward quest. That quest, in Bresson's case, is (this is not too strong) to honor God's universe by using film to render the reality of that universe, and, through its reality, both the miracle of its creation and the mystery of its being.

An Interview with Robert Bresson

The following interview took place at Bresson's home on Ile St. Louis in Paris shortly after *L'argent (Money)* shared the 1983 Grand Prize for creative cinema at the Cannes Film Festival.

BERT CARDULLO: What place do you give to cinema among all the arts?

ROBERT BRESSON: I don't know its place. But it may be able to capture this thing that words can't describe, that shapes and colors alone can't render, by using several combined means.

BC: Could you comment on what you have called your "separation" from the theater?

RB: I think the cinema is misguided, that it has its own language, its own means, and that it has gone wrong since its birth. That is to say, it's trying to express itself by using tools that are those of the theater. Now there are wonderful actors in the theater. Believe me, I get such a hard time because I don't use them; but such performers are not really my pleasure. I believe in the very particular language of cinema, and I think that, once you try to express something through mimicry, through gestures, through words and vocal qualities, you can no longer have cinema. It becomes filmed theater.

Cinema is not that, however. It has to express itself not through images alone but through their relationship to one another, which is not the same thing at all, just as is the case for a painter, who does not use colors by themselves but in their correlation to each other. Blue is blue in itself, but next to green, red, or yellow, it is not the same blue anymore. It changes. The aim of a film should be such a correlation of images. You

151

take two images, and each of them is neutral; but all of a sudden, next to each other, they vibrate as life enters them. And it's not really the life of the story or of the characters, it's the life of the *film*.

So what I am looking for is expression through rhythm and a combination of images, through their position, their relation, and their number. Before anything else, the purpose of an image must be some kind of exchange. But for that exchange to be possible, it is necessary that these images have something in common, that they participate together in a sort of union. That's why I try to give to my characters what amounts to linkage, and I do this by asking my actors—all my actors—to speak in a certain way, to behave in a certain way, which is always the same way. Yes, for me, the image is like a word in a sentence. Poets themselves use desperately common words despite their ability to elaborate on the vocabulary we all use. But it's precisely the common word, the most commonly used one, which, because it's in the right place, all of a sudden shines extraordinarily in sound and meaning.

BC: Doesn't your description of cinema border on mysticism?

RB: I don't know what you mean by mysticism. I think that in a film, there is also what you did not put in it. You have to put things in without actually doing so; I mean that everything which is important must not be there at the start, but end up being there in the end, or beyond the ending. So what you just called "mysticism" must come from what I feel inside a prison, as the subtitle of *A Man Escaped* indicates: *The Wind Blows Where It Wishes*. I'm talking about those extraordinary currents, the presence of something or somebody—call it what you want—or of a hand that controls everything. Prisoners are very sensitive to this strange atmosphere, which is not a dramatic one. It is on a higher level that some have called "symbolist." There is no apparent drama in prison. You may hear someone getting shot, but this is normal, part of life in a prison. That is, the subject is not in the finger that pulls the trigger or the hands that strangle; it's somewhere else, in the currents that are flowing. At such a moment, something quite odd occurs: Objects become more important than characters. That terrace up there, this wall over here, a curtain, the sound of a train—all are more important than what is happening in their midst. Objects and noises, then—in a mystical sense if you want—exist in intimate union with man. And it's a much more serious union, a much more significant one, than the union, as it were, of a man's hands with the neck of the guard he is strangling.

BC: So, paradoxically, in an art that is all about the outside—about things or objects—it is the inside that commands.

RB: Yes, exactly. Only the conflicts that take place inside the characters give a film its movement, its real movement. A film is the kind of creation that demands an inner style: It needs an author, a writer, whose goal is to produce an effect or a series of effects. If he is conscientious, his preliminary work will consist precisely in going back from the effect desired to the cause. Starting from what he wants to engage, the emotions of the audience, he looks for the best combinations of images and words to elicit those emotions. It's a path walked backwards, with selections and rejections, mistakes and interpolations, all of which lead him fatefully to the origins of his composition—that is to say, to the composition itself.

BC: What kind of value do you place on voice-over commentary as you have used it in certain films of yours?

RB: It's a rhythmic element, another element that interacts with all of the other elements in the picture and modifies them. I would maintain that in *A Man Escaped,* the drama unfolded from the meeting of the tone of the film's voice-over commentary with the tone of its actual dialogue.

BC: Of course, you write or adapt everything for the screen yourself.

RB: Because I need, from a film's origin, to be the absolute master of its ideas. All the more so if one wants to improvise . . .

BC: Have you improvised a great deal in your films?

RB: I'm believing more and more in the necessity of improvisation.

BC: Watching your films, I don't find it obvious that a great deal is left to improvisation.

RB: Strangely enough, some of my films seem to have been very planned and weren't at all, like *Pickpocket,* which was written in three months and shot in the midst of crowds in a minimal amount of time. For *L'argent,* I dreaded that the frequent changes in location, with their different group-ings of people, would cause me to lose the picture's thread. But I managed to pass from one sequence to another by means of sonorous—I should say "musical"—transitions.

BC: Why did you choose Bach's "Fantasie Chromatique" for *L'argent?*

RB: Because I didn't want my pianist to play sentimental music. But, then, Bach's music is always sentimental, so I fooled myself a bit.

BC: Some critics, as you know, took exception to your having shown the bottom of pants legs in *L'argent*.

RB: You must be referring to the pants of the passersby in front of the terrace of a café on one of the "grands boulevards." The impression one has, on arriving at one of these boulevards where there is a crowd, is that of a jumble of legs on the sidewalk making a brisk sound. I tried to impart this impression through the sound and the image. I was similarly reproached, you may recall, about the legs of horses in *Lancelot du lac*. But I showed the legs of the horses, without showing their riders, in order to draw attention to the muscular power of their hindquarters when they braced themselves before taking off during the tournament.

BC: Even in D. W. Griffith's time, legend has it, producers complained about doing close-ups, because they had paid for the whole body of the actor.

RB: To show all in a film comes from the habits of the theater, in the same way as the acting of actors does.

BC: Didn't you begin your work on *Pickpocket* by shooting freely in the streets, only to change your method of filming?

RB: Yes. I had been told, "Hide; it's easy." I hid. But I quickly discovered I had to use tricks, because a hidden camera is not precise. Crowds are a mess, for example; and I wound up using some of that mess in a few shots.

BC: What about the sequence at the Gare de Lyon?

RB: It was shot entirely amidst crowds, in July, during the annual vacation departures. I needed the camera to be very mobile, so rails, a dolly, and marks on the floor were required. Nothing like that could be hidden. On top of all that, there was the din and the jostling.

BC: Yet in *Pickpocket* the camera movements are not really visible.

RB: No more than in my other films where the camera constantly moves.

BC: You don't want the movement to be seen?

RB: The camera is not a moving eye but an encompassing vision.

BC: Did you use these dolly shots in *Pickpocket* so that you could more easily maintain the same distance from the subject?

RB: Not the same distance. On the contrary, it's never the same distance. It's the necessary distance. There is only one place in space where something, at a precise moment, asks to be seen.

BC: Why do you impose such difficulties on yourself during your shoots?

RB: So that I capture only reality. In any event, difficulty clings to me, in the same way as speed does. I've often noticed that anything I've not been able to resolve on paper, if I resolve it on location, while filming, that's the thing I do best.

BC: Was it difficult, in *Lancelot du lac*, to film with horses, knights in armor, and an enormous cast of extras? You had not previously done anything like this.

RB: Contrary to what people think, when you can do it with a little, you can do it with a lot. Besides, having bigger means doesn't relieve you of the responsibility of capturing details, suggesting rather than showing, giving prominence to sound. The tournament sequence was staged for the car in this picture, as were virtually all the other sequences. Nonetheless, I didn't have the luxury of enormous amounts of money in the making of *Lancelot du lac*. Usually, such expense doesn't bring good luck to the cinema, anyway.

BC: Still, for you, this film was a "super-production."

RB: But as anachronistic as possible.

BC: Anachronistic?

RB: You need to remove the past to the present if you want to make it believable. And, don't forget, the Holy Grail, the Christian symbol that the knights seek but do not find—the Grail, which represents the absolute in God—it already figures in pagan Celtic legends. So why can't we extend the quest for this holy cup or platter into contemporary life as you and I know it?

BC: What is piquant in Tolstoy's novella *The Counterfeit Note*—from which you adapted *L'argent*—is its contemporary detail: the high school students, the seller of picture frames, and so on.

RB: I wanted to keep this point of departure because it is apt. But I Gallicized it: I made it Parisian and modern.

BC: *A Man Escaped* is also "modernized," like a new version of *Robinson Crusoe*. The hero sets himself technical problems, so as not to let himself be led into metaphysical despair; he tries to find within himself the spiritual resources necessary for survival.

RB: My heroes seem like shipwrecked men, leaving to discover an unknown island, which is something we encounter as early as the creation of Adam. My next film is *Genesis*, for which I will be undertaking preparations over the next few months.

BC: Where will you shoot your next film? [*Genesis* in fact was never filmed.]

RB: I don't know yet. Not in Palestine or in any of the Middle Eastern countries. I don't want to typecast countries—and, besides, landscapes have never been very important to me. And animals are animals all over the world.

BC: Speaking of animals, what is affecting in the quadruple murder sequence in *L'argent* is that the emotion comes from the cry of the victims' dog.

RB: Many animals have an exquisite sensitivity that we don't try hard enough to know. I myself would like to make more use of it. It's like a doubling, an extension, of our own joys and sufferings.

BC: In *L'argent* you have a very harsh view of the bourgeois world. The likable characters are Yvon—the fuel-oil deliveryman—and the exploited old woman.

RB: *L'argent* is not an antibourgeois film. It's not a question of the, or of a, bourgeois world, but of particular instances in it.

BC: Yet Yvon is to some extent the exterminating angel of this world.

RB: Society abandons him, and his carnage is therefore like the explosion of his despair.

BC: To finish up, how did it come about that you dropped actors in the conventional sense and began to use in their place "models," as you say—people taken from everyday life?

RB: From the first seconds of my first full-length film, my actresses—there were only women in the picture—suddenly were no longer people, and there was nothing left, absolutely nothing, of what I had imagined.

BC: How so?

RB: Because, I suppose, of their very exterior way of speaking and their useless gesturing.

BC: It's been said that you hate actors.

RB: That's absurd. It's as if one were to say, "He's a painter, therefore he doesn't like sculptors." I like the theater, and I like actors. Some are good friends of mine. But I wouldn't be able to work with them. I don't ask anyone to follow me, nor do I wish to follow the way of theater and dramatic acting.

BC: How do you look for the people you call your "models"?

RB: Formerly, I looked for and chose them on the basis of their moral resemblance to my characters. But this approach cost me a great deal of time. Today, as long as nothing appears in a potential "model" that is contrary to my general conception of the character, my decision is made.

BC: Why?

RB: Because characters of our own invention are all too much of a piece. As you know, people are full of eccentricities that often don't appear until much later, or until a particular set of circumstances presents itself. Above all, I rely in casting on my flair for doing it and on chance. Nonetheless, there is the voice, which is a divine thing. Taken apart, separately from any physical aspect, it doesn't permit you, or nearly doesn't permit you, to be misled. So I have to choose very carefully when it comes to the vocal quality of anybody who is to appear in one of my films.

BC: What about your direction of actors, or I suppose I should say "models"?

RB: It isn't a question of directing someone, but of directing oneself. The rest is telepathy.

Filmography of Feature Films

Angels of the Streets, 1943
Les Dames du Bois de Boulogne, 1945
Diary of a Country Priest, 1951
A Man Escaped, 1956
Pickpocket, 1959
The Trial of Joan of Arc, 1962
Au hasard, Balthasar, 1966
Mouchette, 1967
A Gentle Creature, 1969
Four Nights of a Dreamer, 1971
Lancelot du Lac, 1974
The Devil Probably, 1977
L'argent, 1983

Lonely People, Living in the World

The Films of Aki Kaurismäki

THE FINNISH DIRECTOR AKI Kaurismäki sees humor as a black, defensive response to the bleakness of a particular type of human existence, as well as to the way that this existence has been charted in previous (mostly American) films. "Existence" for Kaurismäki in *Ariel* (1988)—as in the two films with which it forms a loose trilogy, *Shadows in Paradise* (1986) and *The Match Factory Girl* (1989)—is limited to the down-and-dirty, proletarian variety: No seamstresses or bakers here, but miners and maids, all of whom are nonetheless lonely people seeking if not finding life companions or finding if not seeking them. Thus does the trilogy play on the conventions of movie romance, the sad as well as the happy kind. In *The Match Factory Girl*, for instance, the pregnant factory worker, deserted by her well-to-do lover, buys rat poison, only to use it on the "rats" in her life instead of herself!

Like his earlier films *Crime and Punishment* (1983) and *Hamlet Goes to Business* (1987)—Kaurismäki made eight or nine features (all with screenplays by him) in his first decade of filmmaking, and he and his older brother, Mika, also a director, continue to be responsible for over one-third of the output of the meager Finnish film industry—*Ariel* immediately refers us, not to studio movies, but to a major work of Western literature. But the reference is ironic, as it is in the two earlier films, since *Ariel* is not in the least about a character who resembles the airy, magical, liberating spirit of *The Tempest*, nor is it about any kind of Jerusalem. (*Ariel* means "lion of God" in Hebrew and is a name applied to the Holy City in the Old Testament.) Regularly lifting his storytelling from classic literature—from Dostoyevsky and Shakespeare, to name only two

I Hired a Contract Killer (1990). Directed by Aki Kaurismäki. Shown from left: Jean-Pierre Léaud, Aki Kaurismäki. *(Courtesy of Photofest)*

authors—Kaurismäki reduces their grand dramatic upheavals and transcendent philosophical concerns to the context of the drab, hemmed-in, nearly hermetic existences led not only by miners and maids but also by assembly-line workers, restaurant employees, and garbage men.

Taisto Sasurinen (Tasi for short), the main character (played by Turo Pajala, who looks like Dan Aykroyd but whose acting is not nearly as "busy" as the American star's), has no religion, no relatives, and no work. The moment we see him, he loses his job as a miner in snowy, cheerless northern Finland. The mine has closed down, and a middle-aged miner bemoans this fact, and his life, over a drink with Tasi in a nearby tavern. Then, after giving his young friend the keys to his car, the older man goes into the men's room and shoots himself to death. Tasi quickly opens the lavatory door, dispassionately observes the miner's body on the floor, and leaves to pick up his car, an old, white Cadillac convertible (in the snow!), which he plans to drive down to Helsinki. After he backs it out of its wooden shed, the structure collapses. Tasi motors on; just as he did not stop for his coworker, he does not stop for the shed: In Kaurismäki's darkly comic world, man and object become moral equivalents.

On the night Tasi gets to Helsinki, he is beaten and robbed of his life savings by two thugs; the next morning he hires on as a day laborer at a warehouse in order to pay for his bed that evening at a flophouse. At work he finds a needed overcoat in the trash, only to be told that it belonged to a man who was run over by a forklift. But Tasi does not complain. He just goes through the motions of his life, smoking one cigarette after another in the process. Even his entering into a relationship with Irmeli Pihlajas (Irmi for short) seems to be just another "motion": They meet as she is ticketing his car. (Irmi is not only a meter maid but also a hotel maid, a meat cutter, and a night watchman at the Bank of Finland—a kind of proletarian ad infinitum, played with just the right mixture of feeling and numbness by Susanna Haavisto). They have dinner (we see only the unappetizing food on their table during this scene); they matter-of-factly go to bed; he smokes. When Irmi tells Tasi that she is divorced and has a son, he replies that he would rather marry into a ready-made family than raise one of his own; when she asks if he will disappear in the morning, Tasi answers without a touch of irony or emotion, "No, we'll be together forever." So they will be, even though we get a scare in the morning when the eleven-year-old boy, Riku, shoves a Luger in Tasi's face after Irmi has left for one of her jobs. The gun does not work, Riku declares; then, without missing a beat, he offers Tasi breakfast.

The same day, after unsuccessfully looking for work at a number of businesses, Tasi retreats to a café where he watches *High Sierra* (1941) on television. Unlike Humphrey Bogart, however, he is no excon planning one last heist before he goes straight. Tasi *is* straight, yet he goes to prison all the same, for what appears to the authorities to be attempted robbery but is really his attempt to recover his life savings from one of the men who mugged him, whom he accidentally spots on the street. The sentence is a year and eleven months (two years in any other film!). Together with his cellmate, Mikkonen—a bespectacled, unassuming (and sedated) man in his late thirties who is serving an eight-year sentence for manslaughter—Tasi quickly plots an escape, which Irmi makes possible by concealing a file in a cake she has baked for him.

No sooner have they married (even marriage places an obstacle in Tasi's path, since he needs two witnesses and initially has only one) than the police are on his trail, even as he and Mikkonen are planning a heist so that they can afford passports and passage out of the country. The heist succeeds, but confederates betray them, mortally wounding Mikkonen and in turn being killed by Tasi, who has to load his gun before firing, since he had deliberately unloaded it before committing armed robbery. He buries his friend at the local dump, as requested, then he, Irmi, and Riku drive to the docks with all the loot. As they row out near dawn to meet their ship, which will take them to Mexico, the camera pans gently to their left until the ship's name, *Ariel*, comes into view, and a male voice sings "Over the Rainbow" in Finnish on the soundtrack.

Unlike the Bogie of *High Sierra*, then, Tasi is neither shot to death for his crimes nor deprived of reunion with his moll. He gets to live, and he gets to love, but his happiness and the happiness of *Ariel*'s ending are tempered by both the accidental quality of its narrative—by the way in which Tasi meanders out of rather than repudiates the life of a loner, as well as by the way in which he falls into rather than chooses even a life of crime—and the chilly darkness (a darkness that becomes wanness during daylight scenes) of Timo Salminen's cinematography, not to speak of the fatuous optimism of Kaurismäki's playing "Over the Rainbow" over the final scene and naming the getaway ship *Ariel*.

What lingers in the mind after a viewing of *Ariel*, in any event, is not the final image of Tasi, Irmi, and Riku looking up from their rowboat at the ship of their dreams, but the image of Tasi alone and exposed to the world, yet somehow also inured to it, as he drives down the open road in his white Cadillac, its top down (because he either does not think to put it up or does not know how to) and its radio blaring. When the top finally gets put up—by another loner, Mikkonen, just before he dies in the backseat—Tasi is sitting up front with Irmi and Riku, his world now more secure, more ordered, but also more circumscribed and more insistent. It is as if his life were beginning anew, this time within the confines of the classical Hollywood cinema.

His life, but not his acting, for the acting in *Ariel*, as in *The Match Factory Girl*—indeed, as in this Finnish director's numerous films to date—may seem superficial, but it is not. ("Numerous" may appear to be an overstatement in the previous sentence, but it is not. In his productivity as well as his presence, the fiftyish Kaurismäki could become to his generation of Finnish filmmakerts what Jörn Donner was to the previous one.) This is because Kaurismäki's characters tend to lead dead-end existences that have naturally deadened their spirits, and they are not offered very many emotional outlets or stimulants. Playing such characters, as Kati Outinen sympathetically has done first in Kaurismäki's *Hamlet Goes to Business* and next in *The Match Factory Girl*, itself may appear easy but is in fact difficult, for it requires intense concentration, the subtlest of suggestion, and rigorous self-control, even self-denial. In other words, such acting calls for more than simply "doing nothing," and all the more so, paradoxically, in a film like *The Match Factory Girl*, where the characters talk so little.

Not a word is spoken by them for the first fifteen or twenty minutes, and for the rest of this seventy-minute movie, which includes a number of accentuating long takes, conversation is limited to brief utterances or fleeting exchanges (the longest of which occurs in a letter the heroine "writes" in voice-over). Indeed, most of the speech we hear comes, not from the characters, but from the televisions and movie screens they watch together with the radios and jukeboxes they listen to. These are people who not only are isolated within the frame, even when they occupy it along with someone else, but whose bodies are also occasionally fragmented by the frame into anonymous limbs, torsos, or extremities, and who are regularly excluded from it altogether.

Such exclusion occurs during *temps mort*, or "dead time" when the camera photographs an empty room or street, prior to a character's entrance into the frame, or holds on a location after the character has departed—which Kaurismäki uses in this film, often before as well as after the same scene, more than in any of his others and more than any director in recent memory with the exception of Jim Jarmusch (who coincidentally was one of the actors in Kaurismäki's *Leningrad Cowboys Go America* [1989]). Unlike Ozu, Antonioni, Bresson, and lately Jarmusch, Kaurismäki uses dead time less as an anti "action" device—as a way of making his fiction give up some of its screen time to the world from which it was drawn, for the purpose of calling attention to the mystery, inviolability, and ultimate stasis of that world—than as an antihuman one. That is, so insistent is his use of dead time (at least once creating nearly an entire sequence out of it: the opening one depicting the mechanized matchbox factory) that he seems intent, not only on registering the sublime indifference of the physical world to the problems and needs of his characters, but also on positing this people-free world as a comically serene alternative to the deadly one defiled by human cruelty, imperfection, and torpor.

The Match Factory Girl is the third film of the trilogy that chronicles the dour existence of the Finnish working class, after *Ariel*. Kaurismäki's minimalistic style in these films, in which he shoots one (uninflected) action or movement or gesture, one (suppressed) emotion, one *inaction* at a time in uninterrupted time, and where he limits his focus to a small cast of characters, fits the pared-down lives of his people in a way that seems obvious—now that this Finn has realized it. But it is Kaurismäki's darkly comic, subversively hilarious tone that, more than anything else, has drawn attention to the trilogy and that, combined with his unostentatious minimalism, lands him somewhere between Robert Bresson and Buster Keaton.

To be sure, Kaurismäki does not glamorize his workers by planting them in heroic plots (as Martin Ritt did in *Norma Rae* [1979]), but neither does he portray them as the pathetic victims of an oppressive socioeconomic system (as Lars Forsberg did in *The Yankee* [1970]). What he does is use humor as a mocking response to the dreary existence of the bare economic integer, the average worker, in a Scandinavian society

Leningrad Cowboys Go America (1989). Directed by Aki Kaurismäki. Shown: The Leningrad Cowboys. © Orion Pictures. *(Courtesy Orion Pictures/Photofest)*

defined by averageness. And he complements that humor with station-ary camera placements, mostly in the medium-to-full range, which keep us somewhat at a distance from his characters. Kaurismäki's purpose, as I imply above, is not to make the proletarian life seem either more courageous or more miserable than it really is, but rather to get us to think about just what constitutes such a life and to get his characters to collaborate, not in their own ridicule, but in their metacinematic libera-tion from a ridiculous existence. Theirs is a life without hope, without horizons, without contest or contrast, and Kaurismäki finds these people precisely at the moment when they are consciously or subconsciously waking up to this fact.

Iris (Kati Outinen) is the match factory girl, except that she is no longer a girl. Rather, she is a woman in her late twenties or early thirties who lives with her mother (Elina Salo) and stepfather (Esko Nikkari) and appears to be their primary, if not sole, support. Iris works at a drab match factory in Helsinki, where the only color seems to come from the matchboxes and where her only job is to make sure that their labels are firmly attached as they roll past her on the assembly line. Her life outside the factory is just as monotonous as her life inside it (as her home address, 44 Factory Lane, suggests): She cooks, she cleans, she reads, she sleeps. This is a woman who is washed out in look and outlook and whose wanness is matched by Timo Salminen's cinematography, which seems to drain the light from each scene despite the fact that the film takes place in June or July (when Helsinki receives its annual ration of sun).

Iris is ready for a change, however, which she decides to effect one night by buying a bright red dress and going dancing, much to her parents' surprise and disapproval. (The first line of dialogue in *The Match Factory Girl* is spoken by Iris's stepfather, who calls his stepdaughter a "whore" and slaps her upon discovering the dress and the consequent missing money from her pay envelope.) Dancing for Iris is a means to an end, not an end itself, and that end is finding a man. She finds Aarne (Vesa Vierikko), a sleek businessman with a sports car and posh apartment, who promptly takes her to bed and leaves her some money in the morning. She leaves him her phone number, not realizing that this womanizer has no intention of seeing her again. When Aarne does not call, the worried Iris—who has just passed another birthday—marches to his place and more or less coerces him into another date, after which he dumps her outright. By this time she is pregnant, in response to which her parents kick her out of the house and Aarne mails her a check for an abortion, even though she has expressed a desire to keep the child as well as him. The mortified Iris then goes to live with her brother, who may offer her shelter but offers nothing in the way of consolation: not a word or a hug, nor even his mere presence together with her in the same apartment. It is here, alone in a living room dominated by a jukebox and a pool table, that Iris decides to take revenge on humanity.

Her first step is to buy rat poison at the drugstore, in a dryly humorous scene that belies the desperateness of her design. "Large or small?" asks the clerk, as if her customer were purchasing a medication instead of a toxin. "What does it do?" inquires Iris, trying to gauge how much of the substance she'll need to accomplish her mission. "It kills," responds the slightly incredulous clerk. The match factory girl's first victim is, of course, Aarne, to whom she returns his check before methodically dispatching him by pouring rat poison into his drink. Predictably, Aarne is in another room of his apartment when Iris does this. Unpredictably, and therefore comically, she poisons her next victim—an anonymous man who comes on to her at a bar—as he sits next to her and watches. He thinks she is spiking his drink; she knows she is murdering him. Both smile.

Iris's last stop is her parents' house, where her mother lets her in, and the daughter begins dutifully fixing supper as she always has, except that this time she pours rat poison into the water pitcher. Iris sits, smoking, in the living room as her mother and father dine in the kitchen; we watch her, in a long take, not her victims. We do not even see them drink their drinks. Moreover, we do not observe any of Iris's prey in their death throes, for such a scene if serious would disturb *The Match*

Factory Girl's wryly humorous tone by creating sympathy for the victims, and if comic would send the film into the savagely satirical realm of a Monty Python movie.

To be sure, *The Match Factory Girl* has its savage, even nihilistic side, but that side is kept in check, for Kaurismäki's intent is not to sacrifice the humanity of Iris or his other characters to his vision of a mad, cruel world. Instead, he aims to document Iris's sacrificing of her *own* humanity to such a world, her decision to match its casual inhumanity with her own, deliberate inhumaneness—to go her society one better, in other words, by going it one worse. And it is the memory of her *self*-sacrifice that we take away from this film, not the sacrifice of her victims, not her victimization by an exploitative patriarchy, not her droll manipulation by a Kaurismäki set on taking his own revenge against the numbing, morose sameness of life lived without possibility of enrichment or escape. By her homicidal acts, Iris has chosen to live the rest of her life in a literal prison instead of a figurative one, and the last scene of *The Match Factory Girl*— shot in deep focus, with no cutting—shows her silently being removed from her place of employment by the police. They enter at the top of the frame; Iris labors at the bottom. After she is gone, the camera continues to hold on the same space as another worker busies himself in the background. On the soundtrack we hear the same kind of saccharine love song that Iris has listened to alone throughout the film—in cafés and bars, at home, and at work—and that seems to have influenced her idealized conception of romance.

Iris is not dancing with anyone, then, at the end of *The Match Factory Girl*. Aarne is dead and was keener for sex than dancing, anyway. She has desired the sociability of dance and the intimacy of romance but instead has met first with objectification and then rejection, even by her parents. Part of the problem is Iris's plainness bordering on unattractiveness, but there can be little question that what happened to her could just as easily happen to a more appealing woman. Iris's looks clearly exacerbate her situation, but they are not its cause. We must look for that to the drudgery of her working as well as family life and also to the remoteness, even solitude, of the Finns (especially the men), which has something to do with their severe Scandinavian climate but more, I suspect, with their fuzzy (inter)national identity. (Finland was a part of Sweden until 1809 and an autonomous Grand Duchy within Czarist Russia from 1809 to 1917. In other words, for generations the Finns existed under the political dominance of the Russians and in the cultural shadow of the Swedes—a condition made worse by their "isolating" language, the only one in Scandinavia that is not Indo-European in origin.) All of this is small comfort to Iris, who can now look forward to her own life of solitude behind bars—at least until her baby is born, at which time the authorities will have to decide whether to grant her clemency or separate this mother irrevocably from her child and thus even further from her fellow human beings.

As opposed to living in oblivion, like Iris and many another Kaurismäki character, oblivion is the state into which the protagonist (if that is the word) is pummeled at the start of Kaurismäki's film *The Man without a Past* (2002), the second entry in his "Helsinki trilogy" after *Drifting Clouds* (1996). (The final member of the trilogy, *Laitakaupungin valot [Lights in the Dust]*, was released in 2006.) "M," the only rubric (for *mies*—the Finnish word for man—not for "Mörder" or murderer as in Fritz Lang's *M* [1931]) ascribed to this character in the credits, wakes up in a hospital without a scintilla of memory of the man he used to be; but, unlike countless other amnesiacs in any number of forgettable Hollywood B movies from the 1940s or 1950s (such as *Man in the Dark* [1953], itself remade from *The Man Who Lived Twice* [1936]), M does not embark on a manic search for the life he used to lead or the places he used to know. But, then again, Kaurismäki has never been one to borrow a plot structure, movie genre, or dramatic device (and, among such devices, amnesia has long since been consigned to the great and growing slag heap of exhausted conventions) and leave it unaltered.

The writer-director of twenty-four features and shorts since his 1981 début picture, the music documentary *Saimaa-ilmio*, Kaurismäki achieved, in *The Man without a Past*, American distribution for one of his films for the first time in ten years. It may also be the last, given the facts that Kaurismäki boycotted the 2002 New York Film Festival in solidarity with the State-Department-banned Iranian director Abbas Kiarostami, and that in the same year he absented himself as well from the Academy Awards (where *The Man without a Past* was the first Finnish nominee for best foreign-language film) to protest the Anglo-American invasion of Iraq. The disappearance of his work from American screens would be a pity, because, not only has Kaurismäki been a European film-festival favorite for around two decades—particularly at Cannes, where *The Man without a Past* won the Grand Prize in addition to the award for best actress—he also belongs to a small group of European filmmakers who have been able to eke out international careers.

The reason Kaurismäki's possible "disappearance" would also be a pity is not just that he hails from Finland, an underrepresented minority on the international cinema scene, but also that his style and tone, if not his subject matter, are unique. That subject, again, is the working class, which in Finland can consist of the most dull and laconic of human creatures. But, as I have indicated, it is primarily his dryly humorous, deadpan ironic tone toward, or "take" on, his fellow Finns that has made Kaurismäki's cinema stand out and that, combined with his pared-down style, has landed him in the past somewhere between Keaton and Bresson. Not in *The Man without a Past*, however, where Preston Sturges or Frank Capra replaces Bresson and whose final shot comes right out of Charlie Chaplin.

Thus, as he has sometimes done in previous films, Kaurismäki takes a narrative from popular cinema and puts his own seriocomic spin on it. Indeed, *The Man without a Past*, he has said, is an attempt to pay tribute to Finnish silent melodrama of the 1920s as well to rework the hackneyed plot of a typical Hollywood B picture. (*The Man without a Past* even has intimations of the skid-row internationalism found in 1920s European proletarian novels like B. Traven's *Death Ship* or Victor Serge's *Men in Prison*.) Similarly, Kaurismäki's previous film, *Juha* (1999), was a black-and-white silent movie (save for its musical score and a few other sounds, like that of a door closing) of peasant woes that repositions a silent classic of Finnish cinema—Mauritz Stiller's 1921 *Johan*, itself based on a 1911 novel by Juhani Aho—somewhere at the intersection of farce and melodrama known as Aki World.

We begin with grimness as M arrives in present-day Helsinki by train in the early morning hours, carrying a suitcase that may contain everything he owns. Almost immediately after falling asleep on a park bench near the train station he is savagely beaten, robbed, and left for dead by three thugs. (Compare this beating-cum-robbery with the one near the start of *Ariel*.) Although anyone else hit over the head with a baseball bat, like M, would at least be unconscious, this man is able to rise up shortly thereafter and stagger to the men's room at the railway station, where he collapses—a bloody mess taken for dead by the porter. We find M next on a gurney, where an emergency-room physician pronounces him dead at 5:12 a.m. and a nurse covers his corpse. Promptly thereafter M rises once more, his head swathed in bandages (like Claude Rains in *The Invisible Man* [1933] or Boris Karloff in *The Mummy* [1932]), and stumbles out of the hospital, only to collapse again near the Helsinki waterfront. If, after twice watching the image of an apparently deceased victim abruptly getting up from his deathbed, we needed further evidence that Kaurismäki was beginning his version of a Christian parable-cum-proletarian fable, we get that evidence in the next scene when M is resurrected for a third time.

Asleep or comatose on the coast of the Gulf of Finland, M has his boots stolen by a bum (who leaves his sneakers in exchange), then is noticed by two boys who pass by carrying a litter with an upside-down white (gas or water) container attached to it. They wonder aloud whether M is dead, and they go for help in the form of their mother, whom we subsequently see feeding soup to a revived M outdoors as her sons watch.

These two look uncannily like the boys in the painting *The Wounded Angel*, by the Finnish symbolist Hugo Simberg (1873–1917); Simberg's two boys also walk next to a shore carrying a litter, but theirs has a winged yet stooped angel atop it with a head wound.

The connection between someone like M and an angel certainly would not have been tenuous in Simberg's work. He painted pictures primarily of death and devils—ever-present characters of Finnish folklore—in an ironically humorous manner; Simberg's poor, crestfallen devils suffer the hardships of fate just like the much-afflicted Finnish people of his time, for whom death itself was an accepted part of everyday life and even a comforting friend. But Simberg treated angels in almost the same way as devils: as vulnerable beings who could accidentally hurt themselves or intentionally be hurt by others. Thus did this symbolist painter and graphic artist connect the netherworld or the otherworldly, as well as the forces of nature, with the fates and dreams of ordinary Finnish people. And thus does Aki Kaurismäki—whose work average Finns find as strange today as they did Simberg's a century ago—do the same in his cinema, for the first time.

With no memory of his identity or his past life, the (extra)ordinary M is nursed back to health by Kaisa and Nieminen, the parents of the towheaded boys who found him. They are squatters living in a shantytown on the forlorn urban periphery of Helsinki where the rail yards meet the harbor (also the setting of *Laitakaupungin valot*, which literally translates as "lights on the outskirts of town")—except that this shantytown consists not of ramshackle huts or makeshift cabins but of abandoned freight containers. M gets one for himself with the help of a security guard named Anttila, who fashions himself the landlord of this postindustrial wasteland. And because M is unable to recall his name or social security number, which makes finding a regular job and an apartment impossible, it is here on the margins of society that he must find a new life—must experience a kind of rebirth, that is, which will be touched by its own form of grace. "Life goes on," he gnomically declares, "not backwards," so it is to the future M shall look, to which he senses he has no choice but to look, for the creation of his identity and society.

That future consists of a world where the helpless and homeless must help each other as well as themselves, thus creating something like a society of the disenfranchised. Nieminen, a part-time watchman at a coal yard, introduces M, for example, to the Salvation Army soup kitchen, where he not only gets some soup (and eventually a job loading trucks) but also meets a girl, a Salvation Army officer by the name of Irma, who has infinite trust in God's mercy. Like M, she is a stylized creature with a solemn, weathered face, a curiously formal manner, and a telegraphed inner life that belies the bland conformity of her surface "style." In Irma's case, that inner life—the warmth of which strongly attracts M—is awakened late each night when she returns to her lonely dormitory room, lies down on a narrow bed, and listens to a mid-1960s version of "Do the Shake" by the Anglo-Finnish rockabilly band The Renegades.

In M's case, the revivifying or redemptive music is Blind Lemon Jefferson's "Crawlin' Baby Blues," which he hears on a jukebox salvaged for him from a junk pile and provided with power by a charitable electrician. In this particular land of diminishing returns, the electrical worker asks M only for the promise of one future consideration in return for his favor: "If you see me lying face down in the gutter, turn me on my back." Perhaps he wishes to be placed in this position so that he can be a bit more comfortable as he listens to popular music—rock 'n' roll, rhythm and blues, or Finnish tango—which has always been a salve for Kaurismäki's downtrodden characters. In *The Man without a Past*, the balm of music meets the analgesic of religion when M transforms the Salvation Army Christian band into a swinging pop combo whose open-air concerts attract large crowds.

Their début occurs, not by chance, on the Midsummer Day of June 24—the feast of the birth of John the Baptist, the forerunner as well as baptizer of Jesus Christ—and features a song about memory and the past sung by the venerable Finnish tango singer Annikki Tähti. (She also plays the role of the manager of the Salvation Army thrift shop where M gets a "new" set of clothes.) That song, her 1955 gold record titled "Do You Remember Mon Repos?" is a doubly nostalgic lament in this film, for it refers not only to M's previous life but also to the Finnish province of Karelia (where the spacious park Mon Repos, or "my repose," is located), which was annexed by the Soviet Union in 1944 and remains part of Russia today. The song may also refer to Kaurismäki's previous films, in which the late lamented actor Matti Pellonpää (who died prematurely in 1995 and who himself is resurrected in a photograph that appears on the wall of a bar in *The Man without a Past*) was frequently featured in roles, like that of M, that required a sad-looking, hangdog, even canine-featured type of character.

Save for this little musical scene with Annika Tähti, however, *The Man without a Past* does not dwell on the past. M's own memory of the past, however, is revived by two incidents in the film: At the shipyard near his "home," he sees a man cutting metal with an acetylene torch, knows that he can do this, too, and thus remembers that he used to be a welder; and news coverage of a bank robbery that M witnessed has put his face in all the papers, with the result that a woman in the northern town of Nurmes recognizes M as her missing husband, one Jaakko Anttila Lujanen. But M wants no part of his married (welded?) past, and neither does his wife, for she was in the process of divorcing him—in part on account of his gambling habit—when he left home to look for a new job in Helsinki (where we first catch up with him).

Returning to the capital after traveling north to confirm his divorce, M encounters the three unwise men who beat him up near the train station, but this time he routs them with miraculous, last-minute assistance from his fellow down-and-outers. In return, they will be the sole beneficiaries of the new potatoes M has recently harvested from a patch of black soil he turned into a garden amidst the twisted metal, decrepit boxcars, and assorted trash heaps that surround his living area. Just so, exemployees of the bank robber were the gratified beneficiaries of money from his robbery, which he charged M the witness with distributing before shooting himself to death. (He explained, somewhat disingenuously, that the cash he stole was his own: assets that the bank had frozen when his company went bankrupt.) And Irma, who tells M that he is her first love, will be the continuing beneficiary of his love as, happily united, she and her man walk hand-in-hand away from the camera, only to have our view of them abruptly obscured by a passing freight train until the image then fades to black.

Is this a happy ending? Yes and no. Even though that hurtling, even obliterating train at the end ought to tell you something, certainly there is a strain of sentimentality here to go along with all the whimsy, as there has been throughout *The Man without a Past*. (By contrast, there is no whimsy to go along with all the sentimentality in *Regarding Henry* [1991], or *The Man without a Past* written from the point of view of high-end Americans.) But the real miracle in this movie is not that M offers deliverance to the human refuse of Helsinki or that they offer it to him; it is that M does not see any reason, once "recovered," not to treat everybody in the kindly way he was treated when he was down. That includes representatives of officialdom, Finlandia-style, who are less Dickensian villains here than soulless victims of their own faith in bureaucratic regulation.

As for the real villains, the muggers, they beat up M again in Kaurismäki's alternative, unfilmed ending to *The Man without a Past* and throw him into a trash can. According to the director, "Then comes the garbage truck and picks him up. In the last image, the woman [Irma] is in the garbage field with a stick, trying to find him" (Kaurismäki quoted in the *New York Times*, April 6, 2003). This ending may be an indication that the fairy-tale-like plot structure of *The Man without a Past*, as filmed, should be taken as the vision of a distinctively Finnish afterlife (subsequent to M's beating death in the film's first five minutes) or paradise with a proletarian twist.

Indeed, such a vision seems to have been inspired by the ending of Vittorio De Sica's *Miracle in Milan* (1951), if not by the whole of this neorealist comic fantasy that is simultaneously a veristic social document. For, in *The Man without a Past* Kaurismäki wanted, he has said, "to make a film about homelessness without making it so socially declaring" (*New York Times*, April 6, 2003), even as he made a similar picture about unemployment in *Drifting Clouds* (in which a hapless, down-on-their-luck husband and wife somehow manage to stumble into a happy ending that is as unlikely as it is pleasing.) And De Sica himself appears to have had the same intention in *Miracle in Milan*, which followed such grim, nearly mirthless neorealist dramas of his as *Shoeshine* (1947) and *Bicycle Thieves* (1948), only itself to be succeeded by the melancholy starkness of *Umberto D.* (1952).

As I have stated in the chapter on De Sica's neorealist films, the famous finale of *Miracle in Milan* implies that the poor-in-body but pure-in-soul have no choice but to soar to the skies and seek their heaven apart from the hopeless earth—which is to say, only in their imaginations or in life after death. Thus, to the criticism that this picture's use of the fanciful, even the burlesque or farcical, increasingly overshadows its social commentary about the exploitation and disenfranchisement of the underclass in an industrialized nation, one can respond that there is nonetheless an element of political despair or pessimism, as well as open-ended spiritual quandary, in the fairy-tale happy ending of *Miracle in Milan*. In fact, the entire film can be seen as an extended metaphor, or hymn, to the role of illusion, fantasy, and myth in life as in art. In a way not dissimilar to Kaurismäki's, then, De Sica tells us that the human impulse to creativity, invention, or fabrication, in the secular and religious realms as well as the aesthetic one in-between, is capable of transcending social problems but not of resolving them, like the broomsticks that carry the poor over the Cathedral of Milan, or the two Simberg-inspired boys who help bring the wounded M back to life in *The Man without a Past*.

Miracle in Milan takes place somewhere at the intersection of farce and pathos, however, whereas the pathetic is absent from Kaurismäki's films in general and from *The Man without a Past* in particular. It is not necessarily *inherently* absent from Kaurismäki's subjects (particularly as they might be treated by another director), but pathos is certainly absent from all the acting in this auteur's cinema. The reason is that his characters, living in a deadeningly glacial environment, tend to lead dead-end existences that appear to have blocked their emotional outlets. So, to have such characters acted in a self-conscious, emotive style would be artistically dishonest (not to speak of being psychologically untrue to the Finnish national character as I know it from extended, firsthand experience in this quasisocialistic country).

Watch Markku Peltola as M, for example, as he walks into a café, orders a cup of free hot water, then slowly extracts a dry, much-used tea bag from a matchbox, ready for redunking, and you will see what I mean: acting that is true to the man, his circumstances, and his experience. Chaplin would have transformed this moment into a miniature ballet of self-pity—into the extraction of *our* pity—but Kaurismäki prefers to stake his comedy in the glum, the offbeat, and the cool or detached. Peltola may not be lovable or even pitiable as a result, but he may be more characteristically human. His acting, moreover—like that of Kaurismäki veteran Kati Outinen in the role of Irma—may appear one-dimensional, but it is no such thing.

Understated is what it is, figuratively speaking, and such understatement is clearly the opposite of the externalizing of emotions—of laughing, shouting, crying, or pouting—that we see all the time in conventional, or commercial, narrative cinema. The dialogue itself in *The Man without a Past* could be said to understated—literally understated, as when Kaisa rhetorically asks M, "So you can talk, then?" after he had failed to speak for the first several hours of their acquaintance. "Sure," M replies. "I just didn't have anything to say before." And he means what he says, as in this exchange between him and Irma before he leaves briefly for Nurmes:

M: Will you stay and help me pack?

Irma: But you have nothing.

M: That's why: Let's sit and be silent.

You can find similarly understated dialogue, and acting, in the films of Kaurismäki's contemporaries, the American Jim Jarmusch and the Japanese Takeshi Kitano, as well as in the cinema of his closest artistic ancestor, the German Rainer Werner Fassbinder. (In a possible culinary reference to Kitano, Kaurismäki includes an incongruous sequence on the train back to Helsinki from Nurmes in which M, seated in the restaurant car, eats sushi with chopsticks and drinks sake. In his *Mystery Train* [1990], Jarmusch himself included an entire narrative strand devoted to precisely the kind of young Japanese couple [here on a visit to America] that we find in Kitano's films.) But Kaurismäki's northern European sensibility is finally his own, and it seems to be growing sweeter as he grows older. I mean by this not only that the good end happily and the bad unhappily in *The Man without a Past*. I am also referring to the fact that there is no use of "dead time" in this film, as there is in Kaurismäki's darker pictures—particularly *The Match Factory Girl*, where, as I have already indicated, this device dominates the narrative.

There is no such alternative, unpeopled, nonnarrative world in *The Man without a Past*, not because human cruelty, imperfection, and torpor have miraculously disappeared from the earth, but because they have been divinely transcended. And the idea that they have been transcended is suggested not only by Kaurismäki's eschewing of his usual long takes for an insistently oppositional pattern of cutting (particularly in scenes with authoritarian figures such as a malignant police inspector and an unsympathetic unemployment-office manager). Such transcendence is also suggested by Timo Salminen's summery cinematography, whose wind-scrubbed blue drawn from the Nordic sky and generally warm pigmentation in place of chilly wanness are to be equated with divine lumpen solidarity rather than grim proletarian sameness.

The Man without a Past thus posits a social problem but eschews any direct or critical treatment of it. Does this picture thereby imply less that such a problem cannot be solved than that human nature or fallibility will make it recur in some other form? Probably, though this is clearly not the major theme of the film. That theme has more to do with the passage of time, the process of memory, and the creation of self out of the contingencies of existence, as well as the operation of subjective consciousness on the objects of the material world—not to speak of the role of Christianity in the organizing of all our fleeting perceptions.

The Man without a Past may not be a social-problem picture, then, but to my mind it is something better or more permanent: a meditation on the fundamental solitude of the human condition, sporadically interrupted as it may be by attempts at infinite solicitude on the road to death's final embrace. Aki Kaurismäki's evolving worldview in this film may thus be summed up in a bit of dialogue from its predecessor in the "Helsinli trilogy," *Drifting Clouds*: "Life is short and miserable. Be as merry as you can."

An Interview with
Aki Kaurismäki

The following interview took place on November 15, 2003, in the Restaurant Elite, Helsinki, Finland.

BERT CARDULLO: Your name *Kaurismäki* has an interesting ring. Is it your
real name, and has it been in the family for generations?

AKI KAURISMÄKI: It is the same name I was born with, yes, but my grand-
father changed his name from something Russian. It means "Deer Hill."
Nobody in Finland has this last name except my family, and now my wife.
She's the one who lately always insists that I write a part for my dog,
Tähti, in each of my films. Can we get to the real questions now?

BC: Okay. Is it true that you began as a film critic?

AK: Yes, but I was a bad one. For me it was only masterpieces or shit, and
that's not the right way to be a critic. The correct way is to be honest and
not pretend anything—the same stuff as it takes to be a good filmmaker.

BC: Why did you start making films?

AK: Because I wanted to. Film schools wouldn't let me in. I was too
stubborn. So I learned by watching films from the archives and reading.
You can learn a lot about the cinema if you read a lot.
    Before I shot anything on my first film, I went with a friend and his
camera inside a slaughterhouse—a hall of dead cows. It was completely
silent. And my friend explained what sort of lenses we had, the differences
between his camera and an ordinary still camera, and so on. Once I
understood, I said, "Fine, but never mention this discussion to anybody!"

175

And so then I was able to go out on the set and command, "Camera here! Give me 50 millimeters!"

BC: For you, filmmaking is pretty much a straightforward affair, isn't it?

AK: Yes, all you need are some actors and a camera. You get them to walk about and talk and the camera to shoot. That's all. The magic comes later, in the editing. This is the part that interests me most, so I almost always do it alone—really alone. I shut myself in a room for days and days. What I especially enjoy is mixing the music; I always have some tunes in my head and then I take a pile of records into the editing room.

I use a Steenbeck editing machine so that I can really handle the material—none of this digital equipment. Nowadays people think that technology solves all the mental or intellectual problems, which it doesn't. Everything has to be based on a human story and technology doesn't help with that.

BC: The Leningrad Cowboys are themselves a story. Were they a singing group before you made your 1989 film about them?

AK: Yes. They had changed their name from the Cold Slippers about a year before *Leningrad Cowboys Go America* was made. They had the hair before I worked with them. When I saw them, I felt they had a problem, but for a long time I couldn't figure out what it was. Finally I realized they needed the shoes—cold slippers!—so they would not appear to be blown away on a windy day. They still perform together. Some day, I plan to make an epic about the Leningrad Cowboys meeting Ulysses.

BC: What's your relationship with your regular cinematographer, Timo Salminen?

AK: Timo does the lighting, and I frame the picture. But, again, I do my own editing, I select the music, and I supervise the mix.

BC: What about the use of color as opposed to black and white, as in your 1999 black-and-white film *Juha*, a remake of the classic Finnish peasant drama. Your version of *Juha* even eschewed the use of sound!

AK: I am in love with colors that remind me of Hollywood films of the fifties. But Technicolor has disappeared, so I cannot make the same thing anymore. Yet it is true that some movies, such as Victor Fleming's *Gone with the Wind* and Douglas Sirk's *Written on the Wind*, deeply influenced me in the way that they played with backgrounds. Which is much more difficult to express in black and white. I sometimes carry swatches on the set, you know, comparing colors to obtain a satisfactory color scheme. Some stories call for color, others for black and white—never in between. I am a realist, but you have to be successful in making colors become surreal, or nonrealistic. So I guess you could say that I try to use color poetically, that I am more a poet than a social or political commentator—as in *The Man without a Past*, which is a film about homelessness without being too openly declarative about the problem. After all, you do not make films about ideas, you make films based on stories and the people in them.

BC: You cast the people, or the parts, in your films yourself, don't you?

AK: Of course. I find my actors in bars, where I spend a lot of time myself. Seriously, they're all professionals, but people say I never let them act. Well, many of them are from the theater, where they are taught that the art of acting is shouting. My relationship with my actors has never changed. I hold my finger up when I want them to say the line. They say it and then I say, "Thank you very much." If they want more detailed direction, in that case there is always the door.

BC: Is there any relationship between your theory of acting and Bertolt Brecht's?

AK: I guess so, in the sense that I believe that "acting" should be avoided in films and that actors should avoid identifying themselves too deeply with any role they play. When I was a student, there was a lot of interest in Brecht's theater, and it's likely that his idea of an epic or dialectical theater, as opposed to a dramatic and illusionist one, influenced me. I like Brecht's idea that the actor should regard himself as a narrator who only *quotes* the character he is playing. In this way, audiences are provoked to draw intellectual conclusions instead of just becoming emotionally attached to what they see.

BC: As Rainer Werner Fassbinder did, you work with a regular troupe of actors. Why?

AK: Go ask John Ford and Howard Hawks why they filmed so often with this moron named John Wayne. You know why? For his walk. Jean-Luc Godard once said how much he hates John Wayne when he's a villain and how much he loves him when he takes Natalie Wood in his arms at the end of *The Searchers*; be that as it may, the walk always stayed the same.

So why bother with new actors when the ones you have can do the job? Why replace a good actor just because you are making a new film?

BC: Do you shoot more than one take?

AK: No. Normally, I shoot the rehearsal and then I pretend to shoot the first take. Nowadays, I can afford to shoot the first take, too, but I always print the rehearsal. I don't use too many takes because, in my opinion, each time the actors are less fresh. That is why I don't even let them read the dialogue before we shoot. You see, I like acting when I see it in other people's films, but for me it isn't suitable. I have another rule, by the way, in addition to the one that forbids shouting: no laughing. And I use a very formal Finnish speech. I tried to do films in street Finnish, but it never worked. As I'm sure you realize from your own experience, people in Finland don't really talk as precisely as they do in my movies.

BC: Which directors reign supreme in your pantheon of influences?

AK: Robert Bresson, for one: I made *The Match Factory Girl* in order to make Bresson seem like a director of epic motion pictures. Godard—he created his own filmic revolution. Then there is Ozu, whom I discovered at age nineteen when I saw *Twilight in Tokyo*. What moves me in Ozu's work above all else is his humanity, his honesty, his rectitude. In a sense, I am very Japanese in my own work. No ornamentation; the basis for all art is reduction, simplicity. You go from an initial idea or narrative that you progressively reduce until it is sufficiently bare enough to be true. Then, and only then, are you finished.

BC: I know that you are also attracted to the poetic realism of French cinema of the 1930s, particularly the films of Jean Vigo.

AK: Yes, his last picture, *L'Atalante*, is one of the most important movies ever made. I saw *L'Atalante* for the first time in the late 1970s at a film club in Helsinki. It was made by a man who knew he was dying, and for that reason he showed the beauty of life as he was never going to experience it again. I especially admire sequences such as one in which the young husband, distraught at his wife's desertion, leaps into the river and swims underwater to search for her. That is the sort of cinema which is quite close to painting. I don't know how the hell they did it in the late 1920s, but scenes like those in *L'Atalante* come as close to poetry as anything else in art. I'd sacrifice three hundred Hollywood directors in return for Vigo's being able to return to life and make more films like that, and that's an overestimate because they don't have any real directors in California anyway!

BC: Speaking of Hollywood . . .

AK: I'd rather not, but I know you want to hear something on this subject, so I will say a few things. Hollywood is the reason I make the films I do. Because I hate the place. And I would never go there or waste my time watching its current offerings. I may make a bad film, but I refuse to make shit of the kind that Hollywood produces every day. I love the old Hollywood, but the modern one is just a dead rattlesnake that does not even know it's dead. I am like a dog, always barking about Hollywood because with its power, it could make some really good films. Instead, sixty-year-old men are creating boy-scout-level—and boring—violence; crass commercialism is killing the cinema. Why should people go out and pay money to see such bad movies when they can stay at home and see bad television for nothing? I just have no esteem for films in which people are slaughtered with guns (and more), and this is called "entertainment."

Look, a film is always drawn on a certain scale. If you start to shoot brutality at random and play with explosives, then nothing will be enough. In the old days, you had one murder, and that was enough; now you have to kill three hundred thousand people just to get the audience's attention. If the film is tuned on a minimalist level, however, even the sound of a cough will be dramatic. In such a picture, if the main character slips and falls into a gutter, the viewer is already worried about what will happen to him, even though in other films people are dropped from airplanes yet survive without a scratch. But not in my films and not in *The Man without a Past*, which begins with violence but violence that is honest—which is to say, as it really is, fast and ugly. In Helsinki, the violence is not glamorous, it's nameless. If people want to see violence that looks good and is prolonged, they are sick in the head.

In any event, you know my work: I prefer to make a deep impact on one spectator rather than a superficial impact on two million people. In fact, if I ever got a huge audience worldwide for one of my films, I would know I had failed. I am just a medium-class director, in the end, but if I make a number of decent-to-good pictures, together they may add up to something.

BC: A "medium-class" director but not a middle-class one?

AK: No. I have absolutely no interest in making films about the family problems of the middle class. Middle-class life just doesn't interest me.

Losers do, because I'm a middle-class loser myself. I spent a few years back in the 1970s, you know, when I too was hungry and homeless. For a while there, my only company was my sleeping bag. But things were different then: You could be a bum and come in from the cold later, when you finally found a job. Now you just die in the cold.

BC: So your subject matter became the Finnish working class?

AK: Yes. The people who are hidden, the "ugly people," as some critics have called them. But then who is good-looking? I think many Hollywood stars are ugly, horribly ugly. And I wouldn't want to see some of the women without their makeup. Totally unable to act, these people, *and* totally ugly. So I will stick with my own ugly people, of whom there are more and more in Finland, where, if you smoke a cigarette, you don't eat. Or if you drink a bottle of beer, you don't eat *or* smoke a cigarette. We have started to lose an entire generation, which never got work; we have twenty-year-olds over here who are already out of the labor system forever, yet at the same time the government is talking of raising the retirement age to seventy.

BC: Let's get back to contemporary cinema. What films do you like, other than your own?

AK: Well, I don't watch too many new films anymore. To be very honest, I don't want to waste my time watching fifteen lousy movies just so I can find one that is more or less okay. The really good films, I've seen them all a hundred times before. Nevertheless, I liked the Dardenne brothers' *Rosetta*, which I would compare with Bresson's *Mouchette*. I remember Ken Loach's *Riff-Raff*. And I appreciate the work of my friends Idrissa Ouedraogo, Jim Jarmusch, and Abbas Kiarostami.

BC: Are there any young Finnish directors who interest you?

AK: Not really. There have been great Finnish filmmakers, but never at the same time; I'm particularly fond of Teuvo Tulio and Nyrki Tapiovaara. It is a kind of curse: I have been waiting for a long time for someone to come and surpass me because I am too old and tired, but nobody has arrived. So I have to do the job. The young are too lazy.

BC: What do the young filmmakers, Finnish or otherwise, lack other than industry?

AK: Humility. Above all it is necessary to forget oneself. Start with the beginning, meaning that you are nothing—only dust. Then you watch hundreds of movies, during which you stay absolutely silent. Next you walk alone in the forest while telling yourself that you're nobody. After that, you must concentrate, which means you must watch a hundred more movies. Then you can start to work.

BC: What do you think of Finnish culture in general?

AK: It's the strongest one I ever met. It almost killed me. I also think it's the most beautiful culture in the world. Its problem, though, is the same as that of European culture in general: American culture, which remains the most important one in Europe, on the surface—meaning that it smothers, or tramples, everything that exists at a deeper level.

BC: I know that you boycotted the 2002 New York Film Festival because the United States denied a visa to the Iranian director Abbas Kiarostami. Any comment?

AK: I have to make clear that I didn't boycott the New York Film Festival; I like this festival very much. I boycotted the United States government. I was at the airport with my ticket in hand when I heard that Abbas wasn't being allowed to enter the United States, and I thought, "Okay, if the American government doesn't want an Iranian filmmaker then it won't want a Finnish one, either. And I will not go where I am not wanted."

BC: I laughed out loud when I heard that you had issued a statement in which you denounced American foreign policy and invited Defense Secretary Donald Rumsfeld to go mushroom hunting with you in Finland. All the same, given your fondness for rock 'n' roll, old Westerns, and American cars from the fifties and sixties, there has to be some ambivalence in your bemoaning of American imperialism, particularly as it currently exerts itself in the Middle East over the issue (some say) of oil.

AK: Yes, but the America I like is the America of Franklin Roosevelt, not the one led by that clown George Bush, with the boy scout Tony Blair at his side. Because I think with these two maniacs in charge, we don't have a lot of hope. To be honest, I think the clown and the boy scout will bring us to the end of the world. Goodbye.

BC: Let's move to a less explosive subject. The public, or international, fantasy about Finns is that they are a taciturn and lonely people, frozen into numb silence by the arctic chill. Are there a lot of people such as this in Finland—like Iris in *The Match Factory Girl*, for example?

AK: The country is full of them. Deep inside, I'm like that, and so are all my friends. Never accept a drink offered by a Finnish character.

BC: In *Ariel* and several of your other films, your characters are allowed to escape, as opposed to meeting their end as Iris does in *The Match Factory Girl*. Why not Iris also?

AK: I was tired of watching my characters leave while I remained in Finland. So in *The Match Factory Girl*, my central character stayed, and I moved afterwards—to Portugal, in southern Europe, where I spend half the year growing grapes, making wine, and then drinking it. This doesn't mean that I don't love Finland. Even if you love your native country, a small holiday from it . . . like a lifetime . . . doesn't do any harm.

BC: Why, if you generally feel as glum as I think you do, do films of yours like *The Man without a Past* have a low-key but insistently optimistic streak?

AK: Well . . . I believe that the more pessimistic I feel about the situation in the world, the more optimistic my films should be. This is the way I think about it, in any case. Life is too sad to bear, and there is no hope for anyone. So, now, let us drink to happy endings. And let's at least die laughing.

Filmography of Feature Films

The Saimaa Gesture, 1981
Crime and Punishment, 1983
Calamari Union, 1985
Shadows in Paradise, 1986
Hamlet Goes to Business, 1987
Ariel, 1988
Leningrad Cowboys Go America, 1989
The Match Factory Girl, 1989
I Hired a Contract Killer, 1990
The Bohemian Life, 1992
Leningrad Cowboys Meet Moses, 1994
Take Care of Your Scarf, Tatiana, 1994
Drifting Clouds, 1996
Juha, 1999
The Man without a Past, 2002
Lights in the Dust, 2006

PART III

Anglo-Nordic Temperaments

Early versus Later and Latest Ingmar Bergman

W E LIVE IN A SECULAR, NARCISSISTIC, even hedonistic age. Is there anyone out there who still doubts this? If you do, have a look at a film made by Ingmar Bergman over forty years ago—*Winter Light* (1962)—and you'll see what I mean. This is not to say that something like *Winter Light* could not be made now. We are dealing here with the rule and not the exception, the middle, not the extremities. Obviously, none of this is intended to denigrate Bergman's film as a mediocrity, or a priori to privilege contemporary films over it. Still, "men are as the time is," as Edmund declares in *King Lear*, and no artist in any medium—particularly one so popular, or immediate, as the cinema—can claim exemption.

Winter Light takes place on what used to be a day of rest and devotion—the Sabbath, in this case one wintry Sunday in a rural clergyman's life, between matins and vespers. The middle entry in Bergman's "faith trilogy," *Winter Light* suffers far less from the defect of the other two parts, *Through a Glass Darkly* (1961) and *The Silence* (1963): such an excess of symbolism that each picture breaks down into a series of discernible metaphors for spiritual alienation rather than an aggregation of those metaphors into an organic, affecting work. Though, apart from its literarylike piling up of symbols, *Through a Glass Darkly* relied on almost none of the arty legerdemain that marred *The Magician* (1958) and *The Seventh Seal* (1957), *Winter Light* is even starker and more circumscribed, so much so that this film, noticeably more than the one that immediately followed it, makes one feel that the (ir)religious vision Bergman had been formulating in all his major pictures up to now has finally shed its excrescences and become as simple and direct, as pure and honest, as it is possible to be.

Winter Light is only eighty minutes in length compared to the ninety-one of *Through a Glass Darkly* and the ninety-six minutes of *The Silence*;

185

Ingmar Bergman, circa 1951. *(Courtesy of Photofest)*

and it uses relatively few actors and settings, like those "chamber" works. But they at least have musical scores (in both cases by Bach), whereas the only music in *Winter Light* occurs during church services in accompaniment to Swedish psalms. Such economy of means, of course, is a matter of great artistry, of artistic *refinement*. And no filmmaker, not even Michelangelo Antonioni, was ever Bergman's superior when it came to knowing what to leave out (one can almost divide true cinematic artists from mere moviemakers on the question of such exclusion), the absences in *Winter Light* being as significant as what is presented. They in fact contribute in the most central way to the picture's theme, as well as to its visual architecture, since Bergman is dealing here with an image of spiritual darkness and desolation, with an "absence" in the soul.

That absence is a crisis in, almost a loss of, faith, and it is a middle-aged Lutheran minister who is in its grip. To describe his condition in this way is entirely accurate, for his anguish is experienced like a violent seizure, the "silence of God" being a palpable thing. Since the season is winter, the days are short, and the light is sparse and sterile—a counterpart to the weather, the climate as well as the level of illumination, in the pastor's soul. The planes and angles of the camera's investigations (black-and-white cinematography by Sven Nykvist) mark out this universe of gray emptiness within a framework that makes it even more austere or stringent. And the "gray area" here, the study in varying shades of gray, is entirely appropriate, because the clergyman's crisis is a continuing one; nothing is resolved either for or against religious belief. In a different film, a different life, we would abide in the expectation of answers; in *Winter Light*, we can only take heart from a continuity of questions.

The minister is accompanied, in his clerical vocation, by a school-teacher who loves him and wants to marry and whose presence he accepts but whom he cannot love in return. For it develops that when his wife died some years before, his capacity to love died with her, and it becomes clear that for him such a loss is itself a demonstration of God's absence or indifference. Thus does Bergman, in the most delicate, unrhetorical, yet profoundly moving way, link the realms of natural and supernatural, diurnal and supernal love, keeping the tension between them at a high pitch and never resorting to cheap or arbitrary solutions. For him life's special agony is just such a rending of the loving bond between God and man. Unlike Antonioni, whose work also concentrated on this subject, he does not believe that man invented God but now must be manly enough to admit it and destroy him. Bergman is concerned to find a way of living with—at the very least—the memory of God, and the only way to such divinity is through affinity: if not the loving marriage between two human beings, then fellow-feeling of the kind that is contained in the very idea of "ministration."

Or so this Lutheran minister learns. One of his parishioners, a fisherman with three children and a pregnant wife, is in a state of depression, deepened by the immanence in the world of nuclear-bomb threats. Brought by his wife, the fisherman talks to the pastor after morning service, and the pastor's own spiritual bankruptcy is glaringly revealed in their talk. Later comes word that the fisherman has committed suicide, which brings the minister face to face with the truth that his own worst suffering—as well as that of his flock—is now caused by his inability to fulfill his vocation.

But through the instrumentality of another character, a hunchbacked sexton with a wry, mordant, yet exceptionally deep commitment to faith, he is shown the glint of possibility, of light whose very promise or idea is contained in this picture's title. That glinting possibility consists in going on, in living through the aridity and absence, in making continual acts of faith precisely where faith is most difficult or even repellent. The film ends at twilight with the pastor beginning the vespers service (even as *Winter Light* began with a communion service), in a church with only one or two parishioners in attendance. On the one hand, this clergyman is slipping back almost desperately into clerical routine; on the other, he continues to minister to the faithful, and the darkness of winter night has not yet come.

This summary fails to do justice to the mastery Bergman revealed over his materials in *Winter Light*. For one thing, his actors—Max von Sydow as the fisherman, Ingrid Thulin as the teacher, Gunnar Björnstrand as the pastor—could not be bettered. They had by this time become the perfect instruments of Bergman's directorial will, forming what was undoubtedly the finest cinematic acting company in the world, one that the stage (where Bergman began and, to some extent, remained) might still envy, or envy even more, today. Here, as elsewhere in the "faith" trilogy, their work was especially difficult, for they had to give human gravity to a stripped-down exercise in God-famished theology.

The film's effect depends on the penetration *in us* of the minister's doubt, as well as the teacher's hopeless love and the fisherman's boundless despair (which are meant to reflect, in their way, on the central problem of religious belief). The spiritual problem is not merely stated in *Winter Light*, as some commentators continue to assert; it *is* visualized or externalized, as I described earlier. Still, to deal in physical film terms with the complex metaphysical question of the existence of God and the equally difficult-to-sustain phenomenon of human isolation or alienation requires performances of a freshening, even frightening kind. And Bergman got them in *Winter Light*, to create a solemn, spare, severe artwork that is nonetheless full of strange, harsh beauty.

Another requirement of an authentic spiritual style is that it be grounded in naturalistic simplicity, even abstraction—as *Winter Light* is—not in widescreen pyrotechnics of the kind found in such sand-and-sandals epics as *Quo Vadis?* (1951), *Ben Hur* (1959), *King of Kings* (1961), and *The Greatest Story Ever Told* (1965). The spirit resides within, in internal conviction, not in external trickery. Everything that is exterior, ornamental, liturgical, hagiographic, and miraculous in the universal doctrine and everyday practice of *Catholicism* (as opposed to Bergman's unaccommodated Lutheranism) does indeed show affinities with the cinema—conceived, with its spectacular iconography, as a kind of miracle in itself akin to the miracle of the Sacrament or the saints. But these affinities, which have made for the commercial success of countless movies, are also the source of the religious insignificance of most of them.

Almost everything that is good in the domain of religious film, then, was created not by the exploitation of the patent consanguinity of Catholicism with the cinema but rather by working against it: by the psychological and moral deepening of the spiritual factor as well as by the renunciation of the physical representation either of the supernatural or of God's grace. In other words, although the austereness of the Protestant sensibility is not indispensable to the making of a good Catholic motion picture, it can nevertheless be a real advantage, as evidenced by films such as Robert Bresson's *Diary of a Country Priest* (1951) and *The Trial of Joan of Arc* (1962) as well as Pier Paolo Pasolini's *Gospel According to St. Matthew* (1964). As for the thing-in-itself, good Protestant cinema, you have Bergman's "faith trilogy" and the picture of his that directly preceded it, *The Virgin Spring* (1960), in addition to such films of his fellow Scandinavian Carl Dreyer as *Day of Wrath* (1943) and *The Word* (1955).

My reservations about the secularity and hedonism of our age, as opposed to the one that produced these "faith" films, are those of an aging critic who sees an increasing number of "faithless" movies coming along, yet who continues to hope (if not believe) that there is more to love than lust, that the spirit is greater in importance than the body, and that romance has as much to do with religious rapture as with sexual transport. For all their white heat, in other words, the giddy fantasy of most romantic movies (let alone porno pictures) leaves me alone in earthbound darkness, coolly and contractively contemplating the state of my own connubial bond. Whereas the sober mystery of *Winter Light* may have left me ice cold, but it is glistening cold that seeks out the expansive warmth of divine solace. And everything that so rises, naturally, must converge.

Bergman began his film career, alas, not with *Winter Light* but with a somewhat paranoid invention salvaged by Alf Sjöberg, who, from the sketch submitted by Bergman, put the Swedish cinema on the map in 1944 with the film known in the United States as *Torment*. The germ of this movie was Bergman's fear that he would be flunked on his university entrance examination; his revenge in advance was his creation of a tyrannical schoolmaster whom he aptly named Caligula. (Sjöberg added a political implication by having the actor made up to resemble Himmler, chief to the Reichsführer SS.) Over the years, Bergman's compulsion to nourish every slight, every adverse criticism, grew into his now familiar, never subdued war against Father. (His own purportedly once punished him by locking him into a closet.) From this image of the despotism of the Father—and, from a (more revealing) reverse angle, the fallibility of God (which we see on display in his "faith" films)—he extrapolated the second of his twin obsessions: the fatality of the couple.

Among the other obsessions of Ingmar Bergman that American critics have failed to note, or failed to question closely, is his pervasive resentment in his art of the achieved man and occasionally the career woman—doctor, lawyer, professor, business executive. From the evidence of his numerous films, Bergman may resent every professional except the artist. Predictably, his defense of the artist as somehow sacrosanct has engendered a feedback of guilt: Periodically, having enshrined the creative personality in one context or another, he seems driven to follow up with a self-accusation of the artist as charlatan or as detached and inhuman being, as in 1968's *Shame* and *Hour of the Wolf*. You may be sure that Bergman in his heart does not believe this, but he nonetheless needs to hear an answering echo from time to time that somehow absolves him of his own accusation.

Thus *Autumn Sonata* (1978) is characterized by the same kind of ambivalence that undermined the artistic veracity of *Wild Strawberries* in 1957. In the earlier film, Bergman's portrait of an old professor, whose egoistic frigidity lost him an idyllic sweetheart and produced an impotent son, was at odds with the visibly sympathetic performance of Victor Sjöström. Just as Bergman was reluctant in *Wild Strawberries* to follow the implications of his own scenario by destroying the professor figure entirely, so in *Autumn Sonata* he sets up Ingrid Bergman (in her final theatrical film) as a concert pianist-cum-mother who is supposed to have crippled her two daughters (one child being insufficient for the force of his accusation); then the auteur becomes so enamored of the personality he has given his character that he is hard put to convince us she could possibly be either as indifferent or as ruthless as her articulate daughter maintains.

To synopsize this picture accurately for anyone who has not seen it is almost impossible, since what takes place in *Autumn Sonata* beyond the severely limited action is completely a matter of individual interpretation. Every statement made by the characters is open to question, and the whole moral issue on which the film hinges is never depicted. The damaging relationship of which this mother-daughter confrontation is supposed to be the climax is not visualized in flashbacks so that the viewer can judge for himself; it is, rather, wholly summarized in verbal terms through the daughter Eva's accusatory retrospect.

At the beginning, reading her diary while she awaits the visit of her celebrated mother, Eva (Liv Ullmann) seems pretty clearly, in her spinsterish appearance and manner, to be a manic-depressive type, melancholy and retentive but prone to fitfulness as well. We glimpse her husband hovering in the background, from which he scarcely emerges during the subsequent encounter, and we learn that since her son, aged fourteen, drowned some years ago, Eva has kept his room as it was when he died and moons over photographs of him. This morbid devotion to the irretrievable contradicts the leading statement she reads from her diary: "One must learn how to live. I work at it every day." We further discover that, before her marriage, Eva had lived with a doctor and that she had once had tuberculosis. Not until later in the film do we become aware that she is looking after her bedridden sister, who suffers from a degenerative disease that has affected her speech and movement and whom her mother believes to be in a nursing home.

When the mother arrives at this outpost of Ibsenism (Bergman's set-ting, during this period of his self-exile from Sweden, is among the Nor-wegian fjords), it is not too surprising that, after the first affectionate exchanges are over, as Eva listens obediently to her parent's necessarily self-absorbed chatter (she has come, after all, from the world of professional music as practiced in European capitals), the daughter all the while regards her with mingled amusement and suspicion. In no time at all, suspicion has become hostility, and step by step Eva rebukes her mother's self-secured authority in a crescendo of bitter reproaches that mounts steadily into the realm of hysteria. The younger woman makes the distressed elder respon-sible for all the ills of her life and blames her, besides, for the condition of the drooling sister upstairs, whose presence in the house is an unwelcome shock to the fastidious visitor.

Following a long sequence of passionate denunciation by her daugh-ter, which she stems only at momentary intervals, the mother, inwardly shaken but outwardly collected, leaves to fulfill another musical engage-ment. Then, after a few solicitous suggestions from her husband—who, again, has passively remained on the sidelines of this internecine struggle being waged under his roof—Eva writes a letter to the departed woman in which she retracts the burden of the accusation she had hurled and makes a pathetic bid for love. This letter is in part read over the image of the mother, traveling south for her next concert.

Critics have generally received this film as if it were indeed a straightforward indictment by the neglected daughter of a selfish par-ent, which means that they accept at face value the allegations of the girl and pay no attention either to the personality or the remonstrance of the mother. In fact we have only the daughter's word that her mother's inattention drove her into a messy relationship with that "doctor" who is briefly mentioned. What part any of this played in her contracting of tuberculosis is never clarified. How satisfactory or unsatisfactory her present marriage is, one is left to infer. Whether her mother had an affair with someone named Marten without telling her husband, Josef, depends on which of the two women you believe, and what bearing this has on anything else is never made clear. The viewer is also left to decide whether or not the mother's absence at a crucial hour was the impelling cause of the sister's disabling condition.

It is possible to take the other view, that Bergman intended the Liv Ullmann character to reveal herself unmistakably as a self-pitying neu-rotic, whose charges are patently canceled by the clearly delineated supe-riority of the mother. (One of the most telling moments in the film would then be Ingrid Bergman's correction, at the piano, of her daughter's play-ing of a Chopin sonata: If the girl is to give the piece an authentic interpretation, declares the mother, she must avoid sentimentality and understand that the music should express "pain, not reverie.") However, even this view of Bergman's strategy may be ingenuous; it is much more in his line to establish an impeccably distinguished persona, poised against an unattractive spinster who is nonetheless married, in order to make the latter's accusations appear at first unlikely, then the more convincing, precisely because the accused has the more sovereign air. (This mechanism was invented by August Strindberg in his play *The Stronger*, from 1889.)

In truth, near the end of *Autumn Sonata*, Bergman loses confidence in his own gambit. He cuts, in the most excruciatingly obvious way, from the sick daughter writhing helplessly on the floor, to the entrained mother coolly informing her agent that her visit home had been "most unpleasant." In other words, she shrugs it off. Unless we are to suppose she is acting, this is outrageously unbelievable; it totally contradicts the character of the woman we have witnessed, in merciless close-up, for the preceding hour. Evasive or hesitant she may have been when justifying a given response or action recounted by the vindictive Eva, but never for a moment did one feel that she was radically false. Equally unacceptable, as the film ends, is the abrupt change of heart that dictates Eva's remorse for the vehemence with which she has been arraigning her mother—thereby canceling, at the last minute, the substance of the movie's unrelenting inquisition.

There is small point in trying to weigh truth in the antithesis Bergman has contrived for *Autumn Sonata*. At *any* latter-day movie of his, including the slightly earlier *Serpent's Egg* (1977) and the subsequent, appositely titled *From the Life of the Marionettes* (1980), one cannot be sure whether this director-screenwriter is unaware of the dramatic incongruities that he creates through poor motivation, or whether he does not really care. He seems indifferent to plot because a plot is action consistent with the revealed nature of its characters, and Bergman seems unable to perceive consistency; his characters say what he wants them to say, to an end he alone has chosen, as opposed to what they would say if allowed to speak for themselves.

He was, once, a master of comedy, as in his gloss on Renoir's *Rules of the Game* (1939), *Smiles of a Summer Night* (1955), for in secular, and even more so divine, comedy you can give full rein to the improbable. You can also do so in a religious allegory like Bergman's *Seventh Seal*, if not in existential meditations of the kind exemplified by his "faith" trilogy of *Through a Glass Darkly*, *Winter Light*, and *The Silence*, which, along with the earlier *Naked Night* (1953) and *The Magician* and the subsequent *Persona* (1966), secured the reputation of Ingmar Bergman in America. Even he seems to agree, however, that the enigmas of *Autumn Sonata* represent a parody of his earlier, better work, as he put the matter in *Images: My Life in Film* (1990): "Has Bergman begun to make Bergman Films? I find that, yes, *Autumn Sonata* is an annoying example ... of creative exhaustion." By 1992's *The Best Intentions* and *Sunday's Children*, both of which he wrote if not directed—actually even before them in *Fanny and Alexander* (1982)—his exhaustion had turned into self-absorption, as he became a purveyor of the probable or consistent only through the form of autobiography.

It may be worth remarking here that while *Autumn Sonata* postulates the destructive consequences of perfectionism in life as in art, Bergman the recreant preacher has, in his own way, been aesthetically pursuing the absolute or the ideal like mad: by not-so-coincidentally choosing a central character with the primal name *Eva*; and, most important, by creating immaculate cinematic compositions that achieve their immaculateness at the expense of worldly or natural conception. (Almost all of this film was shot inside a studio.) With this in mind, we should not expect the mundane inventions of *Autumn Sonata* to have objective credibility; the characters' motives are flimsily explored, the actualities of their lives not dramatized but reported after the fact. If Eva knew so much about her own victimization at her parent's hands, she would long since have ceased to be a victim—or at the very least she would have remedied those absurd outer signs of her condition thrust upon her by Bergman via his wardrobe department: I mean the old maid's provincial hair bun and the disfiguring eyeglasses. Women's faces, preferably under stress, are what Ingmar Bergman likes to photograph; objective coherence he no longer cares, or is no longer able, to cultivate.

Like many other films in his canon, then, *Autumn Sonata* is a private tribunal. Bergman himself is the confessor, prosecutor, plaintiff, and as neutral or uncommitted a judge as he can risk being. Critics in America consistently underrate this Swedish inability of Bergman to commit himself to the terms of a moral choice he has ostensibly initiated. And the sympathetic link between this Swede and the Americans is the fundamental puritanism we culturally share; Bergman's Nordic damnations, like Strindberg's, are taken far less seriously, for example, by the Italians, the French, or even the English. Indeed, Strindberg is perhaps the only authentic father figure to whose authority, aesthetic or otherwise, Bergman has consented.

Incidentally, one could couple Strindberg not only with Bergman but also with Eugene O'Neill. For Strindberg was the artistic stepfather of O'Neill, who successfully transplanted the Swedish dramatist's suffocating (Lutheran) ethos into Irish American (Catholic) settings and who, for his part, like the Bergman of *Smiles of a Summer Night*, managed to write only one comedy (*Ah, Wilderness!*, 1932) among his many works for the theater. The Swedes flattered O'Neill and his solemn sensibility back by staging all his plays at Stockholm's Dramaten, in addition to awarding him the Nobel Prize in 1936 (before he had written his greatest, realist-naturalist dramas *The Iceman Cometh* [1939] and *Long Day's Journey into Night* [1941], I might add). Though Strindberg may also be the single most influential figure behind all of Bergman's work, the filmmaker seems to substitute excessive love for women for the dramatist's extreme antipathy toward them.

As for that Strindbergian influence on the Bergmanian, the "rehearsal" in *After the Rehearsal* (1984) is of one of Strindberg's plays (*A Dream Play*, 1902), a number of which Bergman himself has directed for the theater. And *Autumn Sonata* may derive its inspiration from that mad master's chamber drama-cum-dream play *The Ghost Sonata* (1907), not least because Bergman says in *Images* that he initially conceived his film like a dream in three acts, with "no cumbersome sets, two faces, and three kinds of lighting: one evening light, one night light, and one morning light." For all its avant-garde theatrical devices, this early twentieth-century dramatic work is related in theme to its Bergmanian namesake, for Strindberg attempts in his autumnal *Ghost Sonata* to penetrate the naturally deceptive or mediating façade of verbal language, as well as of bourgeois exteriors—not only through the visual eloquence of scenic design, but also through the abstract purity of musical form.

Moreover, Strindberg composed *The Ghost Sonata* not long after the five psychotic episodes of his "inferno crisis," even as Bergman wrote *Autumn Sonata* immediately upon recovering from a nervous breakdown that resulted from his arrest in Sweden on charges of tax evasion. A major difference between these two artists, however, is that Strindberg's psychiatric crisis restored his religious faith, and that faith gave much of his postinferno work a mystical cast in which benevolent or judicious transcendental powers were operative—expressing themselves even during the most everyday of occurrences. Bergman's breakdown, by contrast, had no such effect either on the director or his films, which from *The Seventh Seal* to *The Virgin Spring* (1960) to *The Silence* had led progressively not only to the rejection of all religious belief but also to the conviction that human life is haunted by a virulent, active evil.

If without knowing anything whatsoever about the work of either director, one had seen Bergman's *Autumn Sonata* right after Woody Allen's *Interiors* (1978), one might easily have concluded, however, that the Swedish filmmaker had attempted to imitate the American rather than his own Swedish forebear. For these works share the same cinematographic and editing style, the same concentration on a handful of overwrought characters, and the very same subject—namely, maternal domination. Of course, the reverse sequence is the correct one: Since 1971, if no farther back, the otherwise comedic Woody Allen had yearned to make what he thought of as a serious or tragic "European" film, preferably in the monastic style of Ingmar Bergman yet in an urban American setting. Finally, with *Interiors*, he made it, and fortuitously if not felicitously it resembles (at least in outline) the particular Bergman number that happened to be released in America at almost the same time. (In 1992, Allen managed to make two films derivative, not so much of Bergman, as of Godard and Kafka, respectively. *Husbands and Wives* and *Shadows and Fog*.) Would that each man, in this instance, in the coincidental year of 1978, had opted instead to remake the "merely" entertaining Hollywood love story known as *Intermezzo* (1939), itself remade from the Swedish *Intermezzo* of 1936—with none other than Ingrid Bergman starring in both pictures as a young pianist in love with a renowned, but married, violinist.

As for the Bergmanian cultural puritanism or hunger for the High Serious that O'Neill himself shares in such plays as *Desire under the Elms* (1924), *Strange Interlude* (1928), and *A Moon for the Misbegotten* (1943), and of which Allen unsuccessfully attempts to partake in films such as *September* (1987), *Another Woman* (1988), and *Alice* (1990) in addition to

The Seventh Seal (1957). Directed by Ingmar Bergman. Shown: Bengt Ekerot as Death. *(Courtesy Photofest)*

Interiors, such aspirations toward spiritual austerity and moral rigor are not particularly evident in the American cinema. (One possible exception that comes to mind is *Five Easy Pieces* [1970], but even this work—about a promising pianist who turns his back on classical music and the concert-cum-recording world—has less in common with *Autumn Sonata* than with movies such as *Bonnie and Clyde* [1967], *Midnight Cowboy* [1969], *The Wild Bunch* [1969], *Mean Streets* [1973], *Badlands* [1973], and *Chinatown* [1974].) In American movies, more than in our other arts, popular entertainment is the major enterprise, and it is rarely austere, seldom rigorous, and insufficiently moral—except, that is, insofar as it is at the same time miserably sentimental, blindly self-satisfied, callowly romantic, self-righteously melodramatic, or spuriously religious. We may have our puritanical strain, then, but apparently we prefer to indulge it through the avenue of European cinema—in other words, by going back to its source

So much is this the case that, to judge from the laudatory reviews, Americans may make up the only appreciative audience for Ingmar Bergman's final film: *Saraband* (2003). To be sure, when he finished *After the Rehearsal* in 1983, Bergman had said that he would not direct again. He did subsequently write some (autobiographical) screenplays, but others directed them (more later on one of them). However, in 2002 Bergman turned again to the Stockholm couple Johan and Marianne (now thirty years older) from *Scenes from a Marriage*. For this postlude to *Scenes*—*Saraband*—he directed as well as wrote. Again he said he would do no more directing, and this time he was telling the truth.

First, the good news: Bergman's hallmarks are notable throughout. The calm surety, the simplicity yet pointedness, the Bergman envelopment of drama in a carapace of quiet—all of these qualities are soon evident, as is the Bergman gift of immediacy when, at the start, as she did in *Hour of the Wolf*, Liv Ullmann comes in, sits down, and addresses the audience (which she will do occasionally throughout), thus enlisting us as confidantes. From time to time, as in the past, Bergman's camera even gently closes in on a speaker as if to suggest that it is—or would like to be—convinced about what he or she is saying. In an early scene, moreover, we hear the ticking of a clock, Bergman's familiar hint about human mortality. Later, too, there is a scene in a country church that, with its paradoxical blend of chill and solace, remoteness and refuge, reminds us of *Winter Light*.

The cinematography is at the Bergman level—or, rather, the level of Bergman's regular cameraman in the past, Sven Nyqvist—as well. He used three people in this instance, all of whom give *Saraband* a painterly, composed look without making its images appear arty and calculated.

Per-Olof Lantto, Sofi Stridh, and Raymond Wemenlöv provide any number of moments that simultaneously render the surface and the quintessence of faces and places (which is one definition of realist cinematography). The primary faces belong to the two leading actors, Ullmann and Erland Josephson, the original Marianne and Johan. Their very presence here is moving, for, despite what we know of other films that these two have done since 1973 (for Bergman as well as other directors), the effect is almost as if Ullmann and Josephson had interrupted their own lives elsewhere and consented, for the sake of these two characters, to return to the screen.

There are just three other actors—one of whom appears only in the very last scene and is silent—so once again a film by Bergman, in this auteur's long homage to his venerated Strindberg, has the feel of a chamber play. Johan has a sixtyish son, Henrik—incidentally, the most intricate figure in the picture—a musician and professor of musicology (encompassed, in this character's control of his complicated nature, by Börje Ahlstedt, who once played Claudius in a Bergman [theatrical] production of *Hamlet*), whose mother was Johan's wife before Marianne. And Henrik, whose wife died two years earlier, himself has a nineteen-year-old daughter named Karin (played by Julia Dufvenius, who brims with the mercurialness of such a young woman), whom he is instructing in the cello. (On the soundtrack, accordingly, Bergman uses, along with other classical music, the melancholically beautiful, almost morbidly introspective, "Saraband" from Bach's Fifth Cello Suite—the same piece he used in *Cries and Whispers* [1972].)

Now for the bad news: The screenplay, the sine qua non of any good narrative film, is dissatisfactory in the same way as was that of *Autumn Sonata*. For some, *Saraband* begins with a burden: its antecedent, *Scenes from a Marriage* (1973). But not for me, as I do not regard the earlier film, to quote one admirer, as "one of the last century's major dramatic works about conjugal life." This is hyperbole, intended for a work that is ultimately vitiated by its autobiographical overtones. After all, Bergman did write in the preface to his screenplay of *Scenes from a Marriage*, "This opus took three months to write, but rather a long part of my life [part of it spent, off-camera, with Liv Ullmann] to experience." Furthermore, he scripted the Ullmann-directed film *Faithless* (2001), a de facto epilogue to *Scenes from a Marriage* before the fact of *Saraband*.

Faithless features a couple named Marianne and Markus, instead of Marianne and Johan, and, as in *Scenes from a Marriage*, its subjects are marriage and betrayal—except that in this instance Marianne (here an actress instead of an attorney, to her spouse's orchestra conductor as opposed to the doctor in *Scenes*) is the unfaithful one (and with a movie director, no less), not her husband. The film's unabashedly autobiographical nature is tipped off by the tale that frames the body of its narrative.

It is about an elderly filmmaker named Bergman (played by, guess who, Erland Josephson), who is trying to write a script about infidelity and who invites an actress—perhaps a figment of his imagination, perhaps not—to breathe life into the character of Marianne. She then tells or lives Marianne's story through a series of flashbacks.

Faithless is a chore to watch, not least because of its overlength: At 154 minutes, it is slightly shorter than Scenes from a Marriage (168 minutes) yet more than half an hour longer than Saraband (120 minutes). Its relative brevity does not help Bergman's final picture, however. Not only is Saraband quite different from both Scenes from a Marriage and Faithless, it is less than even these two lesser works. (Therefore, it should come as no surprise that Saraband—which is divided into ten parts that are preceded by a prologue and followed by an epilogue—was originally made for television, even as Scenes from a Marriage was first a six-part television serial whose nearly 300 minutes Bergman then condensed into a single feature film and in 1981 further cannibalized in the form of a theater version.) And I, for one, refuse to condescend to the Ingmar Bergman of Persona, Through a Glass Darkly, Shame, and The Passion of Anna (1969) by arguing, as at least one veteran critic has done, that "the very making of Saraband is one more Bergman marvel," that "the making of the film itself [not the finished product, we are left to infer] gives us one last glimpse of a genius."

The narrative of the film gets under way when Marianne, a sixty-three-year-old lawyer who is still practicing, decides to visit her eighty-six-year-old exhusband, now retired and living in a country house. Since they were divorced three decades earlier, the sheer idea of Marianne's visit is exciting. But from the first moment of their reunion on a beautiful autumn day, the pitch wavers. When, for example, Marianne wakes Johan, who is dozing over a book on his veranda, the scene seems like a rough draft of what it ought to have been. The reason is that, though thirty years or so have passed, neither of these two comments with much perception, affection, or concern on how the other one looks. Then, after some nestling in character tics and quirks, mostly Johan's, the film settles down to its real subject, which has less to do with Johan and Marianne than you would expect.

To wit: Saraband is almost completely devoted to Henrik's relationship with his daughter and, in some measure, Johan's relationship with both. Henrik, an organist in addition to being a cellist, is rightly fearful that Karin will leave him. For he is a volatile man who several times races through a dizzying spectrum of emotions; and he bullies Karin despite the fact that he loves his daughter. There is even a hint of incest between them—he and she sleep in the same bed, and one of their kisses is not exactly familial—but nothing is made of it. (Nothing is made, either, of a cross on a chain that Karin wears around her neck, since, so far as we can tell, religion is of no special importance to her.)

Karin, for her part, is suffering not only from Henrik's moods but also from his dependence on her in the permanent absence of his spouse. Domestic complications are further deepened because Johan loves Karin yet despises Henrik, and the latter seethes with hatred of his domineering father; all that these two appear to have in common is their attachment to Henrik's late wife, Anna, a woman of such beauty and love that her loss has completely devastated her family. The final "complication," the film's climax—Henrik's suicide attempt—arises out of a potential move in Karin's musical career to a conservatory, which would mean departure from her father. And this last possibility fixes *Saraband*'s basic oddity: The climax and all that surrounds it have nothing to do with Marianne. Indeed, very little in the whole narrative has involved her, even though she is sometimes an empathetic listener to the other characters' troubles.

Nonetheless, at the beginning, when Marianne decided to revisit Johan, we had hoped—understandably—for the continuance of, and perhaps an artistic improvement upon, their story after a lapse of three decades. But the picture is not really about them: Marianne's visit only provides a means, or a catalyst, for telling the Johan-Henrik-Karin tale. To be sure, a concluding scene is tacked on to let Marianne reveal what she has learned from her visit to Johan, but it has the feeling of belated repair and forced symmetry. In addition, a photograph of Henrik's deceased wife—Karin's mother—figures prominently in *Saraband* and at the end is even seen in Marianne's personal photo album. (This photograph, incidentally and obtrusively, is actually of Bergman's fifth and last wife, Ingrid von Rosen, who herself died in 1995 and to whom the film is dedicated.) Now why in the world would Marianne have a copy of that photo—of the late mother of the daughter of her exhusband's son from Johan's first marriage—among her pictures, except to buttress a film director's hope for continuity or coherence through the repetition of just such a visual motif?

So, however long it may have taken Bergman to write *Saraband*, it does not reflect Marianne's experience of the thirty-year schism in her relationship with Johan, nor does the movie reflect Johan's experience of the same schism—or anyone's else's, for that matter, including Bergman. This is obviously not to argue that an auteur must literally have experienced what he writes about—indeed, when Bergman has done so, as in the case of *Scenes from a Marriage*, the danger not only is a loss of perspective or objectivity but also an excess of self-dramatization. But it is to say that the screenplay of *Saraband* feels concocted—an abstraction before the fact, as it were—not absorbed from life in feeling and form and *then* abstracted or refined, like the best of Bergman's work from the fifties and sixties. The film consequently produces little of the customary awe we have felt in the past when he plumbed what were, or could have been, our secrets because they were *someone else's*, in life or in art drawn from life. In *Saraband*, as in the case of Woody Allen's *Interiors*, it is as if someone had merely summoned a group of elements—tormented people, mainly— that would make a script in the Bergman style. Ironically in this instance, that someone was Ingmar Bergman himself.

Would that his scenario had lived up to the quality of *Saraband's* cinematography. Cinematographers are not artists, however, and films are not paintings. Yes, images can "mean" as complexly as words, but these images move, motion pictures tell a story, and that story depends on its drama and dialogue as much as, if not more than, its pictorial style. Bergman knows this—all the more so because he has frequently directed (and sometimes written) for another narrative art form, the theater, where language and action (*action*, not spectacle) take on even greater impor- tance than they do in the cinema—or he once knew it. At one time, in fact, not only did he have the makings of a cinematic poet, in the verbal as well as the visual sense, he *was* a poet of the cinema—but one who should have quit at the top of his form. Now he has only the habit of creating poetry; now he can only reflexively stammer at film art. That stammer is not his native eloquence, as it was for Eugene O'Neill in his late, faithfully realistic period: It is his ghostly rattle. And I choose to remember him by his eloquence.

An Interview with
Ingmar Bergman

The following interview took place in August 2004 in Sweden, after Bergman had announced his retirement from both the theater and film and had made his retreat to Fårö Island (where I met him). He passed away three years later, in the summer of 2007.

BERT CARDULLO: I'd like to limit our discussion today to general matters concerning film, theater, and directing, as opposed to treating your films individually. Is that acceptable to you?

INGMAR BERGMAN: That's fine. I don't want to talk about my films anymore; I've talked enough about them. They are in the past, even *Saraband*. What's new?

BC: The same old questions, I'm afraid, about the nature of film and filmmaking, in contrast with other art forms. Could you define the term *film direction* concretely for me?

IB: Film direction? Well, there was a director who once said that a film director is a person who never finds the time to think because of all the problems connected with filmmaking. That is the closest I can come to defining the term. Of course, one can also say that film direction is the transformation of visions, ideas, dreams, feelings, and hopes into pictures that can convey them to audiences in the most efficient manner. There is a technical definition as well: Along with an awful lot of people, technicians and performers, and a tremendous lot of machines, one produces a product. It's an everyday product or a work of art, depending on the circumstances.

But you know what moviemaking really is? Eight hours of hard work each day to get three minutes of film. During those eight hours

there are maybe only ten or twelve minutes, if you're lucky, of real creation. And maybe they don't come. Then you have to gear yourself for
another eight hours and pray you're going to get your good ten minutes
this time. Everything and everyone on a movie set must be attuned to
finding those minutes of genuine creativity. You've got to keep yourself
and the actors in a kind of enchanted circle. An outside presence, even a
completely friendly one, is basically alien to the intimate process taking
place in front of him. Any time there's an outsider on the set, you run the
risk that part of the actors' absorption, or the technicians', or mine, is
going to be impinged upon. It takes very little to destroy the delicate
mood of total immersion in our work; we can't risk losing those vital
minutes of real creation. The few times I made exceptions during my
career I always regretted it.

BC: Did you develop any uniform ideas as to the way to work on a film,
as to how to realize your films? Or did those ideas about how to work
change from project to project?

IB: No, they didn't change. I had a very carefully developed method that
took shape over the years. Let me give you an analogy. Here on Fårö I
saw an old boat one day that had been built a hundred years ago. It was
terribly beautiful, but those who owned it also spoke about how inde-
scribably seaworthy it was. This boat was built in the same way as all
boats had been built a century ago. It was constructed according to a
special prescription, which, of course, had been developed through centuries of experience as to how a vessel weathers the climate and the severe
sea conditions in this part of the world.
      One can say that during my many years as a film director, I built
myself a ship on which I could sail through the problems of direction. I
constructed a practical machine, a method that I used from one picture
to the next. Naturally, this method had to be suited, under all circumstances, to the difficult themes with which I dealt in my work. But in
principle I had a carefully worked out system, and it worked.

BC: Where did you get the ideas for your films?

IB: That is less important than the fact that I had ideas, intentions, passions—even obsessions. Creativity is a tremendously irrational process
that is different every time, for each film; the final picture can even be the
result of seemingly unimportant impulses or stimulants. The idea for
Persona, for example, came from an image. One day I suddenly saw in
front of me two women sitting next to each other and comparing hands.

I thought to myself that one of them is mute, and the other can speak. This little idea returned time and again, and I wondered: Why did it return? Why did it repeat itself? It was as if this idea, this picture, returned so that I would start work on it.

But during my career, if I had no such impulse, if I didn't have anything to say and just wanted to make a film, I didn't make the film. The craftsmanship of filmmaking is so terribly stimulating, so dangerously obsessive, that you can be very much tempted to start doing it even if you don't have any plan. But if you have nothing to bring to the table, so to speak, try to be honest with yourself and don't make the picture. If you have something to bring to the table, if you have emotion or passion, a picture in your head, an intellectual tension—even if you aren't technically minded—the strange thing is that after having worked on the script and having worked with the camera for days on end, suddenly, at the end of the editing process, the story you wished to tell, the images you wanted to evoke, the characters and feelings you endeavored to portray—they are all there.

I have a very good example of what I'm talking about: Antonioni's *L'avventura*. This picture is a mess. He had no idea where to put the camera; he had no money; and the actors went away. I think he had enormous problems the whole time, but he wanted to tell us something about the loneliness of human beings. I can see this picture time after time, and I don't know what touches me more: how Antonioni succeeds without really knowing how to do so, or what he wants to say in *L'avventura*. And that is the most important thing of all: You have to bring something to the table; you have to have something you want to express to other people.

Picturemaking is some sort of responsibility; that is what I think. Antonioni took that responsibility seriously, but he never properly learned his craft. He's an aesthete. If, for example, he needed a street to look a certain way in *Red Desert*, then he got the houses repainted on that damned street. That is the attitude of an aesthete. Antonioni took great care over single shots, but he didn't understand that a film is a rhythmic stream of images, a living, moving process; for him, on the contrary, it consisted of this particular shot, then that one, and then yet another.

BC: Could we continue a bit with your views on the work of other film directors?

IB: Of course. One of the greatest of all was certainly Japan's Kurosawa, but the one I always felt closest to in spirit was Fellini. His *La dolce vita* seemed to me very fine, very exciting. Fellini the artist is wonderful. He is everything I'm not. Indeed, I should like to be Fellini. He is so baroque. His films are so generous, so warm, so easy, so unneurotic.

BC: Was Carl Dreyer, the Danish director, ever an influence on your work?

IB: No, never. I find myself quite remote from him, so much so that his films have never touched me. If we're talking about those filmmakers whose work has really affected and inspired me, we have to begin with Victor Sjöström, with him first and foremost. I used to make an effort to see Sjöström's *The Phantom Carriage* at least once a year; it became a tradition in my family to begin my cinema season—the period during which I made movies each year—with *The Phantom Carriage* and to end it with *A Girl from the Marsh Croft*. I'm enormously attached to these two films. To see them again and again became, in a way, a drug or, if you like, a vice. When it comes to Sjöström's Hollywood pictures, people tend to mention *The Wind* first, and it certainly is a marvelous work. But personally I find *He Who Gets Slapped* even more remarkable. Isn't it incredible how he could adapt to Hollywood yet still be innovative?

Sjöström was also a wonderful man, generous with his advice, simple but wise. "Don't make unnecessary trouble when you direct," he used to tell me. "Don't create too many problems for yourself and your crew. Elaborate camera movements—you don't know yet how to control such things, so don't bother yourself with them. And don't complicate matters for your actors. Keep the sets simple and spare." Invaluable advice for a young iconoclast longing to experiment!

BC: Do you respond to any contemporaries of Sjöström's in the film world?

IB: Oh yes, I think I have a particular weakness for silent films from the second half of the 1920s, before the cinema was taken over by sound. At that time, the cinema was in the process of creating its own silent language. There was the German Murnau and *The Last Laugh*, with Emil Jannings, a film told solely in images with a fantastic suppleness; then came Murnau's *Faust* and finally his masterpiece, *Sunrise*. Three astonishing works which tell us that Murnau, at the same time as Stroheim in Hollywood, was well on his way to creating a magnificently original and distinct cinematic language.

Swedish cinema, you know, was on its way to becoming a remarkable art form unto itself when sound arrived and then everything had to start over from scratch. Swedish film had to retrieve its secrets because, with the arrival of sound, the country's strong theatrical tradition began to dominate moviemaking, with a consequent sterility in cinematic form.

The silent Swedish masters, imitated in their own time by the Germans, inspired me from the first, especially the great Sjöström.

BC: Weren't you once supposed to make a film together with two of your favorite directors, Fellini and Kurosawa?

IB: Yes, that's true. The idea was that we would each make a love story, which would be part of an anthology film produced by Dino De Laurentiis. I wrote my story and flew to Rome, where Fellini was finishing *Satyricon*. For three weeks we had a great time together while we waited for Kurosawa to recover from a severe attack of pneumonia. But finally De Laurentiis gave up and said that there would be no film. And, to be completely honest, it was difficult to get Federico to decide what story he wanted to tell. My own script was very detailed, whereas Fellini had a three-page synopsis that he wanted to develop into a screenplay with one of his regular collaborators. For all I remember, maybe they did actually write something together, but everything fell through because Kurosawa couldn't travel on account of his illness. While we waited in vain for him, I spent some time with Fellini at his studio, watching him work on *Satyricon*. I am very sorry that this project involving the three of us never saw the light of day, but I did get to visit with "Maestro" and his wife, Giulietta Masina. Fellini and I liked each other a lot. He used to call me "fratello mio."

BC: Did you, or do you, feel any affinity for the directors of the French New Wave?

IB: I admired Resnais's *Hiroshima, mon amour*, found it very interesting, but with no bearing whatsoever on what I was trying to do. I did like Truffaut enormously, however; I esteemed him, in fact. His way of relating with an audience, of telling a story, is both fascinating and tremendously appealing. It's not my style of storytelling, but it works wonderfully well in relation to the film medium—particularly in a magical film like *La nuit Américaine*. I can see some of Truffaut's movies again and again without growing tired of them. Like *L'enfant sauvage*: Its humanism made a huge impression on me.

   On the other hand, I've never been able to appreciate any of Godard's films, nor even understand them. Truffaut and I used to meet occasionally at film festivals, and we had an instant understanding that extended to his films. But Godard: I find his films affected, overintellectual, self-obsessed, and, as cinema, without interest and frankly dull, endless, and tiresome. Godard is a desperate bore. I have always thought he made films for critics. He made one here in Sweden, *Masculine-féminine*, so boring that my hair stood on end.

No, I'd prefer to speak of another director from the high point of the New Wave, the one who specialized in crime dramas: Claude Chabrol, a marvelous storyteller in a specific genre. I've always had a weakness for his thrillers, just as I have for Jean-Pierre Melville, whose stylized approach to the crime drama is accompanied by an excellent sense of how to light each scene. I love seeing his pictures. He was also one of the first directors who really understood how to use CinemaScope in an intelligent and sensitive way.

BC: Wouldn't you say that your early films, like *Secrets of Women*, were influenced by the pre–World War I French school of poetic realism?

IB: Yes, when I was eighteen I admired Carné and Duvivier very much. Their films had the charm of the exotic to us Swedes. Carné and Duvivier were decisive influences in my wanting to become a filmmaker. Between 1936 and 1939, I saw Carné's *Quai des brumes*, *Hôtel du Nord*, and *Le jour se lève*, as well as Duvivier's *Pépé le Moko* and *Un carnet de bal*, and they had a huge impact on me. I told myself that if I ever managed to become a director, that was how I wanted to make films, like Carné especially! Those films affected me tremendously.

BC: Do you have any American favorites?

IB: As far as American dramaturgy is concerned, none of its exponents mean more to me than that late Viennese Billy Wilder. I can see the greatness of John Ford as a filmmaker, but his movies have nothing to say to me. With Wilder, it's the opposite. He had a genius when it comes to actors. He always made the perfect choice, even in the case of Marilyn Monroe. I met him when he was filming *Fedora* in Bavaria; I was in Germany at the time preparing *From the Life of the Marionettes*. I've always loved this man's films.

As for Orson Welles, I have always thought he was a phony, overrated. He was shallow, not interesting. *Citizen Kane*, of course, is the favorite of all the critics, always put at the top of the best-films-ever-made lists. But I don't understand why at all. Take only the performances in this picture: They're terrible.

BC: Let's talk about the performances in your films, in particular about how you worked with actors.

IB: How I worked with actors—that can be a very complicated question, and it can be a very simple one. If you want to know how exactly I worked with my actors, I can tell you in one second: I just used my intuition. My only instrument in my profession, really, was my intuition. When I worked with my actors in the theater or at the film studio, I just *felt*. One thing was very important to me: that an actor always had to be a creative human being. And what your intuition has to discover is how to free—do you understand what I mean?—how to free the creative power in the actor or the actress.

I can't explain how it works. Excuse me, but I see this question in your eyes. It has nothing to do with magic; it has everything to do with experience. But I think when I worked together with my actors I tried to function like radar—I tried to be wide open—because we had to create something together, through mutual cooperation. I gave them some suggestions and stimulation, they gave me some in return, and if this fantastic wave of giving and taking was cut off for any reason, I had to sense it and I had to look for the reason—good heavens, what happened? And I knew that if we tried to work with this wave cut off, it would be terrifying; it would be a tough, fruitless job, both for me and the actors. Some directors work with aggression: The director is aggressive, and the actors are aggressive, and they get terrific results. But for me that way of working was impossible. I had to be in contact, in touch with my actors the whole time. What we created first when we started to work together was an atmosphere of security around us. And I was not the only one who created such an atmosphere; we created it together.

You know, all those situations, all those decisions, all those very difficult choices—I had to make hundreds of them every day, yet I never thought about it. It was never an intellectual process for me; once again, it was a matter of intuition. *Afterwards* you could think everything over, not before. What was this? Why was that? After the fact you could think over every step you had taken.

Let me add, with regard to performances, that the first take is almost always the best one. After that the actors become impatient or tired: Their gestures and their intonations show the effect of this. That's why, whenever possible, I preferred to confine myself to one or two takes.

BC: You used women as your main characters a lot; your male characters often aren't in the foreground of your films. Did this have anything to do with men's and women's working habits on the set, how you related to them?

IB: Absolutely. I liked working with women more. Filmmaking is a job that tests your nerves, believe me, and I think that women have far better nerves than men. God forgive me, but I have the feeling that the prima donnas are always male. I think it has to do with our whole social system, the male parts and female parts that have to be played. It's very difficult for men to be actors in our society—to play the male role as it has been formulated—but it's not so difficult to be an actress.

BC: You have been widely praised for your sympathetic depiction of, and insight into, the feminine protagonists in your films. How is it—

IB: You're going to ask, "How is it that I understand women so well?" Women used to interest me as subjects because they were so ridiculously depicted in movies. I simply showed them as they actually are—or at least closer to what they are than the silly representations of women in the movies of the 1930s and 1940s. Any reasonably realistic treatment looked great by comparison with what was being done. Over the years, however, I began to realize that women are essentially the same as men and that they both have the same problems. I now don't think of there being women's problems or women's stories any more than I think of there being men's problems or men's stories. They are all human problems and human stories. It's people who interest me these days, even if I am not going to make films any longer.

BC: Was your way of writing similar to the way you worked with actors?

IB: Yes, yes, yes. The best time in my writing, I think, was when I had no ideas about how to do it. I could lie down on the sofa and look into the fire, or I could go to the seaside and just sit down and do nothing. I could just play the game, you know, and it was wonderful; I made some notes and could go on for a year just making notes. But when I had finally made a plan, the difficult job started: I had to sit down on my ass every morning at ten o'clock and write the screenplay. Then something very, very strange happened: Often the personalities in my scripts didn't want the same thing I wanted. If I tried to force them to do what I wanted them to do, the result would always be an artistic catastrophe. But if I left these personalities free to do what they wanted and what they told me was right, everything was okay.

So I think that this is the way to handle writing, like acting: All the intellectual analysis has to come afterward. You have seen *Cries and Whispers*, yes? For half a year, I went around and just had a picture inside my head about three women walking around in a red room in white clothes, and I didn't know why. I couldn't understand these damned women. I tried to get rid of them; I tried to get them down on paper; I tried to find out what they said to one another, because they whispered. And suddenly it came out that they were watching another woman who was dying in the next room, and after this revelation everything began to come into place. But this took about a year. It always started for me with a picture like this, with some kind of tension in it, and then slowly things developed.

I always spent approximately a year on each script that I did. First of all, I wrote much more than I could use, and after the first draft was finished I cut and cut, until everything was trimmed away except what seemed essential. I did the writing either at my villa near Stockholm or at my country place in Dalarna in central Sweden. I rose early, usually by five-thirty or six; the writing was done in longhand and typed up for me afterwards.

I would probably have gone mad if I had had to write a script as screenplays are usually done—that is, by putting in long shots, close-ups, and other camera directions. Such technical notations in a script are unnecessary, at least for me. It would be boring for everyone, including the actors, to have a script full of such details. All of us who worked on my films had a communal feeling about the story, and we knew what we had to do without being prompted every minute by the scenario. I discussed the entire script in advance with my photographer, anyway, and we achieved a rapport that lasted throughout the shooting and that could only help the actors. I should mention here that there is one kind of detail that I did find it helpful to include in a script—sensory details, even odors, anything that would help to suggest the mood.

Years ago, I have to tell you, I was hesitant about publishing four of my screenplays in book form—mainly because it seemed to me difficult for the general reader to appreciate an individual work that was not so much literary as a kind of score for the director, the cinematographer, and the actors.

BC: After you had finished writing a script, did you continue to develop the characters during the shooting?

IB: No. You know, I have always worked with trained actors; I have never worked with amateurs. An amateur can be himself always, and you can put him in situations that give the scene a third dimension, as Vittorio De Sica did in *Bicycle Thieves*, but if you work with trained actors you must know exactly what you are going to do with each of the characters, at every point. We had all our discussions prior to shooting and then we worked in the studio or on location. We gave each other suggestions or advice, but the whole time we kept in mind what we had already decided was our goal. It's very dangerous to go away and suddenly start to improvise. Of course you can improvise on the set; but if you improvise, you have to be very prepared, because to improvise on an improvisation always produces shit. If you are very prepared and know how to do it, you can return to your original form or structure if the improvisatory spirit suddenly one day fades away, which it will. It certainly will. Inspiration, enthusiasm, everything like that is beautiful, but you can't work solely on such a basis. Once you are on the set you have to be very strict.

BC: What was your relation to the camera during filming?

IB: If intuition is our mental instrument, the camera is our physical instrument. I myself think the camera is exotic. It is the most exciting little machine that exists. To me, just to have worked together with my cameraman, Sven Nykvist, so as to see a human face with the camera and with a zoom to come closer to it, to see the face changing before our eyes—this was the most fascinating thing. The choreography of the actors in relation to the camera is very important. If the actor feels that he is in a good position, in a logical position, he can be with his back to the camera, and it doesn't matter. The camera has to be the actors' best friend, and the actors have to be secure in the director and the cinematographer's handling of the camera. They must feel that we are taking care of them.

We who are directors must never forget that we are behind the camera, and the actor is in front of the camera; he is nude, his soul is bare. If he has confidence in us, he has given us an enormous responsibility. We have something fantastic in our hands: someone we can destroy, or someone we can help in his quest to create. To be behind the camera is never difficult, but to be in front of it is always a challenge, a difficulty: to be there with your face and your body and all the limitations you feel in your soul as well as in your physical being. We must not lie to the actors, moreover. We have to be absolutely truthful with them. Better actors like the truth more.

BC: Did you rehearse with the actors on the set before you planned your shots?

IB: No, never. That is a very good question. Because if you rehearse with trained actors, they go from the mood of intuition to what they are trained to do, to stage acting on a nightly basis. If you go on rehearsing with the actors too much, if you rehearse with them for several days, some new process takes over the actors' minds. An intellectual process, I think, and that process can be very good, but it's very dangerous for filming because then you have something in the actor's eyes suddenly, some sort of "Now I do this" and "Next I do that" and "Afterwards I do that." He's conscious of what he's doing, whereas he should be doing it intuitively.

BC: Along similar lines, can you say something about the similarities and differences of working in the theater and the cinema?

IB: Oh, it's absolutely different. Filmmaking is a neurotic job; it's abnormal to every creative process I know. It's some sort of craftsmanship, and it takes a lot of physical power to work in this craft. As I said earlier, we make only three minutes of the picture each day—if we are lucky. If you are in the theater in Sweden, you get about ten to twelve weeks of rehearsal. We start slowly at ten-thirty in the morning and then we go, and if it's very lousy we just sit down and relax. Everybody feels that "this is not a good day but perhaps Monday will be better, and in the middle of next month we will see how far we have progressed." The creative process in the theater is thus natural, unneurotic. Theater is a drawn-out, methodical operation that allows for difficult components of all kinds; whereas film is a continuous downhill race in which you have to know each other very well in order for everybody to reach the goal in time and intact.

And when you are a film director who has written the script yourself, you have to be some sort of Dr. Jekyll and Mr. Hyde, because if Dr. Jekyll has written the script, Mr. Hyde has to direct it—and I tell you that they don't like each other so much. I think this is a very schizophrenic situation.

In the theater, we were a group of artists who just came together; we came together in a house that was built for us to work in. We came there like very effective, very efficient little children with our books. At ten-thirty a bell rang and we all went to our rehearsal rooms and then we were there together with our thoughts, our emotions, and Strindberg, Ibsen, Molière, Shakespeare, or any of those other old, marvelous gentlemen. We had the opportunity to live with the drama and to try to understand its wisdom.

If I had had to make a choice—God saved me from that—if somebody had come to me and said, "Now, Ingmar, you have made both film and theater for long enough; you have to make a decision about which one to pursue singly," I am sure I would have chosen the theater. Because in the theater if you grow old and stuffy and dusty, you still have a lot of experience, and if you can just distill that experience into some crazy yet illuminating words, the artists will understand you, and you will have a wonderful time with them. My teacher in the theater, in

Göteborg, was a director who was eighty-five years old and could hardly speak, but he still was able to create wonderful, incredible, larger-than-life productions because his soul was young. This man was absolutely a physical wreck, however, and you can't be a wreck when you work on a film—especially when you are on location. If you are, you are courting real danger.

When I was a teacher in the national theater school of Sweden, with the pupils of the first class we started with a discussion of what you need to make theater. On the blackboard we wrote down many things: stage, actors, tickets, costumes, money, spotlights, footlights, makeup—more than a hundred different things that we thought we needed. And then I said to the students, "Now take away everything that you think is not necessary." And we went on and on and on; we even took away the director. And three things remained. What do you think they were?

BC: The actors.

IB: Yes, *an* actor, that's true.

BC: An empty space, a stage.

IB: No, that's not necessary.

BC: A script.

IB: A script or scenario, yes. That's two. And the third essential ingredient?

BC: An audience.

IB: That's right, an audience. The class wasn't sure that the audience was necessary, but I thought it was absolutely necessary. And that is my theology of the theater: What we need is actors, some type of script, and an audience. If we have those three things, we have a performance. Because the performance is not on the stage alone; it is in the hearts of the audience. It is very important to know that. Theater fascinates me for these reasons. For another, it's so much less demanding on you than making films, as I have suggested. You're less at the mercy of equipment and the demand for so many minutes of footage every day. It's primarily between you and the actors and, later on, the audience. It's wonderful—the sudden meeting of the actor's expression and the audience's response. It's all so direct and alive. A film, once completed, is inalterable; in the theater you can get a different response every time you do the same play. In the theater there's constant change and always the chance to improve, to renew the piece's essence yet again. I once thought I could never live without it.

BC: The more you talk, the more I begin to realize, in fact, how different theater and film are.

IB: Yes, I find it easier to compare film not to the theater, or even the novel, but to music. In fact, I think of film and music as equals of a sort. In pure film and pure music there is feeling that goes directly to some deeper level of the listener or viewer, and only afterwards is it possible to analyze such an experience. Not that music and film are the same. Film has its own rhythms, its own manner of pulsation. Yet, if I found myself adding less and less music to my films, perhaps it was because what I was doing seemed to me a little like adding music to music. The practice of adding a musical score to a film after it has been made—I can't see that at all. I have heard that a musical score can sometimes "save" a movie, by producing emotions that the film itself hasn't produced. But, for me, that would only make matters worse.

It's important for me, when people see a performance in the theater, that they are completely aware they're sitting in a theater. By contrast, when they see a film, it's vital that they appreciate the great miracle of cinema and its unique quality, the human face in close-up. The cinema is a fantastic medium, because, just like music, it passes through your intellect and goes straight to your emotions. Yet, to arrange a scene so that it has maximum effect, so that it works in the most perfect way, is a very hard task for the film director. He knows that the right close up, at the right moment, can have an enormous effect, but he has to select the right close-up and the right moment. If a close-up is sensibly shot, well composed, adequately lit, and focused upon a good actor or actress, you can let it continue on the screen for as long as you want! While I was still active as a film director, my big dream was to make a whole feature in one single close-up.

That said, in both filmmaking and theatrical production, you are part of a group. If you are a relatively inhibited, shy, and timid person like me who has difficulty establishing deeper relations, it is wonderful to live in the collective world of filmmaking or to be part of a group in the theater that is working on a play. The reason is that nothing but the work is of importance to the group; you devote yourself completely—no less is acceptable—you stake your soul, for better or for worse, on what you do, and you have to accept the possibility that people will laugh at you. But through making films and staging plays you constantly come into contact with other people. The nature of the work is such that one intrudes into the lives, and the problems, of others. Performers, the members of the crew, everyone is forced into a form of emotionalness that is very worthwhile and even quite amusing. Constantly fascinating, too, because the great stimulation one has all the time is that one is in the company of other people, living, creative people.

BC: How long does the theater season in Sweden last?

IB: At least seven months and sometimes as long as the whole year. Every winter I used to direct plays for the municipal theaters in Malmö and Göteborg. To be sure, I explored Strindberg's plays in particular. As for the French repertory, I have great admiration for Molière, especially his *Don Juan*. I also have a great passion for Racine, but no translation of his plays into Swedish is really satisfactory. Our language remains very awkward when it comes to alexandrines. On the other hand, we possess excellent translations of Shakespeare. I've directed *A Midsummer Night's Dream*, *The Merchant of Venice*, and *Macbeth* each three times, and every revival had an entirely different mise en scène. Of all the plays by this dramatist, I prefer *Macbeth* without a doubt.

BC: How many plays have you written yourself?

IB: Dozens, the first one at the age of seventeen. But I've only had a relatively small number produced or published, among them *The Day Ends Early*, *To My Terror*, and *Rachel and the Cinema Doorman*. As for the rest, I prefer to keep them in my drawer.

BC: Does the theater sometimes operate for you as a kind of prolonged rehearsal or preparation for a film that is already embryonic in your consciousness?

IB: I guess you could say this, although it has never been a conscious plan on my part. In 1954, I directed Franz Lehár's *The Merry Widow* for the municipal theater of Malmö. The next year I wrote and directed the period comedy *Smiles of a Summer Night*, which utilizes—for my own rather savage purposes!—the atmosphere of romantic light opera. In 1956, I published the short, impressionistic play *A Medieval Fresco*. The title in Swedish translates literally as *Wood Painting*. This play was not produced, but it did form the basis for *The Seventh Seal*, which I wrote and directed in the same year. So there must be some truth to your supposition.

BC: What's your view of film criticism?

IB: I have long since given up reading what's written either about me or about my films. Most film critics know very little about how a film is made and have very little knowledge of film or culture in general. That's changing, of course, and you, as a critic, are one example.

BC: Your films have been unfavorably reviewed for, among other reasons, the private meanings or even total obscurity of many of their episodes and much of their symbolism. Do you think this criticism has any validity?

IB: Possibly, but I hope not, because I think that making a film comprehensible to the audience is the most important duty of any moviemaker. It's also the most difficult. Private films are relatively easy to make, but I don't think that a director should make easy films either for himself or for his audience. He should try to lead his audience a little farther with each succeeding film. It's good for the public to work a little. Still, the director should never forget for whom in fact he is making his film. In any case, it's not as important that a person who sees one of my films understands it here, in the head, as it is that he understands it here, in the heart. This is what matters. I never wanted to make merely intellectual films. I wanted audiences to feel, to sense, my pictures.

BC: Whatever the nature of their understanding, a great many international critics still concur in ranking you foremost among the world's filmmakers. How do you feel about this approbation?

IB: Success is transitory; that's how I feel. It's such a flimsy thing to be in fashion. Take Paris: Years ago I was their very favorite director. Then along came Antonioni. Who's the darling of the critics these days? Who knows? I'm less interested in approbation than in sincere criticism, even when it's unfavorable to me. Let me give you an example. Long before your own unfavorable response to *Autumn Sonata*, a French critic wrote, with regard to the same picture, that "Monsieur Bergman has begun to make Bergman films." It wasn't meant to be a compliment. But I still think it was a very intelligent and perceptive comment, which I really took note of because I knew exactly what he meant. He was absolutely right. And such self-imitation—I hesitate to say self-parody—is what a director must make an effort to avoid at all cost.

BC: What would you like to be said about Ingmar Bergman in twenty or thirty years? What would Bergman himself say?

IB: That's something I've never really thought about, because I'm so one-hundred-percent convinced that I made useful things, both in the theater and on film. I am totally indifferent to whether they survive me or not or whether people will be praising or damning my work three decades from now.

BC: Do you think that film itself has a future?

IB: Oh yes, an enormous one. The technical and formatting changes are going to continue, of course, but they aren't as important as people think they are. Movies as channelers for dreamers and distributors of dreams, of audiences' dreams and hopes and most secret longings—such movies will always exist, because there is no better medium for that purpose.

BC: What do you think of the fact that you're already part of everyday language? For instance, when you read a novel by V. S. Naipaul, you come upon two people talking in the African night, and one of them says to the other that this is a Bergman landscape.

IB: Well, as I like to say, all that seems to be about someone else. Some-how or other it has nothing to do with me. Even though I'm world-famous and widely written about, and people are immensely nice to me, the only thing that meant anything to me when I was working was the work. The work had to be meaningful to those who were carrying it out, and it had to be alive. That's the only thing I was afraid of—God knows, I was dead scared of it—that my ability to make things come alive and be effective would be taken away from me or that I might lose it, that suddenly I wouldn't know how do it, or perhaps worse, that I would be left with people doing what I said only out of politeness. You know, I never had so many nightmares during my life, but I did have one recur-ring bad dream: of myself, doing things that were stone-cold dead. The idea that I could no longer put any life into what I was doing—*that* was what terrorized me.

Filmography of Feature Films

Crisis, 1946
It Rains on Our Love, 1946
A Ship Bound for India, 1947
Night Is My Future, 1948
Port of Call, 1948
The Devil's Wanton, 1949
Three Strange Loves, 1949
To Joy, 1950
This Can't Happen Here, 1950
Summer Interlude, 1951
Secrets of Women, 1952
Summer with Monika, 1953
The Naked Night, 1953
A Lesson in Love, 1954
Dreams, 1955
Smiles of a Summer Night, 1955
The Seventh Seal, 1957
Wild Strawberries, 1957
Brink of Life, 1958
The Magician, 1958
The Virgin Spring, 1960
The Devil's Eye, 1960
Through a Glass Darkly, 1961
Winter Light, 1962
The Silence, 1963
All These Women, 1964
Persona, 1966
Hour of the Wolf, 1968
Shame, 1968
The Rite, 1969
The Passion of Anna, 1969
The Fårö Document 1969, 1970
The Touch, 1971
Cries and Whispers, 1972
Scenes from a Marriage, 1973
The Magic Flute, 1975
Face to Face, 1976
The Serpent's Egg, 1977
Autumn Sonata, 1978

The Fårö Document 1979, 1979
From the Life of the Marionettes, 1980
Fanny and Alexander, 1982
After the Rehearsal, 1984
Saraband, 2003

The Committed Cinema
of Mike Leigh

I N *HIGH HOPES* (1988), CYRIL AND Shirley are proletarian lovers in their midthirties whom the director and screenwriter Mike Leigh (previously represented in the United States only by *Bleak Moments* [1971]) contrasts with two caricatured couples: Valerie (Cyril's sister) and Martin, vulgarly consuming, newly arrived members of the middle class; and Rupert and Laetitia, yuppies who affect the status of gentry and have gentrified the house next to Mrs. Bender, Cyril and Val's mother, in a once working-class neighborhood of London. Unfortunately, the caricature is at times so broad that it nearly discredits the seriousness and amiability of *High Hopes*. But the film is saved by the wryly affectionate relationship between Cyril and Shirley and especially by their relationship with his seventy-year-old, widowed, and senile mother—one that is comically foreshadowed in the opening scenes by their solicitous dealings with a baffled, boyish newcomer to London, who promptly returns home to the country to his own mother, with whom he had had a row, rather than confront the cold, hard ways of the city where even his sister has not welcomed him.

Actually, *High Hopes* revolves around the relationships of all three couples, all childless, with the often immobile and taciturn Mrs. Bender, whose immobility and isolation Leigh several times emphasizes by holding the camera on her expressionless face when others are present. Val and Martin do not want to be bothered with her, except to give her expensive, tactless presents on the appropriate occasions; Rupert and Laetitia consider her an embarrassing nuisance who should sell her home to people like themselves; so it falls to Cyril and Shirley to look in on "Mum" from time to time and to be there for her in moments of crisis. Shirley takes these actions out of kindness and love, Cyril out of guilt and duty, for he believes that "families fuck you up." Philip Larkin speaks for him in "This Be the Verse":

> They fuck you up, your mum and dad.
> They may not mean to, but they do.
> They fill you with the faults they had
> And add some extra, just for you.

The last two lines of Larkin's poem read, "Get out as early as you can, / And don't have any kids yourself." Which is also Cyril's philosophy, expressed a bit more succinctly when he says, "Two's company." He and Shirley have been keeping company for ten years (though they are un-married), and she wants a baby, which Cyril does not, not only because of what he perceives as the pernicious influence of parents on their off-spring, but also because of the world into which he would be bringing a child. Prole that he is (he drives a motorcycle for a messenger service, even though his mind is equipped for more challenging work; Shirley is a groundskeeper for the city), Cyril is nonetheless no wide-eyed Marxist. During a visit to Marx's grave in Highgate (complete with camera-toting Japanese tourists!), he reads aloud the epitaph that Brecht was so fond of quoting as the rationale for his plays ("The philosophers have only inter-preted the world in various ways. The point, however, is to change it"), then queries, "Change what? The world's a whole new place now." And shortly afterward he contemptuoulsy responds to the revolutionary blather of a friend with the line, "There ain't gonna be no revolution."

Cyril is resigned: to living as best he can, to loving Shirley (whose political views are a toned-down version of his), to preserving his sanity in a world whose feverishly capitalistic workings threaten the safety and wel-fare of all. After a harrowing seventieth birthday party at Val and Martin's gaudy home, Mrs. Bender happens to spend the night for the first time at her son's small, somewhat seedy apartment, and that night Cyril and Shirley make love without benefit of her diaphragm. Leigh doesn't make a big sentimental deal out of this: They go to bed, they talk a bit, Shirley reveals that she hasn't put her "cap" in, and Cyril gives his tacit approval after having just expressed his fear of becoming bitter; then, lights out.

The next morning, they take his mother up to the roof of their apartment building, which overlooks St. Paul's Cathedral, King's Cross, and the train line on which the late Mr. Bender used to work. After the old woman declares, "This is the top of the world!" *High Hopes* ends with an extended long shot of her seated center screen in profile, with her son and his girlfriend standing off to the right, holding each other near Shirley's rooftop plant menagerie. All three look out over the city, and not another word is spoken. The London skyline, as shot by Roger Pratt, is a mass of cool blue-gray shrouded in dirty air; Andrew Dickson's music has once again turned from the hauntingly elegiac to the whimsically upbeat; and the acting of Edna Doré (Mrs. Bender), Philip Davis (Cyril), and Ruth Sheen (Shirley) remains what it has been throughout the film: absolutely committed to revealing the unadorned truth about these unadorned but oddly appealing, quietly brave characters.

There is plenty of good acting on display as well in *Secrets and Lies* (1996), the film by Mike Leigh that won the Palme d'Or at the 1996 Cannes Festival. Leigh is celebrated in English theater, television, and cinema for his method of collaborating with actors and developing scripts. He and each of his actors choose a real person from the actor's life, on the basis of whom they construct a fictional character in improvisations with other cast members, whose characters have been similarly created. The performers are forbidden to discuss their roles or motivations with one another so that none of them will have an overview of the story or an awareness of what is happening outside their own scenes. Himself trained as an actor at the Royal Academy of Dramatic Art in the 1960s, Leigh believes that this approach liberates the actor's creativity, because he is thereby freed from the pressure to produce "results"; he has only to experience truthfully what his character is undergoing in the moment— as in real life. From the improvisatory sessions as well as his cast's "life-drawing," or drawing characters from actual people, Leigh develops ideas from which the narrative of the piece is negotiated, so to speak, slowly constructed, then reworked over months of rehearsal. Only at the end is anything written down in the form of a script.

This method of moviemaking has been compared to that of the late John Cassavetes in such films as *Shadows* (1959), *Faces* (1963), and *Husbands* (1970), but the differences are that Cassavetes seemed concerned in his pictures more with getting the actors to spill their guts or finger their own psyches than with penerating the essence of the world as we all think we know it; and that the Greek-American director lacked a sense of humor about himself as well as his work. Leigh has been trying since 1971, in 16-millimeter movies made for BBC television as well as in full-scale theatrical releases, seriocomically to investigate a particular aspect of his part of the world: the lower rungs of British family life, the more anguished corners of the post-World War II English working class. And he has managed to conduct his cinematic investigation without the political tendentiousness bordering on religious affirmation of Ken Loach (at his worst) or the passionate self-regard approaching masochistic exaltation of Terence Davies (at his best), the two countrymen of Mike Leigh who are best known for treating the same central subject on film.

Leigh's titles vacillate between ironic comment upon that life-class, let us call it—*Who's Who* (1978), *Home Sweet Home* (1982), *High Hopes*, *Life Is Sweet* (1990); trenchant observation of it—*Meantime* (1984), *Naked*

(1993); and straightforward remark about it—*Bleak Moments, Hard Labor* (1973), and *Secrets and Lies*. Moreover, his deemphasis on the machinations of plot—the result of his workshop approach to creating character first and foremost—seems peculiarly suited to some of the peripatetic, even random or aimless, lives he studies, such as that of the abrasive drifter Johnny in *Naked*. Similarly, Leigh's focus in rehearsal primarily on the life of character or the character of life, on the artistic examination in detail of people's existences, is unusually germane to the subject of *Secrets and Lies*: the search of an adopted child for her biological mother. For the movie's questions are "Who am I?" and "How are these people related to me?"—which are exactly the questions an actor asks in the exploration of a character and his life.

Secrets and Lies opens with the funeral of the adoptive mother of Hortense Cumberbatch, a twenty-seven-year-old, single, black Londoner, whose adoptive father is also deceased. Hortense is an optometrist, and therefore it is no accident that this opening scene is cross-cut with one featuring, not her biological mother, but instead her birth mother's brother, Maurice Purley. He is a photographer whom we watch fastidiously yet genially shooting a bride at home in her wedding gown—a "shoot" soon to be followed by a scene in which Hortense amiably examines a little (white) girl for eyeglasses. Leigh thus immediately announces that his film will be concerned with seeing, with the ability to see (through frames) and the desire to be seen (in a frame), by means of the ocular as well as the camera lens. And, naturalistic artist that he is, Leigh will invoke the power of the frame to engage us, the audience, in the act of beholding, and recognizing, the lives of his ordinary human characters: strangers to whom we would not—and could not—normally give more than a moment's consideration in real life.

Furthermore, this director insistently reminds us of his naturalistic mission by five times throwing in a sequence of tableaux—otherwise unrelated to the "plot"—in which mainly everyday people pose for their portraits in front of Maurice's tripod. We see whole families, mothers and children, pets with their owners, groups of friends, various couples, individual achievers (like a black boxer), a few exhibitionists, and, most important, the last photographic subject: a classy young woman with a beautiful yet badly scarred face by which we are simultaneously attracted and repelled. She has the longest session before the probing camera of Purley Photography, and her face becomes the visual conceit of *Secrets and Lies*. It is a corporal metaphor for the beautiful yet badly scarred soul of Maurice's sister, Cynthia Rose Purley, in addition to being a grotesque commingling of two faces or facets of film: the fantastic Hollywood cinema of beautiful people and its opposite number, the naturalistic, in this case British, picture of the down-and-dirty, the nitty-gritty, or the lean-and-mean.

After her photographic session, the lovely but disfigured young lady is harassed on the street by a disheveled drunk named Stuart Christian, who turns out to be Maurice's former partner. He is disgruntled because, he claims, he built their photography business into a success, only to be bought out by his associate. Like Maurice's current photographic subjects, Stuart spends only a small amount of time on screen, and his "story" appears unconnected to that of Maurice, Maurice's sister, and their respective families. However, he is clearly a meaningful "character" in his own right, a lapsed photographer in search of his camera—the great equalizer-cum-immortalizer of the twentieth century (and beyond) and for this reason a kind of god unto itself. Stuart Christian does not find his god at Purley Photography, but it, in the form of Mike Leigh's movie camera, has found him, even as it has found something like his female counterpart in Cynthia Purley.

She is Hortense Cumberbatch's forty-two-year-old, white, unwed biological mother, who supports herself with a factory job assembling boxes. Cynthia gave away Hortense, conceived when she was only fifteen, without so much as looking at the baby, has kept the birth a secret between herself and her brother ever since, and has even forgotten that her early lover was a black man. She lives with her second (white) daughter, Roxanne, the product of a fling the youthful Cynthia had with an American medical student one summer while on vacation in Spain. Although she has the intelligence to be a professional like Hortense, the bitter and angry Roxanne works as a street sweeper in a sort of spiteful revenge on an environment that failed to nurture her. Roxanne's revenge naturally extends to her tippling mother, with whom she has a fuming relationship—literally as well as figuratively, since each of the women smokes!

At the start of the film, it has been two-and-a-half years since Roxanne has seen her thirty-eight-year-old uncle, Maurice, and his wife, Monica; Cynthia herself has not seen her brother and his spouse for about a year, dating back to the day the prosperous yet childless couple moved into a large new home in one of North London's better neighborhoods. But the Purleys' estrangement is about to be cut short with the approach of Roxanne's twenty-first birthday, just as Hortense's long separation from her birth mother will end as a result of the sudden death, in her fifties, of the black, Barbados-born woman (herself a midwife) who adopted her.

This death leaves the otherwise successful and self-possessed Hortense feeling lost, despite the fact that she has two adopted adult brothers, so in the summer of 1995, two months after her adoptive mother's funeral, she decides to find her biological mother. Hortense has known since she was seven years old of her adoption, but only as the result of a British law passed in 1975—coincidentally, the year in which she turned seven—is she now entitled to learn, through a social agency, the name and address of the woman who bore her. The agency advises her not to pursue the matter on her own, to let a case worker handle it, but Hortense disregards this caution and arranges to meet Cynthia, who, somewhat comically, is as startled to discover her daughter's race as the daughter is to discover her mother's.

Their reunion is preceded by that of the warmhearted Maurice with his equally warmhearted sister at Cynthia's gloomy, South London row house, where both grew up, where Cynthia more or less raised Maurice after the death of their mother in 1961, and where she continues to rent despite inheriting, upon the death of her father, the money with which to make a down payment on the place or some other one. She used that money instead to set Maurice up in his own photography business, to finance the acquisition of his neighborhood studio, and her gift is a contributing factor to the deep—and moving—bond between brother and sister.

Leigh cinematically renders this bond through a long take of the weeping Cynthia in the arms of the bearish yet loving Maurice. And he repeats such a held shot at the first meeting of Hortense and Cynthia in a big but otherwise empty tea shop at the Holborn railway station—except that, in this instance, the take lasts a full seven minutes without a cut. The camera "merely" remains fixed on the two women seated side by side in a full frontal shot, gingerly getting to know each other after two introductory, necessarily intercut telephone calls. They meet again a week later for dinner as well as for the celebration of Hortense's July 23 birthday, then yet again the next week for a movie; and in this time Cynthia warms to Hortense to the point of inviting her as a "mystery guest" to Roxanne's own twenty-first birthday party, which will soon be held at Maurice and Monica's house.

I hasten to add here that there is absolutely nothing maudlin about the budding relationship between this mother and her long-lost child or about the accompanying, seemingly resultant détente between the bemused Roxanne (who still does not know of her half sister's existence, but who suspects instead that her mother is "seeing" someone) and the mellowing Cynthia, even though the latter must do a lot of crying in the film. Her tears are earned, however, and they are varied depending on the situation or the cause. So much so that, for once in a movie, crying becomes a device for plumbing character, not for tugging at audience members' heartstrings and making *them* cry—as in such "weepies" aimed at women as *Dark Victory* (1939), *Little Boy Lost* (1953), and *Love Story* (1970).

Secrets and Lies proceeds through the effect that Hortense has not only on Cynthia but also on Cynthia's whole family, gathered in the climactic scene for the party in honor of Roxanne's birthday. I deliberately did not write "the black Hortense" and "the white Purleys" in the previous sentence because this picture is not about race in the way that it would be had it been made in America. Race is a factor in *Secrets and Lies*, yes, but not a hateful, divisive, deeply ingrained one; Hortense's color makes her different and even "other," but it does not make her despicable. Class is more of a factor here, as it is in all English films, in that, ironically or not, the educated Miss Cumberbatch speaks the Queen's English with exquisite diction, unlike her common blood relations. (For a film in which Mike Leigh does to some extent tackle the injuries of race as well as class, see *Meantime*, which is about unemployment and adolescent angst during the Thatcher years and features black, working-class characters who exchange insults with their equally despondent white brethren.) Oddly enough, on the surface Hortense's closest relative among the Purleys is the one to whom she is not related by blood and who loathes the "vulgar," "hysterical" Cynthia whom Hortense is growing to love: Monica, who speaks well, has good manners, and likes nice things, yet who views the world through the myopic eyes of an interior decorator (and an amateur, thriftless one at that), not the expansive ones of an optometrist.

Among the revelations at the birthday-barbecue party, in addition to the chief one that Hortense is Cynthia's biological daughter given up for adoption twenty-seven years before (not her coworker at the box factory, as Cynthia had lied), is the truth about Monica and Maurice's childlessness: She is unable to have children, not selfishly denying them to her husband (as Cynthia had believed), and nothing the desperate couple have done over the past fifteen years has been able to change that fact. Ironically, they have not considered, or have chosen not to pursue, adoption, even though Maurice says that his wife's infertility—together with her chronic moodiness as a result of her condition—has almost destroyed their relationship. Roxanne, for her part, practices the birth control that may have been unavailable to her mother, declares that she never wants to have any children, and initially is none too thrilled to learn—on the anniversary of her own birthday—of the birth of a half sister six years before her; she says besides that she does not even plan on moving in with her long-suffering boyfriend, Paul, let alone on marrying him. Neither Hortense nor her birth mother has a man in her life, yet neither woman seems especially troubled by her "singleness."

What Cynthia and her two daughters have at the end is one another, even as Monica and Maurice have their marriage. These latter two say as much to each other in bed after the party in the film's penultimate

scene, then we get the final scene the next day in Cynthia's modest garden, where Mother, Hortense, and Roxanne have gathered for talk and
tea. The last shot is a long, overhead, slightly off-center take of the three
of them sitting together in the sun, at the end of which Cynthia rhetorically asks, "This is the life, ain't it?" It may be, but the singularity of
Leigh the director's uneasy or unstable aerial camera here causes us, if not
to doubt Cynthia's certainty, then at least to question the tidiness of
Leigh the writer's feel-good ending, all the more so when we remember
that Hortense's persistent questions to Cynthia about her biological father, during the two women's meeting at the train-station café as well as
during their attendance at Roxanne's birthday party (where, ominously,
Hortense's query comprises the last words spoken in the scene), go unanswered. They—the women together with the inquiries about paternity—seem to embody Mike Leigh's belief that "it's necessary for you to
walk away from this kind of film with questions unanswered, and work to
do, and matters to be faced" (*Films in Review*, January–February 1997).

"Welcome to the family," Maurice had comically declared to
Hortense after all the painful truth-telling and exasperating rancor of the
birthday party. However, the comedy here derives precisely from the
double-edged nature of his welcome, not merely from the conciliatory
nature of his embrace after the hostilities that have preceded it, for Maurice
is welcoming Hortense to the pain and rancor as well as the pleasure and
affability of life with the Purleys. Fortunately, secrets have been uncov-
ered and lies untold, but, unfortunately, the Purleys' happiness remains a
fragile one, just as the comparative ease of their acceptance of Hortense
may turn into relative uneasiness.

Maurice himself, the peace-making portrait photographer, the chroni-
cler of subjects coaxed to look and act their best, knows a thing or two
about the common human habit of allowing orneriness and deception, fear
and vanity, to destroy happiness—by which this movie means the closeness
and connection between people, as opposed to their isolation and loneliness. It is Maurice who speaks the film's title as he rails against the destructive power of secrets and lies, to which Leigh opposes the restorative power
of cinematic truthtelling. And it is Maurice who, in his last scene, admits
he is frightened that Monica does not love him anymore, at least not in the
way she once did. Despite her protestation, it is his fear that sticks in the
mind long after a screening of *Secrets and Lies*, just as it is the manner in
which Leigh shoots the concluding scene more than the content itself that
is etched in my memory. Like the reformed alcoholic and country-and-
western singer/songwriter Mac Sledge at the end of that fine American
movie *Tender Mercies* (1983), Mike Leigh seems finally not to trust happiness, and neither does his fictional alter ago, Maurice Purley.

What Mike Leigh does trust is his actors, and he shows this, for example, by not cutting during that long scene between Hortense and Cynthia in the subway station café—a scene in which form is perfectly wedded to content, since its subject is the literal as well as figurative coming together of mother and daughter. The actresses here—Marianne Jean-Baptiste as Hortense and Brenda Blethyn in the role of Cynthia— get to act *continuously* as a twosome, as they would on a stage (and as Jean-Baptiste has done on the stage), without dependence upon close-ups or on the piecing together of segments from different takes of the same scene. And these performers, like their colleagues Timothy Spall (Maurice), Phyllis Logan (Monica), and Claire Rushbrook (Roxanne) from Leigh's informal repertory company, are able to reward their director's trust because they have had the rehearsal time—courtesy of him and his producer, Simon Channing-Williams—to prepare for scenes such as this one.

To be sure, Leigh is not averse to moving his camera rather than holding it steady on the characters, as he does in the tea shop; but he has to have a good reason for doing so, and he does during the opening funeral sequence, where the tracking camera creates a fluid, dynamic language of its own to compensate for the absence of dialogue among the static mourners. Nor is this director averse to cutting between actors in a scene, to the shot-reverse-shot technique of filming, but, again, he uses it when he should, to suggest conflict or tension between speakers, not as the standard method for shooting dialogue.

For instance, the first time we see Maurice and Monica together in *Secrets and Lies*, they discuss Roxanne, about whose future they are worried and whose past seems limited, for them, to the first professional photograph her uncle ever took: of his niece as a smiling, toothy little girl. It sits atop Maurice's mantelpiece in the background of this scene between him and his wife, which apparently does no more than record a solicitous conversation between a couple about a close relative of theirs. But the editor Jon Gregory's incessant cutting between the two speakers, together with Andrew Dickson's somber tones (though not sentimental ones, here or anywhere else in the picture) on the soundtrack, suggests that something else is going on here. That "something else," we will later discover, has to do with the barren Monica's antipathy toward, combined with her jealousy of, her childbearing sister-in-law—Roxanne's mother— whom she regards as little more than a boozy floozy.

Leigh's color film looks pretty good in a subdued or soothing way, making much use of soft blues and even turquoise in the background of the mostly interior shots. One could argue that *Secrets and Lies* might just as easily have been photographed in raw or graphic black and white, like the moving pictures of the British social realists—the "Angry Young

Men"—from the late 1950s and early 1960s. But *Secrets and Lies* is not really as grim, say, as *Look Back in Anger* (1959), *Saturday Night and Sunday Morning* (1960), or *The Loneliness of the Long-Distance Runner* (1962), nor is it making any kind of sociopolitical statement that needs to be removed to the world of proletarian gray; and, unlike John Cassavetes during his black-and-white phase, Mike Leigh has no interest in registering the dreary, grainy side of life for its own sordid sake. What he is interested in is centrally examining the life of an ordinary but affecting human being under a microscope, if you will, and microscopes have a way of both opening up dirty little pores and extenuating, alleviating, or desaturating the big bright colors of life's spectrum. In other words, "microscopic" cinema such as that found in *Secrets and Lies* paradoxically enlarges our humanity at the same time as it reduces us all to our least, or our lightest, common denominator.

Would that I could say the same about Leigh's *All or Nothing* (2001). I cannot, alas, for the acting in this film is all that there is: No novelistic or dramatic source precedes Leigh's screenplay, and the script itself is kitchen-sink naturalism of a low order. So it was "More art, less matter" that I kept repeating to myself as I watched this well-acted slice of lower-class British life. Leigh is one of those directors who feel that acting is the matter, the heart and soul, of cinema, and, although I am suspicious of such absolutist pronouncements in so collaborative an artistic medium, he has almost made me believe this particular *pronunciamento* when his writing has been on the same high level with the performances of his actors—in *Naked* and *Secrets and Lies*, for example. But there is nothing of the kind this time, not at all.

The real truth here *is* in the nakedly truthful acting, but acting such as this, because it resides in a film with little or no thematic import, amounts to little more than simulation. Yes, it is true, and yes, it is convincing, but apparently to no end other than the creation of true and convincing proles from South London. This is the work of illusionists, not artists, and this is an illusion we do not require, given the abiding supply, in abundance, of the real proletarian thing, which in real English life would include blacks, Pakistanis, and other ethnic or racial groups—none of which are in evidence in the housing estate (public housing project) where the movie's assorted Caucasian characters live.

These characters make up three discrete, dysfunctional families. Phil Bassett, heavyset, scruffy looking, and sad-eyed, drives a taxi when he manages to get up in the morning and out to work. He is a gentle, mumbling soul who means well but never quite manages to make those around him happy; trapped in a cabbie's unchallenging job, with its scant earnings, he even has to borrow money from his common-law wife and two children to pay for a pint at the local pub. Penny, Phil's long-suffering, and long-complaining, spouse, is employed as a cashier at the local grocery store—boring, repetitive labor that no doubt pays her only minimum wage. She unhappily puts up with the aggressive, disrespectful rebellion of their hugely overweight, chronically unemployed son, Rory, who spends most of his time stretched out on the couch watching television or slumped over the kitchen table eating his mother's cooking, cursing as he shuttles between his two favorite spots. Phil and Penny's daughter, Rachel, also obese, is employed as a cleaning woman at a nursing home. She's so self-effacing (if not inchoate) that she rarely speaks, seemingly numbed or stunted by the drudgery of her work and the tedium of the Bassetts' domestic life. But at least she is not the layabout with a chip on his shoulder that her brother has become.

Among the neighbors of the Bassett family are Ron, a recklessly incompetent cabdriver; his wife, Carol, an all-day-long, falling-down-drunk alcoholic; and Samantha, their teenaged temptress of a daughter who neither attends school nor has a job. Then there is single-mother Maureen, who works at the supermarket with Penny, takes in ironing to make ends meet, and seems to be the only character in *All or Nothing* who is more or less adjusted and reasonably happy. She manages to keep a sense of humor and optimism despite the fact that her daughter, Donna, is involved in an abusive relationship with a local bad boy named Jason.

Life Is Sweet (1990). Directed by Mike Leigh. Shown: Jane Horrocks and Claire Skinner. © October Films. (*Courtesy October Films/Photofest*)

Donna uses almost as many profanities as Rory, and, like the characters played by Jane Horrocks in Leigh's *Life Is Sweet* and Claire Rushbrook in *Secrets and Lies*, she is a short-tempered, caustic, mousy-haired twentysomething—moreover, one who divides her time, not between her mother and looking for work, but between copulating with her loser of a boyfriend and sitting around waiting for him to show up again. Needless to say, Jason impregnates Donna before abandoning her altogether.

So desperate is Leigh to do something with this congealed mass that he resorts to a worse trick in an attempt to garner sympathy for a character who has not earned it: The obese Rory has a heart attack—but only when he aggressively attempts to bully a boy during a pickup soccer game on the green of the apartment complex where both live. Rory's churlishness does not keep his family from rushing to his hospital bedside, however. He will recover, and his parents, as a result of his crisis, will experience their own in which Phil (like Maurice in *Secrets and Lies*) confronts Penny with his realization that she doesn't love him anymore. He asks her if she does, then they tearfully kiss and embrace—but she never answers his question. It does not really matter, Leigh seems to be saying, for the Bassetts do not have or cannot see any alternatives, and they will stay together because even though family cannot allay the oppressive loneliness, together with the unremitting hopelessness, that pervades their lives, family is all they have.

Clearly, *All or Nothing* is uncomfortably bleak, unleavened by the dark humor to be found, say, in Leigh's *High Hopes*. Yet there is a certain kind of bleakness that, no matter how faithfully it sticks to the hard facts of life, is its own kind of lie, a failure of nerve and of imagination. Those failures are what lead to the somewhat sentimental conclusion of the picture, where Leigh tries to alleviate its melancholy tone with an element of optimism and even of redemption (as Phil, for example, suddenly gets up the next day at 5:00 a.m. to drive someone to the airport for a big fare). This is a filmmaker in search of a subject, but, by the early 2000s, the hardscrabble lives of people on the economic fringes of Margaret Thatcher's ruinous legacy no longer require documentation. There is plenty of it already, artistic and otherwise, and, even at its best, this is all that *All or Nothing* offers to the viewer: a documentation of characters mired in banality if not depravity, without promise of opportunity, change, or escape; with no skills or education to fall back on, nor any professional help to guide them in handling the difficult situations with which they find themselves confronted.

The Bassetts and their neighbors are doomed, then, the only question being in which circle of hell these narrow, thwarted, dull, pathetic figures will wind up and whether they will drag their audience down with them. So, in a sense, the oh-so-truthful acting out of the characters in this movie—most notably by Leigh veterans Timothy Spall as Phil and Lesley Manville as Penny—is an act of condescension by performers who happily get to go home to a far better life. Nonetheless, their simulation of the lives of those less fortunate *is* accompanied by an elegiac musical score (by another Leigh veteran, Andrew Dickson)—primarily for cello—that consistently underlines the essential nature of an underclass existence, as well as unostentatiously low-key, delimiting, and cool-filtered cinematography by Leigh's usual cameraman, Dick Pope.

So there are some things to like in this film, but there is enough not to like, and all the more so because, as I intimated earlier, working-class characters such as the Bassetts have now been a major subject of British art since the mid-1950s. These folk persist in being the focus of so much narrative, dramatic, and cinematic art for two simple reasons: A blooded working class continues to subsist in Great Britain, one that, like the blooded aristocracy in that country, tenaciously defines itself by accent, occupation, and attitude; and British artists' anger at the plight of the lower class—an anger that first expressed itself in Europe during the second half of the nineteenth century under the banner of naturalism—has not subsided. In the second half of the nineteenth century, however, and even in the midtwentieth century, that anger made more sense. Socioeconomic change in the West was both urgently necessary and humanly possible. But does anyone seriously think, in the first decade of the twenty-first century, that the British class system (for all its "improvements") is ever going to go away, that Britons for that matter *want* it to go away, or that a family like the Bassetts would have all its problems instantly solved by welfare subsidy in the form of substantially higher salaries to go along with their already significantly lowered rents?

If Mike Leigh believes this (as does his fellow British auteur Ken Loach), I believe he is naïve or has become so; if he does not, I do not know what he intended in *All or Nothing*—except to create a piece of work that is short on art and long on (slice of) life. *Vera Drake* (2004) itself is short on art, but to a different end than *All or Nothing*. Mike Leigh's latest film is about a kind of violence against women, though I do not think Leigh sees illegally performed abortions in this way, particularly as they were performed at a time, the 1950s, when the term *legal abortion* was an oxymoron. Vera Drake is the eponymous heroine, a middle-aged woman in the London of 1950 who works as a housemaid in an upper-class home. She lives with her husband, an auto mechanic, and their two grown children in an apartment so small that even a word such as *cramped* cannot do it justice. (Thus, as in every Leigh picture, do the homes of the poor become inseparable from the nature of their lives, even the very beings of their characters.)

Vera Drake (2004). Directed by Mike Leigh. Shown on the set: Mike Leigh. ©
Fine Line Features. Photographer: Simon Mein. *(Courtesy of Photofest)*

But Vera has another (secret) occupation besides those of housewife
and maid. After her day's work, she scurries from one working-class do-
micile to another, performing abortions, either on unmarried women or
on wives already burdened with large families. Vera uses a syringe and a
soapy solution of water, does the job, then leaves the patient with a
usually correct prediction of the result. What she is doing is of course
unlawful and, by her method, dangerously unsophisticated even for the
repressed 1950s. An accident inevitably occurs during one of the abortions, followed by Vera's arrest, trial, and sentencing to thirty months in
jail. The last time we see her, she is joining two other female abortionists
in prison, each of them second-time offenders sentenced to three and
four years respectively. The film then closes by showing Vera's family
having dinner, without her.

What are we to think? Vera has been painted as an unflagging angel
of mercy: Devoted to and loved by her family, she helps the sick and the
aged when not aborting the fetuses of the poverty-stricken, and she even
has time for matchmaking—fixing her daughter up with a lonesome neighbor, for example. Furthermore, she does not get a penny for her "opera-

tions." Another woman makes the appointments and takes a fee that Vera knows nothing about. Even when she is found out by the police, this matron worries as much about her family's dismay and its loss of her housecleaning income as about her own travails. As far as Vera is concerned, she was doing what any goodhearted soul would naturally do: provide a desperately needed service to desperately needy women who simply could not get it in any other way.

And, as far as Mike Leigh is concerned, the law stopped Vera from helping indigent women who couldn't afford professional, hospital-shielded care. *They* were risking shame, worsened poverty, or abandonment, and *she* was cruelly blocked by the state in her humanitarian ministrations. To underscore the injustice of Vera's punishment, Leigh even provides us with a subplot in which the daughter of her posh employers is forced by her boyfriend to have sex, becomes pregnant, and then gets a high-priced, psychiatrist-authorized abortion in comparative comfort (in a Catholic hospital, no less)—the first time in one of his films that this writer-director has felt the need to inform us that the rich are better off than the poor.

So openly sympathetic is *Vera Drake* to its titular character that it spends most of its 123 minutes simply following the heroine house-to-house as, unresisted, she performs one abortion procedure after another. Then, in its relatively brief latter portion—the trial sequence—the film is careful to sport lingering shots of saintly Vera's suffering if not tearful face. (The same problem occurred in the similarly abbreviated second half of Leigh's *All or Nothing*, with its mawkish, heavy-handed emphasis on the all-redeeming power of love as opposed to martyrdom.) If one does not believe Vera is meant to be regarded as a saint, one has only to listen to the film's score: The usually restrained and subtly evocative composer Andrew Dickson here provides maudlin music that even features a celestial choir.

My own reaction to *Vera Drake* was not what Leigh intended, for I happen to disagree with his propaganda despite his repeated asseverations that he is a political filmmaker without being a polemical one. He *used* to be an auteur who, in films such as *High Hopes*, *Naked*, and *Secrets and Lies*, was making anything but agenda-driven movies. But he is getting to be a lot like his colleague Loach at his worst: a tendentious, if not downright socialistic, agitator, and one whose tendentiousness is revealed here by Leigh's atypical resorting to diagonals in order to score visual points. (Note, for instance, the shot where Vera exits a client's basement apartment, which is ramparted against the outside world by a spiky iron gate.) Save for such an extra-aesthetic purpose, why else would Leigh have made *Vera Drake* a period or historical piece (a rarity for him, the only previous instance being *Topsy-Turvy* in 1999), instead of a contemporary one in an England where, to put the matter mildly, the law on abortion has changed somewhat? Obviously, in order to beat a dead horse that (as Leigh well knows) some people, in his own land as in ours, would like to see revived.

The prochoice, prolife question aside, my own feeling is that Vera the makeshift abortionist should have been stopped a good deal sooner. Most of her "patients" seemed to come through all right, yet there was always a strong chance that they would not, and some of them did not. The pregnant woman's worry is clear enough, but her own possible death— not to speak of the fate of her embryo or fetus—is not a remedy for her troubles that evokes my sympathy. I am surprised that she, the woman with an unwanted pregnancy, was not the focus of Leigh's film, a focus that might have made it more compelling as well as more complex. However, given the fact that Leigh (born 1943) is the son of a physician and a midwife who grew up in England's industrial north among people of far less fortunate circumstances, the slant of *Vera Drake* is understand- able if in the end lamentable, all the more so for all the time and effort that went into this film's collaborative making.

Imelda Staunton (as the hard-pressed, alternately weepy and chirpy heroine) and the other cast members—including such Leigh regulars as Jim Broadbent, Lesley Manville, and Peter Wright—participated in the forming of their characters through the long process of improvisation and rehearsal (which includes the designers as well as the cameramen) that has become Mike Leigh's standard mode of moviemaking. He sees this coop- erative, communal approach to creating film art as itself an implicit cri- tique of the egotistical, neo-Darwinian, rampantly capitalistic climate of contemporary Anglo-American culture.

I do not disagree with Leigh's characterization of our two respective cultures, but I wish that *Vera Drake* itself—the first of his films that he has ominously anointed with the name of its main character—were a little less ego-driven on the part of its author-enabler as well as its protagonist. In other words, the narrative could use a few more ideas and a lot less ideology to go along with Leigh's otherwise lean and tight directing, not to speak of the severe, wintry pall that the dependable Dick Pope has cast over this film's brown-dominated imagery. Pope proves, in *Vera Drake*, the last thing he wanted to prove: There is no such thing as an artist- cinematographer, there are only good cinematographers who sometimes work for artists. And the artist, in this case, was wanting. Would that he will soon return to form.

An Interview with
Mike Leigh

The following interview took place at Leigh's London office in January 2005, after the release of *Vera Drake* but before he had begun work on another project.

BERT CARDULLO: You've been making films for well over thirty years now. Why do you think they caught on in the United States only in the late 1980s or early 1990s?

MIKE LEIGH: I don't know the answer to that. I suppose if you stick with anything long enough (*laughs*) . . . It's partly because I made a feature film in 1971 called *Bleak Moments*, which was quite successful in a very limited way, though it had no real commercial life. It won a couple of prizes at international festivals. And between that and 1988, which was seventeen years, I, like a huge number of British filmmakers, didn't get to make feature films, but made feature-length films for television instead. And it wasn't until *High Hopes*, in 1988, that I made my first proper, albeit low-budget, theatrical film since *Bleak Moments*. And it's really only since then that the possibility has been there to have any international profile.

BC: What enabled you to make the jump from television to features after all those years?

ML: There was a change in the circumstances in the U.K. They simply changed the rules. They changed the approach to television films and did what we all had been talking about for years, which is to say, make the films on 35mm film, give them a theatrical life, and show them on television two or three years later.

BC: Your films have proven quite popular in America, yet they're distinctly British in subject matter. What do you think American audiences see in them?

ML: I don't know. I just do these films. They are not in any way exclusively English or British or London films. They are in that milieu, obviously, but the issues in the films are issues that I intend to and expect to cross any barriers. As to why they're popular specifically in the United States insofar as they are, because they're only popular in Los Angeles, New York, Seattle, and a few other cities—maybe it's because they're good.

BC: Unlike many Hollywood films, they're about real people in real situations.

ML: I feel that's entirely true, implicitly. Every film I make is implicitly an antiHollywood statement.

BC: Stephen Frears, who also got his start on British television, has become a successful Hollywood filmmaker. Could you ever make that jump?

ML: No. I think it is neither desirable, nor attractive, nor feasible. Stephen Frears does so, and he does it very well, and I admire him for it. But he's a different kind of filmmaker. What defines what I do as opposed to what he does is not a question of budget or scale; it's that I make very personal, idiosyncratic films of a particular kind, of which I am author. He is, in the best possible sense, an eclectic, craftsmanlike, jobbing, versatile director. He can take any kind of screenplay and make it work. I can't do that, and I'm not interested in doing that. It's not my job. I'm an authorial filmmaker. I plough this particular, slightly mad, lone furrow. So there's no logic to my going to Hollywood to do what I do. If Hollywood wanted to hand over the money with no strings attached for me to do the films that I do, fine. That is what they should do, actually. But they won't do that. They can't do that. They're pathologically incapable! But it's not an issue for me, really, provided I can keep getting the money from elsewhere to carry on developing my own particular rantings and ravings.

BC: Your films are developed in a unique way. Can you discuss that?

ML: It boils down to, essentially, that I start with no script. I do a brief treatment of the film for myself, which is usually pretty fluid. Then I work with the actors for an extensive period creating the characters, through conversation, research, and improvisation. Then we go out and invent the film on location and structure it and shoot it as we go. To me, that's what it's all about. It's about using film as a medium in its own right, not as a way of including the decisions of various committees.

BC: Can you elaborate on the process of improvising with the actors?

ML: In essence, the main thing to understand is that when I make these films I say: "Come and be in my film. Can't tell you what it's about. I can't tell you what your character is. We'll invent that as part of the process. And you will never know any more than your character knows." That makes it possible to do long and detailed improvisations that investigate the years and years of people's lives in a spontaneous way. I don't get people together and tell them, "This is the theme. Let's all get together and improvise." It is a much more painstaking process of people getting together and growing. It's a way of building up a world like the real world, with all those tensions. We move out of that and distill things into a structured film.

BC: Who ultimately writes the script? You?

ML: No, I don't go away and write it byself. I write it by working with the actors as they improvise. I then organize it and make suggestions. I put things in and take things out. It's a complicated process. It is scripted sequence by sequence during the shoot. That is only made possible by my having created the whole premise of the film previously and, implicit in that, the whole network of relationships. There is not so much a story at the beginning as a feeling and conception. The journey of making the film is a journey of discovery about what the film is. I only do what all other writers, painters, and novelists do. All art is a synthesis of improvisation and order. You put something down and then you work with it. You discover what it is by interacting with it.

BC: That's certainly a different method of filmmaking than what other filmmakers, especially those in Hollywood, employ. How did you arrive at it?

ML: Maybe I'm wrong, but to me it's entirely logical. How I arrived at it—that's like asking Alexander Graham Bell how he invented the telephone.

BC: Is it the way you made *Bleak Moments*?

ML: Oh yeah, I started developing this method in 1965, in some plays. The difference is, it got more sophisticated. It was born in the first place (and this is still what defines it) from a desire to write and a desire to direct, and a fascination with actors. There are directors who are not interested in actors and acting, and I obviously am. I've tried to advance the whole possibility and scope of what acting can do. I found at a very early age that I was inherently bored by directing scripts that already existed. I also found it inherently arid to sit in a room writing. So add all these things together, and you've got the way I work.

Look, what we're talking about is fine, but it's not really the substance of my style of filmmaking. It's all about what happens creatively with the camera, with the cinematographer, with the editor, with the people on location. Everything that goes on with the actors is very important but only by way of background and preparation. In the end, it's a complete process that grows organically and involves everyone.

BC: Do you have a specific target audience, or are you aiming for a general audience with your films?

ML: A general one. The battle, really, is to get the films across to a popular audience. The problems in making films like mine are exclusively problems of distribution and exhibition. The battle is to try and make films like mine be perceived as commercial films for a wide audience. Because I don't think audiences are stupid. I don't think audiences are congenital idiots and children who need to be pandered to. I think anyone can get *Naked*. My assumption about my audience is that they are an infinite-sized group of people who are at least as intelligent as I am. I think I make populist entertainment films. But that doesn't necessarily mean soufflés and trifles.

BC: So many people go to movies for escapism and light entertainment. Do you really think a film as dark as, say, *Naked* can reach a mass audience?

ML: Yes, I do. I think the only barriers are the prejudice of the exhibitors and distributors about what a film is. I think it would be ridiculous if every single film was a *Naked*. Just as I think it would be ridiculous if all someone ate was steak. You've got to have a mixture in your diet. I think films like *Naked* should sit alongside other kinds of films.

BC: Your films can be quite pessimistic. Are you a pessimist?

ML: Yes, I suppose I am a pessimist, as well as being an optimist. I'm pessimistic about some things; and I find it very difficult to be very optimistic about many aspects of the future given the way the world is today. As a parent, I worry about what the future will be like in ten or twenty years' time. About those things I'm a pessimist. About humanity, on the whole I'm an optimist, which is based on my belief about how people *can* behave toward each other.

BC: As for *All or Nothing*, there appear to be contrasting views. Some people think it's your bleakest film ever, and some say it's the most optimistic.

ML: Well, some people have said that it has bleak moments, which is what my first film did. I feel that this film is entirely about redemption. It's about connecting. I don't think it arrives at completely comfortable conclusions. You certainly don't walk away from it thinking that everything is all tied up and fine. But I do feel that the spirit of the film points toward hopeful possibilities. I feel that *All or Nothing* is a film about potential, really; it's about possible fulfillment.

BC: What interests you most as a film subject?

ML: People relating to each other and the relationships between people and children and work.

BC: British people, right?

ML: Again, I have to say that I don't really personally see my films as being about London, England, Britain, or English things. Obviously, the milieu, the territory, or the landscape, is that, but I am more concerned with the emotional landscape, as I have always been when the chips are down. Although it may sound pretentious to say so, I guess I think my work is about something more universal than just the U.K. So, I don't really see it like that.

BC: Where did you shoot *All or Nothing*?

ML: On an estate right in the middle of Greenwich, with 340 flats and nobody in it. It was great. We had this whole place to ourselves. I could control everything that you could see, and it helped to inform the general atmosphere of the film. This could have been an estate that was boring to look at, but it was a really interesting place.

The whole thing about making films, in an organic film on location, is that it's not only about characters, relationships, and themes; it's also about place and the poetry of place. It's about the spirit of what you find, the accidents that you stumble across. It was great to find this place that had these qualities.

BC: For about two-thirds of *All or Nothing*, your attitude toward the characters seemed a bit smug and self-satisfied. It smacked to me of emphasizing the stupidity of the characters, almost to the point that they were being laughed at. How do you respond to that?

ML: I have nothing to say to that. To me, it doesn't sound like the kind of film that I've made. I can't really respond to that, I'm afraid.

BC: Do you agree that poverty has a strong fascination?

ML: No, because, so far as I understand what you're saying, that would suggest that poverty has a kind of fascination by itself. I think that it's important to look at in the sense that it affects a very large proportion of the world in one way or another. Do you mean that it has some sort of voyeuristic fascination for me?

BC: Yes, because you've talked about the bleak emotional landscape in such a way that it appears to have poverty as the driving force behind it.

ML: I suppose that the implication of your question would be to suggest that maybe people who didn't suffer from poverty couldn't have the emotional problems that *All or Nothing* deals with. But I don't think that's the case. I don't think that these kinds of emotional experiences or break-downs of communication are the prerogative of the poverty-stricken or the working classes. That would be absurd. However, the fact is that this film deals with these people.

There is no question in my mind that, although one could tell stories about other kinds of people, and I'm very comfortable doing that, this film is what it is. And, looking at people as I do, whose life is in some way stripped down nearly to its basics—not absolutely all the way, because that's not what I'm dealing with here—this film relates to the raw-ness of their emotions. But poverty as a subject is not inevitable. It just happens to be part of the whole combination of elements that *All or Nothing* deals with, but it's not what I would call an "exclusive preoccu-pation" or riff of mine.

BC: On the other hand, most of your films have characters who are more or less at the end of their tether, a condition caused by poverty or social deprivation or something like that. And this one certainly has that. Poverty is inescapably part of it.

ML: I don't arrive at those portraits beforehand, though. They are not motivated by a particular kind of fascination with a certain sort of imagery. Huge numbers of people do live these sorts of lives, and I am drawn to deal with them because that's what life is about for a good many people.

BC: Do you think the kind of people that the film is about would appreciate the humor in the film?

ML: It's not a matter of my opinion because I know it to be the case. I know the kind of people who have seen the film. It's always the case that the people whom the film's about love it. Hitchcock famously said that the kind of woman who spends all day washing up and doing the housework does not want to go to the cinema to see a film about someone who spends all day washing up and doing the housework. And Hitchcock, on this thing and many others, was a million miles from the truth. He didn't know what he was talking about.

It is definitely and consistently the case that people love to see a film that reflects their own lives. Because you don't usually see that in the movies. They think it's an absolute gas. They relate to it, and they are moved by it. It's very good news for them. In the 1970s and the 1980s, as I've noted, I didn't make films for cinema but for television, along with many other filmmakers who were lucky enough to get the opportunity. We did films called *Play for Today* on Monday and Wednesday evenings. People loved them. They had huge viewing figures. They were these kinds of films. People were up for it.

BC: I think you once said that movies should aspire to the condition of documentary, and I immediately thought of movies like *Armageddon* and *The Matrix* and wondered if you would do away with those if you had absolute power?

ML: No, no, I wouldn't do away with anything if I had absolute power because I'm in no way that kind of a fascist. So that's to start with, but I certainly wouldn't do that. I didn't actually say that movies *should* aspire to the condition of documentary. What I actually said is that in making a film, one wants—what one thinks when one actually shoots— to aspire to the condition of documentary in the sense that you want to make it happen so that it's completely three-dimensional in front of the camera.

BC: To get back to *All or Nothing*, this picture seems to take quite a negative view of the white British male. And it seems to emphasize the strengths of white British women. Can you comment on that?

ML: It certainly isn't an objective of the film to discredit the white British man as such. I don't really know how to answer that question. Obviously, whatever you see in the film comes from the creative process of making it. It can't come from anywhere else. There are unsympathetic characters in the film. Clearly the most unsympathetic character is Jason, the boy-friend. But I would hope that, for example, Phil comes out at the end of the film beyond being merely discredited. It's not a one-note film. There are a lot of things going on in it. You can only talk about the strengths of women and the weaknesses of men by looking at them together. I don't know how to answer your question. It demands isolating out of the film some kind of national thematic strand, which I don't think is really there. It wasn't my conscious objective to discredit the white British man.

BC: I guess the women in the film are stronger than the men. They seem to have more inner resources ultimately in this particular film.

ML: You can say that's true of Maureen. But you can only talk about the central relationship between Penny and Phil in terms of a symbiotic relationship. It's not about stronger women and weaker men. I don't think that theory stands up in terms of what the film is about or what happens in it.

BC: Do you feel that you have trouble with upper-middle-class characters? They seem to be rather stereotyped in films like *High Hopes*.

ML: I think *High Hopes* has a satirical element to it. But that's not what I normally do. Satire is not my natural tendency. I think *High Hopes* contained that in a very specific way. That results in the satirical portrayal of the upper-middle-class characters. I think all of my films up to and including *Life Is Sweet* had broader comic elements. From *Naked* onwards, I moved on to a different kind of feel and relationship to the characters. I don't find any group of characters more difficult than other groups. *Topsy-Turvy* was full of middle-class characters, and I had no trouble with them. They were Victorian in that film. They weren't even twenty-first-century figures. But I can understand if you found yourself at odds with my broader comic style in those earlier films.

BC: How conscious are you of exploring themes in your films?

ML: Jean Renoir famously said that all filmmakers make the same film over and over again. The truth is that I know that I return endlessly to certain preoccupations, but you're not necessarily aware that you do. If you look at all of my films, you'll find an undeniable preoccupation with pregnancies, being parents, being children, whether to have children. That comes out of a life preoccupation really.

What I try to do is not to worry about that, because I realize that that is the sort of work I do. The important thing is to try to make a different sort of film within the genre and to tell a different kind of story within the overall perameters of the discipline—to confront different things and to deal with different issues, although the underlying themes remain constant.

You like to think that you're getting closer to something, if only because you get older. I'm past sixty now. As to the fatuous notion that I'm arriving at "the truth," I feel that that would be somewhat optimistic.

BC: Did any Hollywood stars, after the success of *Secrets and Lies,* express an interest in working with you?

ML: Yes, they did. And I dealt with it with extraordinary diplomacy and subtlety. There are some people, like Jennifer Jason-Leigh, Willem Dafoe, and Steve Buscemi, whom I know and like and are the "American version" of the sort of actors I work with here, who are feasible candidates to work with on the right project. There are bigger stars than they whom it would be ludicrous to contemplate having anything to do with for a split second.

BC: Speaking of Hollywood, do awards mean anything to you?

ML: Of course they do. I mean, I'm in the movie business. It's important. I don't want to be an obscure name in the middle of the index of some esoteric tome about European cinema. So anything that happens that is part of all that and helps a film along is good news, and I enjoy it, I embrace it, I encourage it, and I want it. No problem. Give me more of it. If any film of mine is nominated for an Oscar, like *Secrets and Lies,* I am thrilled. But the only thing that would help totally would be a film that was a runaway commercial success, and I haven't made such a film. I can get money, but there is a ceiling beyond which people won't take a risk. But that's fine because we make the films we do below that ceiling.

BC: Do you ever get frustrated when your films are shown only at selected cinemas?

ML: I am totally frustrated by that. That's never the intention. The idea that any film I have ever made should be dumped in what are regarded as art-house cinemas isn't acceptable to me. I am not concerned with making esoteric, obscure kinds of films. My films can speak to anybody about real things.

BC: Let me address the representation of these "real things" on the screen by asking whether color is very important to you.

ML: That is the case. What you see in *All or Nothing*, for example, *Topsy-Turvy*, and all our films in fact—I say our films because Dick Pope has shot all my movies since *Life Is Sweet*, and my designers are Alison Chitty, who designed my earlier pictures, and Eve Stewart, who does them now. We work very cautiously and in great detail to create the palette of a film, the color and visual spirit of a film in relation to its feeling and what we feel we want to pull out of it. The most extreme investigation occurred in *Naked*, for which we used a process called "bleached bypass" where you deliberately don't complete the color process in the laboratory. The palette was very restrained. There were no reds, no bright colors at all; it was very muted. In one way or another, that's the kind of thing we've experimented with in all my films.

With *All or Nothing*, we had this sense of people in this gray environment. And it is reflected in the work of the costume designer, Jacqueline Durran, who had worked as the assistant designer to Lindy Hemming on *Topsy-Turvy*. She was therefore very familiar with my approach to working.

With *Topsy-Turvy*, although we made the picture for peanuts given what you saw on the screen, the costumes were quite elaborate and relatively expensive to make. Jacqueline managed to costume *All or Nothing* for next to nothing. She hit the charity shops everywhere. She would go out to get one sweater and come back with two hundred of them. She worked in a room adjacent to where we were preparing the film. You would go in, and she would have dozens and dozens of variations of the same garment in subtly different shades of gray. She was really on top of the quite sophisticated job of squaring the color and palette requirements with the character requirements. In those terms, the harmony of all the different visual elements with the dramatic and character-motivated aspects of the film is very successful indeed.

BC: What about the mise-en-scène in your work?

ML: In *All or Nothing*, for instance, there are lots of shots of people in this particular housing estate. There are choices as to whether you're looking at a big, empty *space* with somebody in it or *somebody* in a space. When my cinematographer and I were discussing how to shoot certain scenes, we would ask: "Is it a man in a room, or is it a room with a man in it?" Those are two different things. It has to do with the idea of what the image means. But we're not talking about a kind of symbolism that can be decoded and translated. That is, there are all kinds of symbolism in *All or Nothing*, but symbolism isn't really the right word. It has to do with a visual language that is organic to what is going on. Occasionally there are things that have some sense of external reference, but that's not what it's about, because that's not what I'm concerned with in telling this kind of story in one of my films. These are not characters in an abstract void; they are in a physical world, interacting with each other and their environment. These things that happen are not random choices. These things become the imagery of the film.

BC: To stay with *All or Nothing* for a moment, how did you edit the film? Did much end up on the cutting-room floor?

ML: Our editing is fairly conventional. What we shot was fairly precise, and therefore what we took to the cutting room was fairly disciplined. No more ended up on the cutting-room floor than does in any feature film one way or another. I do go through and pare down anything that is repetitious, as you do with any film. For example, what happened with the French woman Cecile and the vase—we saw her getting into the car with this vase rather fussily, with the antiques dealer hanging around. But when we stuck it all together, it was clear that the scene was redundant. It didn't say anything interesting, and it made the whole thing take longer than it needed to. The scene outside the antiques shop would have telegraphed to you too obviously that she was going to be important.

BC: What is the relationship between your theater work and your film work? How does the theater influence the films you have made?

ML: I trained as an actor. I also went to film school. I developed my sense of drama in the theater because it was cheap. Movies by definition cost money. They are more elusive or used to be until the invention of new technology. My film work has been influenced by my theater work in some sense. The convention of rehearsing a film for six months, which is what I do now, comes from the theater, as I suggested earlier. And, of course, I wrote plays for the theater before I wrote screenplays. But there is nothing about filmmaking that I don't love. It is a great experience. It is something I am happy to do endlessly and can't get enough of. Film always

seems grown-up compared with theater. There is something rather insular and claustrophobic about people locked away in an airless, lightless
building. I prefer getting out into the open air and real places with a
whole gang of people: It is more enlivening.

BC: Could you elaborate on what you find insular about the theater?
Because it seems, for one thing, that theater actors thrive on the daily
contact they have with the audience.

ML: Well, I think, from an actor's point of view, that is true. And certainly there is something very inspiriting about live performance. Yes. But
there's something very insular about the *institution* of theater, whereas
film gets you out into the street, and you're out there in the world, and
somehow there's something kind of healthy about the whole process of
filmmaking, which I find isn't the case with theater.

BC: Would you like to do something for television now, or are you happy
in cinema?

ML: So far as television is concerned, apart from a few televised studio
plays, which have gone out of fashion, all I ever did was make films for
telly. They were films. The fact that they were shown on TV was a
technicality, although obviously making films for the cinema means that
you can work to motion-picture standards. It's good to work on a big
screen. Going back to television wouldn't mean anything to me, especially not the television of today. Television in the 1970s was a very liberal
outlet compared to nowadays. Nowadays you hear all these stories about
neurotic, nervous bureaucracy. There never used to be this concern about
ratings or the commercial element. In the context of today, television has
no attraction to me at all.

BC: It seems to me that more and more highly touted young directors are
working in a more cinematic, visceral, myth-focused, violent, overtly stylized manner, rather than what you call a "humanist" vein, especially in
American independent cinema. How do you feel about that?

ML: The only way to approach thinking about this is to look at where
various kinds of cinema come from, what are the motivating forces behind them and the prevailing conditions under which they are created.
The fact is that there is a great tradition, which exists in Europe and
plenty of other places, not least of all Japan, of making films about real

life, uncluttered and unfettered and uninterfered with by the kind of disease that you can—broadly speaking—diagnose as Hollywood. This tradition goes back a very long way. It is entirely possible for a filmmaker to go out and listen to the world and sense the world and savor the world and experience the joy and pain of the world, and then express it in a completely pure, honest, interesting, and very cinematic way. There's no question about that, ranging from Satyajit Ray's first film, *Pather Panchali*—which he made absolutely on a shoestring, with no film industry backing at all, and yet it remains a classic—to films that are made just as independently but within a film-industry context.

In most countries, even to some extent in Britain, the film industry has been a system that serves the needs of filmmakers in an organic way. But once you get a film industry that becomes more important than the organic needs of films that look at life, once it becomes a creature unto itself and grows out of all proportion to human scale, which is what Hollywood is, then it becomes impossible.

The fascinating thing for me about going to the States and endlessly talking to filmmakers is that it appears that it's quite simply impossible for people to make independent films in America. The films that are made in most parts of the world aren't "independent" films; they're just films, really. In the U.S., "independent" films means films made in spite of Hollywood. And some get made, but it's tough.

All good cinema, and indeed all cinema in some shape or form, is concerned with style, is concerned with being cinematic, is concerned with form and content and all the rest of it. But because Hollywood is so dinosaurlike in its overweighted industrialization, that whole weight squeezes the humanity out of it all. People are left talking about style and being stylistic, formalistic, and self-consciously cinematic, because that's what people have to hang onto, instead of real integrity, real truthfulness, real getting out there and telling the stories that are out there.

It's not as if you have to walk very far from a studio in Los Angeles to find real life going on. There are still people living lives. But the scale of Hollywood means that everything becomes a commodity, including style. We're all concerned with style. I make very stylistic films indeed, but style doesn't become a substitute for truth and reality. It's an integral, organic part of the whole thing.

BC: Sometimes independent filmmakers try to make movies outside the Hollywood system and about "real life" and "real people," but so often their efforts fall flat. Frequently the impediment seems to be that they feel they need to teach something or have a message.

ML: On your general point, I agree with you. This is the debate about agenda-driven art or ideas. My films are full of ideas, lots of different ones—things working on all kinds of different levels. For me, making a film is an exploration into what we feel. I'm not concerned with making films that are conclusive or prescriptive, and certainly not propaganda. I make films where either rationally or emotionally I tend to ask more questions than give answers. I feel that the audience should have something to work with when the film's over, something to discuss and argue about. But really what I'm talking about is the actual world out there—getting that on the screen. And you're right, somehow that doesn't happen very much in American films. Yet it's not as if the concept is absent from American literature. Although we have to pay—I say this with a note of irony—some of our respects to Robert Altman, who does go as far as anybody there in getting that.

BC: Do you have a Marxist or leftist background?

ML: I don't have a Marxist background. It was, broadly speaking, leftish, liberal, with a quite unavoidable strain of anarchy. I have never been politically involved in any real sense at all. And, unlike my compatriot Ken Loach, I don't make films that have any clear agenda. Certainly you never walk away from a film of mine having a clear political view, because I haven't got one. So, to suggest that my background is Marxist would be undeserved. Of course I have socialism in my background. In my film *High Hopes* I deal with it in an inconclusive way. It's about how difficult it is to face up to the fact that you may call yourself a "socialist," but what are you doing about it? Are we all sitting on the fence? And that's a personal statement, my expression of that sense of my own wooliness at the time that film was made.

BC: What exactly is it, then, that makes your movies different from others depicting ordinary people?

ML: What you're really asking is: Why is it that things that purport to be about real people fail to be actually real? My answer to that would be that the filmmakers are not aspiring to what I have called the condition of documentary; that is to say, they have caused something to happen in front of the camera which is not really researched and doesn't have a reality about it. It isn't three-dimensional; it wouldn't be able to go on if the camera weren't there.

Also, they don't understand it; they don't know who these people *are* really; they haven't asked questions about where they come from, what they had for breakfast, et cetera. I'd say that what I do is work very, very thoroughly indeed and get the actors involved from the word *go* to create a world that really does exist, whether we point a camera at it or not. Huge amounts of what we do, during our five-to-six-month rehearsal periods, never sees the light of day in tangible terms, as action in front of the camera. But we really know who these people are. We know everything there is to know about them socially, economically, and in every detail of their lives. And it all informs what happens. So it begins to do what it seems to me the job is, which is, putting it at its crudest, to reproduce the real world with some kind of semblance of reality.

And not only that, but in looking at it and deciding how to shoot it and what it is I'm trying to say, I actually understand this world. I actually have taken the time and the patience and gone through the pain of the research to know what it is that we're dealing with. I suspect that it boils down to no more than that in the end. If you look at any of the great films from around the world—whether you look at Buñuel's *Los olvidados*, showing those kids on the streets, or at one of Ozu's family dramas—there's no question whether these guys know what they're filming. They know the world; they know the culture; they know who the people are. This other style you're talking about is people making films in a culturally and professionally infantile, naïve, and ultimately presumptuous manner.

BC: It seems that what *you* try to do is capture a reality that you actually believe in, as opposed to directors—many of them American—who want to make movies about regular people but depict their world the way they think it *should* be.

ML: And the question is: What is the source and nature of that notion of the world as they think it should be—the idealized world? It's like the debates over *Naked*, for example. Obviously, the assertions that it was a misogynist film are ridiculous and not even worth talking about. That criticism comes from the kind of quarters where "political correctness" in its worst manifestation is rife. It's this kind of naïve notion of how we should be in an unrealistic and altogether unhealthily overwholesome way.

The decisions one would make about any character, whoever she is when we make her up, *are* implicitly political. In many a movie you've got a character that nobody's ever stopped to think twice about. It's just a character, a woman. But I do. I can't get to it until we've done all that, until these questions are really addressed and have become the life force of the thing.

And the questions that are asked, and the decisions that are made, are political in the sense that by placing everybody in their social, economic, cultural, historic context, we create—in a distilled and dramatic and cinematic and therefore metaphoric way—a world that will contribute something to the way the audience lives their lives. And as far as I'm concerned, that is a political act, as distinct from making a film where you actually stand up at the end, walk straight out of the cinema, and shoot the first policeman you see and man the barricades, which may or may not be a good thing. Making my kind of film is a political act because life is about how you live it in the smallest way from moment to moment as well as in the great moments, which are actually easy to talk about.

BC: To some extent, you combine politics and race in *Secrets and Lies*. Yet the intriguing aspect about race in this film is that it seems as if it's going to be a big issue at the start, but it winds up being less important as the narrative wears on.

ML: As you get to know Hortense, you simply forget that she's black because you get to know her, and it ceases to be an issue. And that's what happens to the characters, too. When it comes to the crunch, on the whole, the thing that worries anybody least is the fact that she's black.
　　Again, the idiots in some quarters came out waving their flags and saying, "Well, the film shirks its responsibility, and why aren't they intolerant towards her, why didn't they behave negatively?"—as though everybody in the world would be racist, which was not the case in 1996, when the film was made. I knew—and this is built into the structure of the film—that a lot of people would make the assumption that Hortense was going to be reacted to in a racist way. But, finally, we made what is a very unequivocal political statement, which is: "We are all people." It seems incredibly obvious to have said that in 1996. It's not a very sophisticated thing to say, and maybe it's sort of a wishy-washy liberal thing to say, but actually that is what the film is all about: that, actually, other things transcend this, and that is as it should be. In that sense, you could argue that I am presenting something as I think it should be. That's how people should behave.

BC: Compared to *Secrets and Lies*, *Life Is Sweet*, and even *High Hopes*, a film like *Naked* has a very distinct quality to it. In the other three pictures, it seems as if all the people could almost live in the same neighborhood.

ML: You could look at it on another level; you might say that all of my films with the exception of *Naked* are about family, but I would disagree with that because I think all of my films, including *Naked*, are about family. The fact that there isn't a family in it doesn't stop it from being a film about people who have a need for family, who are constantly talking about family yet who are constantly in retreat from their roots. All of that is what the film is about. So, in a sense, the actual difference that you identify isn't really such a difference at all. You could, for example, take a male character out of three of these films and line each of them up alongside the others and find some extraordinary similarities. Most obviously Cyril in *High Hopes*, Johnny in *Naked*, and Morris the photographer in *Secrets and Lies* are all very similar and are characters that I would identify with in some way. All are guys with a passionate idea of an ideal world and how we should all be. The first guy, in *High Hopes*, has kind of given up on it and doesn't know what to do, is inert. The second guy is so angry with everything, the failure, that he's turned in on himself. And the third guy deals with it in the opposite way and carries on being as positive as he can. But all of those things relate to each other. I think it's too easy to pull *Naked* out as being different, when in actual fact it comes from the same preoccupations; it's fished from the same sea.

BC: Still, *Naked* explores "badness," and it does so with a destructive character who is simultaneously attractive—even charismatic.

ML: Yes, there was an element in that film that was entirely evil. It was a film about badness as much as anything else. Who wants to make a film about goodness? There are people around who can't do enough to be positive, and I wanted to deal with the opposite, which is also important. And I would suggest that what you see in *Naked*, and in my films generally, you mostly don't see in the movies. As a kid in the 1940s and 1950s, I would sit in movies endlessly —and that's mostly Hollywood and British films, because we didn't see any other films—and think, "Wouldn't it be great if you could see people in films as people actually are?"

BC: That's unusual, since most people go to the movies to get away from reality.

ML: People say, "Ah, yes, but audiences just want to escape." I think that if people see a film like *Secrets and Lies*, where the stuff that's going on relates to things that they really care about, then it's more of an escape. They answer, "Well, yes, but then the audience worries about real-life things," but this is fulfilling; it's enriching; it's not like just eating candy for an hour and three quarters. It's actually really communing with something and feeling as if you've been through something that comes out making you feel better able to go back and worry about the specific things that are your problems.

So I think people are very dumb, very mindless, about escapism and entertainment and all that. They say, "Ah yes, but we're in the entertainment business." Excuse me; I am also in the entertainment business, and I make no bones about it. If my movie ever was not entertaining, it's a turkey as far as I'm concerned. My aim is to entertain, meaning, literally, what the word means. People forget what that word means. It means to make you stay there, to keep you in your seat. One of the things that drives me mad about watching films over in the States is that nobody can sit still for two minutes. Everyone's in and out, like bloody monkeys in a cage, eating and talking. The attention span is dreadful because, well, the films are boring, basically.

BC: Unlike *Vera Drake*, your latest film. As you know, I have my reservations about it, as I did about *All or Nothing*. But we're not here to talk about my film criticism. . . . Is this the most intense subject you've ever tackled?

ML: It's different, I'll say that. *Secrets and Lies* was about someone who brings up a child who doesn't know she has a half sibling somewhere: Secrets, after all, are how we live our lives. *Vera Drake* is darker, because she's doing something she knows is criminal on a certain level. The film poses a moral dilemma that asks questions of you and asks you to see an essentially good person cast in the societal role of a criminal. In the current, immediate context of the fact that the law may be changed in the United States, people should be aware that if you change the law, we will retreat to where we were and go back to the situation that the film portrays.

BC: What made you tackle abortion?

ML: This film isn't a sudden leap into a new subject, if that's what you mean. I have a basic preoccupation with life and how we live our lives. This is the film where I decided to deal with it directly. I remember what it was like before the law was changed in 1967. When I was a child I knew many women who had been to prison, and you weren't sure for what, but you found out later. But mostly it's about an issue we have to concern ourselves with; at least I do, as a parent and as a member of society. The population of the world has increased since the beginning of this conversation by rather more babies than you could get into the top floor of this building, and not all of them are born into loving environments. That has to be confronted in this chaotic society. So I'm only concerned, in the film, to ask questions and to raise them, which is why I hope I haven't made a picture that is polemical and crudely propagandist and bludgeons you about the head.

BC: What was your film stock for *Vera Drake*?

ML: Super-16. We shot it on Super-16 to save money. It was a tough budget of just under $9 million. Super-16 here doesn't look like that because of the brilliant cinematography and also because Kodak developed an amazing Super-16 stock. It's got a great grain-quality for blowing up to 35 millimeter.

BC: How much research did you do for this film?

ML: I did it in all sorts of ways. I talked to medical and legal people and historical people and people with sociological backgrounds. You name it, I did it. But that's what I always do. That's part of the job, and the joy, of creating a total reality.

BC: Given that the abortion law changed in 1967, you set the film in 1950. Why did you choose this period?

ML: Well, first of all it has to be before 1967. I could have set the film in 1966, but the truth is that I think I chose 1950 because it's still in that postwar period, when there's still that sense of the trauma of the war hanging in the recent air, in recent memory. It's still in that functional utilitarian world of rationing, but there's a sense of togetherness as well; there's a sense of putting things back together again, and all of that's in the film. There's almost a kind of innocence or wholesomeness. If the film takes place a moment after 1956, then rock 'n' roll has happened, and therefore it's a different world. That's my perception of it. And so the time period felt right, because it's just on the cusp of things. It's still an old world, but the second half of the twentieth century lies just before it. It just felt right, really, given what has to happen to this family, ultimately, in the story. And remember, this particular 1950s world still exists in many countries where the law remains such that abortion is outlawed.

BC: Do you think you made Vera *too* good a person, too angelic?

ML: No, I reject that premise. I don't think it's true at all. She's a perfectly real person of the kind—and we all know them—who are simply disposed to be helpful. Vera is a *good* person, a good person criminalized by society, such that the film in the end is about good and evil, the good and the bad.

BC: Do you think she would have been able to carry out the abortions if she had admitted that's what they actually were, as opposed to just helping out young girls?

ML: She absolutely doesn't think that it's a criminal activity. To put this matter in its social and historic and universal context, the fact is—whether anybody likes it or not—that there have always been, in all societies, at all times, people, mostly women, who have been there, in your family or in the next street or in the next town, and who know how to deal with this problem. We may not like that but that is a reality.

BC: That's not really an answer to my question. Vera may not view herself as an abortionist, may never even use the term. But she's not a stupid woman, and therefore she would surely know that, with each abortion, she was snuffing out a human life or at least the possibility of one. I agree with you that *Vera Drake* in the end is about good and evil, but I see some of that evil in Vera herself.

ML: And I don't. Denial, yes; evil, no.

BC: Even the police in this film are "good," sensitive and nonjudgmental.

ML: The decision to make the police, basically—especially the detective inspector and the policewoman—good guys and not bad cops was an entirely thematic and dramatic decision on my part, because I felt that to have bad cops come in and just beat her up and give her a hard time wouldn't . . . we'd learn nothing from that. Just as we'd learn nothing if she was a hard, extortionist abortionist. There'd be nothing to learn. There'd be no moral dilemma involved.

BC: But, again, Vera's moral dilemma has to do only with her desire to continue her "helpful" work at the same time that she knows what will happen to her family if she gets caught. The aborted fetus is left out of the picture. Had you chosen to have Vera meet Lilly, her procurer, face to face, perhaps somehow, implicitly, this subject could have been raised. After all, Lilly is the one making money off Vera's abortions, not Vera.

ML: Oh, I see. That's interesting. That, what you're particularly referring to, that moment of their seeing each other, it never occurred to me. The truth is that whilst Lilly the procurer certainly could have been prosecuted under the law, the tendency was to prosecute the abortionists rather than the procurers. And for that reason I don't pursue the Lilly strand. But also, dramatically, to be perfectly honest, I felt that to deal with what happens to Lilly, at the trial stage of the film, would be cumbersome and in a way something of a red herring. But what you're saying is something else, which is quite interesting, which is the notion of their actually, at some point in time, confronting each other or of Lilly's being confronted by Vera. Well, such a scene is not in the finished film, but I am happy to leave it as one of the many things for audiences to ponder. And, though we disagree about some matters concerning this picture, ponder you have. So, from my authorial perspective, that makes *Vera Drake* a success in a way that I hope all my movies are successful. Making people think is what it's all about, isn't it?

Filmography of Feature Films

Bleak Moments, 1971 (based on Leigh's play of the same title)
Hard Labor, 1973; made originally for television
The Permissive Society, 1975 (TV)
Knock for Knock, 1976 (TV)
Nuts in May, 1976 (TV)
Kiss of Death, 1977 (TV)
Abigail's Party, 1977 (TV; based on Leigh's play of the same title)
Who's Who, 1978 (TV)
Grown-Ups, 1980 (TV)
The Five Minute Films, 1982 (TV)
Home Sweet Home, 1982 (TV)
Meantime, 1984 (TV)
Four Days in July, 1985 (TV)
The Short and the Curlies, 1987 (TV)
High Hopes, 1988
Life Is Sweet, 1990
Two Mikes Don't Make a Wright, 1992
A Sense of History, 1992 (TV)
Naked, 1993

Secrets and Lies, 1996
Career Girls, 1997
Topsy-Turvy, 1999
All or Nothing, 2001
Vera Drake, 2004

The Theater of Film of Hans-Jürgen Syberberg

THE FILMS OF HANS-JÜRGEN SYBERBERG (born 1935) are at times annoying, confusing, and overlong, but they are also ambitious and compelling. In no way is he ever conventional or commercial: Critics and audiences have alternately labeled his work "brilliant" and "boring," "absorbing" and "pretentious," and his films today are still rarely screened. Stylistically, it is difficult to link Syberberg with any other filmmaker or cinematic tradition. In this regard he is an original, the most controversial of all the New German directors, and a figure who has long been at the vanguard of the resurgence of experimental filmmaking in his homeland.

Not unlike his (late) contemporary Rainer Werner Fassbinder, Syberberg's most characteristic films examine recent German history: a documentary, for example, about Richard Wagner's daughter-in-law, who was a close friend of Hitler (*The Confessions of Winifred Wagner* [1975]). But especially "historical" is his trilogy covering one hundred years of Germany's past, including *Ludwig II: Requiem for a Virgin King* (1972), which portrays the mad king of Bavaria who was the patron of Wagner and a builder of fairy-tale castles; *Karl May* (1974), which deals with the life of the famous author of Westerns who himself had never seen the American West; and, most famously, *Hitler, A Film from Germany*, also known as *Our Hitler* (1977). Seven hours and nine minutes long, in four parts and twenty-two chapters, *Our Hitler* effects a synthesis of Brecht and Wagner, of epic defamiliarization and operatic pathos. (Brecht's influence began relatively early in Syberberg's artistic life: The latter's 8-millimeter sound film of the Berliner Ensemble at work in the 1950s— a film blown up to 35 millimeter and released in 1970 as *My Last Move*— is the only record of that group during the Brecht period.) Syberberg's Hitler is painted as both a fascist dictator who could have risen to power at any point in time in any number of political climates and a monstrous movie mogul (called "the greatest filmmaker in the world") whose version of Griffith's *Intolerance* (1916) would be *The Holocaust*, with himself in the leading role.

Syberberg unites fictional narrative and documentary footage in a style that is at once cinematic and theatrical, mystical and magical. His films might easily be performed live (*Our Hitler* is set on a stage, and *The Night* [1985] was in fact performed live), but the material is so varied that the presence of the camera is necessary to translate the action thoroughly. Additionally, this director is perceptibly aware of how the events that make up history are ultimately comprehended by the public via the manner in which they are presented in the media. History is thus understood more by catchwords and generalities than by facts; as a result, in this age of mass media real events can easily become distorted and trivialized. Syberberg demonstrates this in *Our Hitler* by presenting the Führer in so many (dis)guises that the viewer is often desensitized to the reality that was this mass murderer.

None of Syberberg's later work has earned him the visibility, let alone the acclaim, of his earlier films. Since *Parsifal* (1983), his version of the Wagnerian opera that was his most widely seen work, he has collaborated with one of that film's stars, Edith Clever. Their artistic ventures have included a number of theatrical monologues, a few of which have been videotaped or filmed. The series commenced with *The Night*, a six-hour examination of how an individual may act or what an individual may ponder deep into the night—the literal night as well as the figurative one that resulted (among other events in the history of the West) from the holocaust of the Second World War. This examination continued into the nineties with *The Bad and Happy Lot of Art after World War II* (1991).

Syberberg's last work of which I am aware, a video installation titled *Plato Cave Memory* (1997), itself continues to pursue his major filmic theme—Germany's collective remembrance of things past—in addition to exploring the important subjects of the interview to follow: the relations between theater and film, and by extension among film, video, and computer-enabled digital technology; the relationship of the *Gesamtkunstwerk*, or "total work of art," to the particular arts of closet drama, literary fiction, and lyric poetry; and the juxtaposition of artistic "shadow worlds," in Plato's cave as in Syberberg's own films, to the material world of transitory reality, on the one hand, and the ideal realm of immutable eternity, on the other.

In this chapter, I would like to examine the two works by Syberberg that best exemplify what I describe in my title as the "theater of film": *Parsifal* and *The Night*. Let us begin with the earlier picture, whose subject should not surprise if you know Wagner's *Parsifal* (1882) and if you have seen Syberberg's *Our Hitler*. (The connection between Wagner and Hitler is the fact that the Führer venerated Wagner's works and saw them as embodying true German ideals.) No, you should not be surprised by Syberberg's choice to make a film of Wagner's work; nor should you be surprised by this director's general approach to his subject. But this *Parsifal*, among its fascinations, does have a surprising new aspect to which I shall return.

Syberberg's obsession with Wagner has long been familiar. The first film of his to be shown in the United States, *The Confessions of Winifred Wagner*, was a 104-minute condensation of the five-hour interview, made for German television, that he conducted with the composer's daughter-in-law. Wagner, musically and otherwise, is present in several other Syberberg films. And one of the most vivid images in postwar German cinema occurs in *Our Hitler*: the toga-clad Hitler rising from a grave that has a stone marked "RW." In Syberberg's view, then, *Parsifal* must be the most representative of Wagner's works, the most beautiful but silly, exalted yet pretentious, noble at the same time it is vicious—all the contradictions that Syberberg patently finds in German character and behavior.

Wagner himself, of course, is prototypical of a great deal that both repulses and fascinates about Germany. On the one hand, there is Wagner, the maniacal, blood-and-iron, anti-Semitic Teuton. On the other hand, there is Wagner, the titanic genius whom the young Nietzsche saw as the new Prometheus restoring Dionysian flame to a pallid civilization. (And the older Nietzsche never really recanted. As Thomas Mann remarked, "Nietzsche's [later] polemic against Wagner pricks on enthusiasm for the composer rather than lames it.") Eric Bentley, in that masterwork *The Playwright as Thinker*, goes as far as to pair Wagner with Ibsen as one of the two great modern exponents of tragedy. Yet this is, inseparably, the same Richard Wagner who inspired Adolf Hitler.

Wagner's score for *Parsifal*, which (I think) Syberberg uses uncut, is a succession of marvels that coalesce into a gigantic marvel; yet the libretto, or "poem" as Wagner called it, is itself less than completely cogent. The atmosphere may be as spiritual as anything in Wagner, but he explicitly intended the work as an Aryan, anti-Semitic allegory. (Further contradiction on that point: The first conductor was a Jew.) Moreover, it is an allegory that idealizes (again) Wagner's view of male innocence beset by the temptations of woman: as in Tannhäuser's enslavement within the Venusberg in *Tannhäuser*; or in Siegfried's cutting open the armor of the sleeping Brünnhilde, in the third part of the *Ring of the Nibelung*, and exclaiming naïvely, "*Das ist kein Mann!*" Be that as it may, the Parsifal-Kundry encounter in act 2 is still one of the most perceptive rites of sexual passage in drama. (Kundry entices Parsifal by speaking of his mother—more than a decade before Freud.) Writing in October 1889 from Bayreuth, for *The English Illustrated Magazine*, Bernard Shaw had this to say on the subject: "And that long kiss of Kundry's from which [Parsifal] learns so much is one of those pregnant simplicities which stare the world in the face for centuries and yet are never pointed out except by great men."

No wonder, then, that Syberberg, only one of a number of German artists who have simultaneously loved and loathed their country, should respond to *Parsifal*. Nonetheless, a question persists, one that leads to the surprise mentioned earlier. Why did he film a work that was already famous in another medium? His previous films had been entirely his own creations. Here, Syberberg did begin with a new recording of *Parsifal*, but, except for bits of music rehearsals under the credits and a few snatches of random voices after the finish, he simply supplied visuals to accompany that recording. Why?

The answer begins to be suggested by the following statement of his, from the originial press kit for *Parsifal*: "Just as the composer [Wagner] was inspired by a legendary evocation of the Middle Ages in his desire to express ideas which were of his own time, I am basing my approach on the fact that the work is one hundred years old and that I can therefore describe its significance through time." Ascribe the hubris of that last phrase to the energy that an artist needs in order to do anything serious at all—no one knowingly creates just for next week—and Syberberg's approach becomes clearer while we watch the film. This view of *Parsifal*, as a classic text chosen by a later artist for contemporary definition, puts his film in a *theater* tradition, not a cinematic one. That is the surprise. And his film derives, fundamentally, from Adolphe Appia.

Appia (1862–1928), the Swiss theatrical designer and visionary, had revolutionary views of production that have hugely influenced Western theater in the twentieth and twenty-first centuries, particularly nonillusionistic dramatic practice. Not only did he emphasize the role of light—to Appia, the visual counterpart of music—in fusing all of the stage's visual elements into a unified theatrical whole, but he also argued that artistic unity requires that one person control all the elements of production, and thus he helped to strengthen the role of the director (especially what has come to be known as the "concept" director) in the theater. Appia's strongest love was for Wagner; all his life, in fact, he worked on designs for Wagnerian productions. And although he participated in only six actual productions of any kind during his entire career, they changed the theater's way of seeing.

Appia was shocked by the old-fashioned staging and design at Bayreuth, which had been prescribed by the composer. He wrote that

Wagner made but one essential reform. Through the medium of music he conceived of a dramatic action whose center of gravity lay inside the characters and which at the same time could be completely *expressed* for the hearer. . . . But he did not know how to make his production form—his *mise en scène*—agree with his adopted dramatic form. (From *Music and the Art of the Theatre*, 1899; published in English by the University of Miami Press in 1962.)

Though Appia never stopped dream-designing for a theatrical revolution of Wagner that would fit the revolution in the music, he did get three Wagnerian production chances, half of his whole practical career. One of them was *Tristan and Isolde* for Toscanini at La Scala in 1923. Neither of the others was *Parsifal*, but his unrealized designs for *Parsifal* figure prominently in the treasury of his work.

Syberberg's film of *Parsifal* does not in any detail come from Appia, but ideationally it is the result of an intent that began with Appia and has since flourished. To wit: Appia was the first conceiver of productions who recreated the inside of his head on stage, rather than reproduce the world outside realistically, classically, or even romantically. What he wanted to

Parsifal (1983). Directed by Hans-Jürgen Syberberg. Shown on the set: Hans-Jürgen Syberberg. © Triumph Films. *(Courtesy of Triumph Films/Photofest)*

reify on the stage was his imaginative response to a work of art. And that, exactly, is Syberberg's basic intent in *Parsifal*, though of course his response is his own, nothing like Appia's.

Syberberg puts before us, then, not just a film of the opera, however symbolic or impressionistic, but absolutely everything that *Parsifal* evokes in him, about art and politics and history, about theater and cinema, about the possible exorcism of the demon Wagner himself. While Wagner's rich, almost extravagant music floods our hearing, Syberberg feeds our eyes with as much as he can crystallize of what that music's very existence has done to him. To be sure, the *Parsifal* story gets told well enough, but this is not a consistent "eccentric version," as a modern-dress or science-fiction adaptation, for example, might be. What we are really watching, in addition to the *Parsifal* narrative, is a cascade of connections, the play of associations hauled out by other associations in Syberberg's mind.

Some of the elements in his film are easily understood, perhaps too easily. When Gurnemanz leads Parsifal to the castle in act 1, for instance, they go backward through German history as represented by an alley of flags, beginning with the swastika. Behind Klingsor in act 2, the watchtower of a concentration camp can be seen. The waxworks-museum heads of Marx, Nietzsche, and Wagner himself are sometimes part of the décor, as is a three-dimensional facsimile of André Gill's famous caricature of Wagner, inside a human ear, hammering away. At one point Parsifal is even seen against a ridge that turns out to be Wagner's face in horizontal profile. Amfortas's wound, moreover, is an entity quite separate from his body so that it seems to be a possession more than an affliction. Syberberg represents it by a thick, folded napkin on a pedestal next to the ailing king's couch: The bleeding gash is in the napkin. (It suggests a vulva, and thus the wound, which he got from Kundry, may be a figure for carnal seduction.)

Most of the film's actions and details, however, must be taken only as phenomena that affect us or do not, not as elements to be explicated. For one thing, most of the roles are mimed with lip-synch. (Two of the performers we see happen also to be singers on the soundtrack; the text is naturally sung in German, with subtitles.) That in itself is neither novel nor troublesome. But Syberberg goes further: He chooses to have Parsifal mimed first by a stripling, adolescent boy and then, after Kundry's kiss, the role is mimed by an even younger *girl*, with Reiner Goldberg's strong *Heldentenor* coming out of the mouth of each Parsifal in turn. At the end, the boy and girl embrace chastely.

I do not believe that this device "means" anything; it is intended to jar preconceptions and provoke new response, not to fill out any pattern, Freudian or otherwise, as is the device of dolls that are suddenly used as characters and then discarded or the one of the Flower Maidens posed

Parsifal (1983). Directed by Hans-Jurgen Syberberg. Shown: Hans-Jürgen Syberberg (center). © Triumph Films. *(Courtesy of Triumph Films/Photofest)*

immobile, against rocks, while they sing of caressing Parsifal. The penultimate image itself is of a skull, crowned with a bishop's miter, lying on the ground. The last image is of Kundry, her arms and long hair embracing or entwining a small wooden model of what I take to be the Bayreuth Festspielhaus. There is much more, all of it intended only to represent Syberberg's visions, or visionary response to *Parsifal*, for us to absorb, to use, if we can and will.

Contrapuntally, as in *Our Hitler*, Syberberg insists on a kind of Brechtian candor throughout, to keep us aware that fabrication is part of his process. Everything is played against a black cyclorama, on which slides are often projected. (Compare this device, used here on a sound stage as it was in *Our Hitler*, with the use of theatrical backdrops in Syberberg's *Ludwig II*, where such scenery crystallizes the theatricality of Ludwig's life and the "performance" of that life, his passion for the theater as well as his devotion to Wagner.) The lighting of a scene often changes while we watch, and almost all the scenery is meant to look like scenery. Sometimes, for example, we see the board floor of the film studio. Near the end, projected on the cyclorama behind one scene, there is even some film footage of the conductor, Armin Jordan, shot during the recording session. (Jordan, who has conducted in many European opera houses, here leads the Monte Carlo Philharmonic Orchestra and the Prague Philharmonic Choir.)

Yet, in the midst of this torrent of images combined with Syberberg's "exposé" of image-making, most of the performances are quite traditional. The Gurnemanz here is much younger than usual, but he is nonetheless the poem's Gurnemanz, beautifully played by Robert Lloyd. (Lloyd also sings the role beautifully; the other singer who appears on screen is Aage Haugland, the Klingsor.) Amfortas is feeling, mimed—by the conductor himself—to the accompaniment of the good baritone of Wolfgang Schöne. And Yvonne Minton sings Kundry powerfully, while that miraculous actress Edith Clever mimes this problematic role with an intensity that holds its tensions in fiery focus. (The recording, by the way, is fortunately in Dolby stereo, but, spatially speaking, Syberberg elects to use the "old" screen size, which is one-third wider than it is high.)

The most significant previous film of an opera, made only eight years before *Parsifal*, was Bergman's *Magic Flute* in 1975, and a comparison of this work with Syberberg's own reveals a paradox. To Bergman, Mozart's opera was a *cinematic* challenge: By means of the camera, he therefore combined a conventional stage performance both with the presence of an audience and with backstage data to create a purely filmic locus for the work. By contrast, Syberberg, who had never worked in the theater until *The Night*, strives in *Parsifal* to make film into theater.

Distant from Appia yet evolved from him, Syberberg puts his "definitive" theatrical production on film because, in several senses, it would not be possible in an actual theater. Aided by designers of exceptional talent, he has created a sweepingly personal, expansively idiosyncratic vision of *Parsifal* that nonetheless places his film in a venerable theatrical line: a director's "statement" of a classic. In spite of a camera that is almost always slowly moving in or away, panning or traveling, this work, then, is much less like pure cinema than a superb (television) film of a production in a hypothetical (but oversized) theater.

Syberberg's final—or perhaps first and foremost—comment on *Parsifal* is that he filmed it all. For *Parsifal* has a unique history: Beginning with its premiere at Bayreuth in 1882, it was zealously guarded as a sacred work, to be performed only in the hallowed atmosphere of Bayreuth, not on profane stages elsewhere. And except for some concert versions, this "edict" was carried out for twenty-one years. Then the Metropolitan Opera in New York took advantage of inexact international copyright law to produce *Parsifal*, despite German cries of profanation, on Christmas Eve, 1903. (A chartered Parsifal Limited train came from Chicago, while the *New York Evening Telegram* produced a *Parsifal* extra.) Other "profanations" followed in other cities, in the United States as well as abroad, until 1914 when the Bayreuth copyright expired, and *Parsifal* became unrestrictedly available to every opera house throughout the world.

One hundred years after *Parsifal*'s original production, Syberberg makes a "mere" film of it, something that can be shown anywhere, at any time. But this fact, too, holds a contradiction. By making his film, and making it in his particular way, Syberberg has utterly destroyed any remaining fake pieties about *Parsifal*. At the same time he has tried, through belief in the pertinence of his vision/version of the work, to consecrate it anew for the present-and-future, protean theater of film.

A true adventurer in film, Syberberg pressed on after *Our Hitler* and *Parsifal*—which teemed with images and characters and devices and fantasies—with *The Night*, which is mostly set in one place and, through all of its six hours, has only one performer. Yet, another contradiction, this film is not a whit less adventurous than the earlier two and, through different modes and stimuli, teems just as plentifully. However, unlike *Our Hitler* and *Parsifal*, *The Night* had fewer theater showings in North America: several in Chicago, some in Montreal, and then four in New York (where I saw it). No regular theater showings followed, then or now, which is a sadness I would rather not dwell on here.

The Night consists of a prologue and two sections, with an intermission after part 1. Following the prologue, of a half hour or so, the credits appear, a number of authors are listed, some album pages turn, and then we move to part 1 and the only setting used thereafter. Part 2 begins with a similar listing of authors, some album pages, and a return to that same setting. (The prologue is in pale colors, as shot by Xaver Schwarzenberger; the rest is in black and white.) From the authors whom he names, Syberberg has culled, touched up, and interwoven with some autobiographical material a skein of language intended to circumscribe the night of his title: the long night of Western culture.

That he includes more than Europe in this night is patent from the start. The prologue, spoken in a large, rubble-strewn room in a battered Berlin building, is the speech of the American Indian chief Seattle when he signed a peace treaty with Washington, D.C., in 1855. His words envision the end of his people and their ways, but Seattle warns the white man that, though the Indians may disappear from view, their spirits will continue to inhabit the land. Syberberg dabs this speech with present-day (mid-1980s) references that ensure topicality and ensure also that the words apply to Europe as well as the United States. The speaker is the great German actress Edith Clever, clad in a simple dress and holding a dark, rough cloth about herself. Only then, after Clever finishes speaking, come the credits.

We now move to a placeless place: a floor of gleaming black gravel, a white circle of light at its center and a small white cloth in the light, with a cloak of darkness surrounding everything. In the light, acutely varied by the cinematographer Schwarzenberger, Clever spends the next five-and-a-half hours, close to us or with the camera at differing distances and angles, her body statuesque or sinuous depending on the angle and the light, her torso curved away from the camera-eye into architectural form, her body self-caressed in recollections of Eros, her presence immediate, her presence godlike, as she speaks, intones, sings, mourns, and eulogizes through the medium of the text that Syberberg has prepared. As far as the film reveals, Clever, or Clever's character, is the sole survivor of a long, glorious, *and* atrocious history, and before she too disappears into the black all around her, she offers a threnody.

The text, often accompanied by sections of Bach's *Well-Tempered Clavier* in Sviatoslav Richter's hands, moves through literature that is mostly German—Hölderlin, Goethe, Heine, and Nietzsche, as well as Schiller, Kleist, Novalis, and Heidegger—but with minglings of other cultures translated into German. (Prospero's farewell to his art, from *The Tempest* but in German, is transfixing.) The tone ranges from Wagner's crawling pleas for help from his patron Giacomo Meyerbeer, to his slimy spewings to King Ludwig about "Jewry in Music"; from the sight of a child's toy in Clever's hand to her sublime reciting of a poem in which humankind asks Jesus if his father is still alive, to which the son of God, his eyes streaming with tears, replies that we are all orphans now.

Courage is one hallmark of Syberberg's film work, and that hallmark is visible in *The Night*. He wants to burst through order and plunge into the unknown, the possibly chaotic, there to forge a new aesthetic order. Since he did this differently in his previous two films—*Our Hitler* and *Parsifal*—no fixed criteria will help the spectator to navigate Syberberg's artistic ventures. Sometimes, I must admit, *The Night* escaped my powers of attention during my sole viewing of it. For the film does not aim at a relentless, concentrated march toward spiritual nakedness and existential nullity like *Acropolis*, the titanic theater production by Jerzy Grotowski from the mid-1960s, which conducted its own requiem. (*Acropolis* took the concentration camp at Auschwitz for its setting, and, for its "plot," the building by the prisoners there of the gas chamber in which they will be consumed.) *The Night*, six times as long, does not march and only fitfully exalts.

Principally, the film *remembers*, but its memories wander in addition to both fondling the past and grieving over it. Certainly it has passages that repeat notes already heard. Certainly, too, it vibrates more fully for someone (like me) familiar with German literature in German. But even such a person would not find every moment in *The Night* tense and fraught with meaning. I, for one, did not. Yet it is a facet of Syberberg's experimental daring—not an excuse for avant-garde idling—that, instead of shaping a drama, he has in effect enclosed a preserve or park, of time, in which to linger and remember and even nod in the last remaining light. One factor in this film, however, did sustain me through its length, and it was surely a part of Syberberg's design from the beginning. *The Night* must have been conceived, that is, with the prospective collaboration of Edith Clever in the principal—and, it is worth repeating, the lone—role.

Clever is known in the United States chiefly through the films *The Left-Handed Woman* (1977, by Peter Handke) and *The Marquise of O.* (1976, by Éric Rohmer) and, as previously mentioned, through Syberberg's *Parsifal*, where she mimed Kundry so intensely that, although it was not her singing voice we heard, it seemed to be. What is not known in North America is her theater career, mostly with the Schaubühne in the former West Berlin. I have never seen Clever on stage, but I know that she has played leading roles in Schiller (*Kabale und Liebe*), Goethe (*Torquato Tasso*), Middleton and Rowley (*The Changeling*), Ibsen (*Peer Gynt*), and Aeschylus (*The Oresteia*), as well as in Gorky, Brecht, and Botho Strauss. In 1983 she played Gertrude in *Hamlet*.

I cite all of these instances prior to Clever's work in *The Night* because they are quite clearly the sources of her spiritual or imaginative endowment (not to speak of her physical resources), the simple majesty with which she makes her very first movement, utters her very first word in this, Syberberg's eighth film. I know of no better actress or actor in the world than Edith Clever, and few are her peers; but *The Night* is not a display vehicle, a "one-woman show" where the woman herself, or generic "woman," is the focus. Clever is completely and wondrously in union with what is happening in the film, so much so that her art *in itself* is as much a manifestation of the culture that *The Night* embraces and indicts, as much both an exhilarating triumph and a profound grief, as any of the words in the text.

Clever performed *The Night* a few times in a small Paris theater in 1984, and in a conversation with Syberberg not included in the following interview with him, I asked if it had been planned as a theater piece, then filmed. No, responded Syberberg, *The Night* had been planned as a film, but when this Paris theater offered to produce it, he accepted. The stage setting was much like that of the film, and French subtitles were projected high above, on the dark wall behind Clever. The production was done in two evenings—three-and-a-half hours, then two-and-a-half hours—each evening without intermission. Syberberg proudly declared that although there was a prompter there, "Edith never needed him; she never faltered." I replied that I supposed the stage darkened from time to time, if only to give Clever a momentary breather, in the way that the film goes to black and then resumes at a different angle or distance. "No," said Syberberg, "and the pauses in the film of *The Night* are there only because the film runs out in the camera magazine."

That Paris engagement was Syberberg's first theater work, and for me it underscored that, volitionally or not, he was further exploring—on screen as on stage—what I earlier called, in reference to *Parsifal*, the "theater of film." Two passages in the film of *The Night* especially mark this exploration: two Wagnerian excerpts, one from Isolde's *Liebestod*, the other from Brünnhilde's "Immolation Scene" in the *Twilight of the Gods*. In both instances, we hear a full orchestra playing as Clever sings. She has nothing like an operatic voice; she merely sings pleasantly. (Syberberg did tell me, however, that a Wagnerian conductor he knew was struck by the accuracy of her entrances and tempi and phrasing.) The point is that, with her modest singing voice, Clever acts those excerpts in a manner that illuminates them as never before.

Wagner himself asked the impossible: wonderful singing *and* wonderful acting. A major Wagnerian production gives you the first, plus passable acting. Clever, who could not possibly do the first, supplies what is always missing from the second. As I watched her perform in *The Night*, I suddenly wanted to see a Wagnerian theater of film in which Clever would give us, in this manner, the missing dramatic element to add to our memory of musically great Isoldes, to name just one heroine—which is not the same (if you think about it) as her miming a character, however convincingly in the case of *Parsifal*'s Kundry, to the accompaniment of another woman's operatic voice.

All of the above is to emphasize that, for me, Syberberg is seeking new empowerment for the arts he inherited in the arts he practices: theater and film, or film and theater. What persists after the long filmic threnody of *The Night*, as after the enduring theatrical conceptualization of *Parsifal*, is that Syberberg's search, in tandem with Clever, is the expression of an austere hope (but nonetheless a valid one) not only for the rebirth of the culture he is mourning, but also for the consecration of a theater of film.

An Interview with Hans-Jürgen Syberberg

The following interview took place in the fall of 1988 in the offices of *The New Republic* magazine, Washington, D.C.

BERT CARDULLO: It seems to me that in your films to date, at least up to *Our Hitler* and *Parsifal*, there is a certain affinity with the work of Adolphe Appia. The question is, Just what is that affinity?

HANS-JÜRGEN SYBERBERG: In *Our Hitler*, it could be seen as the empty space lighted by the projection of a few symbolic objects, which in *Parsifal* became one symbolic object: Richard Wagner's death mask. (This space was, of course, economically outfitted with stairs as well as workable or usable scenery and props.) The case for my affinity with Appia should more likely be made, however, in the realm of ideas, seeing Appia in the context of history; for I myself make (will I soon say "made"?) films, after all, and Appia was a man of the theater.

BC: But you also have become a man of the theater, haven't you?

HJS: Yes, I have directed my own scripts (*The Night*) as well as those of others (Kleist's *Penthesilea*) in the theater—that is, in live theaters—instead of for film. This has resulted for me in the necessary adoption, or better, in the necessary detachment, of an artistic personality that looks to history for guidance, even when grappling with projects from my own era. And that's where Appia enters the picture and, through him, Richard Wagner, the great influence on his thinking.

BC: Could you speak a bit about the historical context of Appia's work?

269

HJS: When Adolphe Appia was thinking, writing, and trying to realize himself as an artist, he first had to do away with the theater dominated by historicism, which was allied with naturalism. Electric light presented new possibilities for the theater, though a retrogressive profession by nature (take Heiner Müller as one example), and for film, which was competing against theater just as photography was competing against painting. Both were calling into question other art forms, were asking what their own unique possibilities were and were not. Was art still to be regarded in the old sense, with photography and film united against it in a sudden, egotistical dictatorship of the masses, which would no longer have any need for qualitative hierarchies? Film began in Germany in the cinematographs of the cinematheques. What has become of it? That is, how have film and theater differentiated themselves from each other as separate expressions of the same longing? How have they influenced each other: fruitfully or faithfully?

BC: One could easily ask the same questions about theater and film in the United States.

HJS: In America, as I see it, the theater is dwindling into mere entertainment, with an interest in nothing but the marketplace. Similarly, American film has for decades been turning itself into a huge factory of boulevard theater, with its time-tested mixture of kitsch and commerce, the most popular example of which is what I call the "throwaway melodrama," intended for the mentality that demands little more satisfaction from a show than a customer does from a visit to a brothel. In Germany, by contrast, expressionistic film arose out of the expressionistic theater and in accordance with old artistic traditions. But after the war such continuity disappeared.

Under the influence of the American (film) occupation, the public theater of today originated—that mixture of ideology, state subsidy, high pretentiousness, and quickly changing fashion. Alongside this public theater sprang up such events as happenings, environmental theater, performance art, and theatricalized works of art containing frozen figures and objects. Josef Beuys should be mentioned in this connection, as should your own Robert Wilson. Along the way there have been several influences, as on any intellectual movement: Wieland Wagner, Fritz Kortner, Bertolt Brecht. But were Leni Riefenstahl's films and Albert Speer's cathedral of light also influences, in that they were attempts to mirror the aesthetic side of the Volk in its adherence to the Führer's will? The living reflection of the masses was the art of Volk become classicism on the screen. Consider, too, the "blood and soil" films of UFA under the Nazis and the neorealist cinema of postwar Italy. All this, I have to say, is very much in accord with my current interests, projects, problems.

BC: Like the work of Appia, right?

HJS: Oh, yes. I would so much like to be a student again, possessing Adolphe Appia's intellectual intensity, and studying his textbook of the modern theater modeled on the work of Richard Wagner; learning how Appia attempted to make the music embedded in a text manifest, through the translation of that text's inner rhythm into an intellectual-spiritual body of gesture and movement; discovering how he attempted to clear the stage, to free it from all the constraints of obstructive technology and the pseudo-wealth of management's budget, as well as from the aesthetic fashions and ideologies of scenic discourse. Coming from film, however, I pursued my own course (which in recent years has escaped American viewers). I still very much stand by my previous ventures, as both a writer and a director (even to the point of letting those films be seen on videotape in other countries, if that is what people want). There was a mixture of theater and film in that work, and it showed itself to be as absolute in its rejection of the status quo as was Adolphe Appia when he envisioned his new stage.

BC: But you're departing from that mixture now, aren't you?

HJS: Yes, that's absolutely true. And therefore a few remarks may help to explain where I stand, may serve for friends of my prior work as an intimate reminder of that which they once knew and as a distant report on what has become of it. Adolphe Appia has something to do with my change in direction.

After *Parsifal*, doubtless the last film of mine seen by American audiences, I decided to clear the studio, to make it into an empty stage, to free my work of projections and meticulous editing and, more and more, of those layers that had previously characterized my films and given them density as one of their qualities: music, sound effects, words, and images, themselves uniquely layered. As it happened, my next work, *The Night*, originated both in theater and on film, but without the characteristic qualities of my films up to that point. And if until now my films have been different from those of other directors, in that they were an expression of my inner worlds, were counterworlds to the world as it exists and to the world as it is ordinarily portrayed on movie screens and theater stages, then what I was presently creating would also be different.

BC: How so? What's different about it?

HJS: Well, I abandoned the character from *Parsifal*, called "Kundry" by Wagner and played by Edith Clever, who at the beginning and the end defined the limits of my film's cosmos, who contained it in herself, and yet who, when everything is over, will still be what she had been before it began. I chose instead a single human being to embody all the possibilities of expression, to express that for which in my films I needed design, music, words, and sound effects. In this human being, herself a different score for each of several texts, worlds were originated and expressed that contained those texts, on stage as on film.

This was more realistic than any reality, but it was realism of the inner sort, expressed through the face and through movement, whose various manifestations represent the coordinates of the spiritual realm, through light changes, through the eyes, and through the props and gestures otherwise necessary to the performance. Everything was in one human being: cutting and close-ups and long shots of landscapes; ubiquity of place and simultaneity of time; stairways and doorways, chases on land and chases on sea, heroes and beasts, nightmares and fantasies—all the images and the figures that populate the arts and with which we fill our films and plays. The same goes for rivers and walls, stones and trees, clothes and the elements, for everything from a storm to deadly silence. It was all able to be encompassed in a single human being.

BC: Isn't this what is often described as "cinematic" in books—the cutting to a close-up and then back to a full shot, which creates a corresponding emotional effect in the viewer, mining his or her psychic depths through the manipulation of two-dimensional space?

HJS: Precisely! But all of this is created here by one human being, by the story contained in that human being's body and face. And if light helped in this process, it was not the kind that illuminates an area of the stage but rather the kind that illuminates the play of spiritual forces on the face and over the body, as they move, figuratively speaking, from light into darkness and from darkness into light, either directly or in a roundabout way. Thus an aesthetic system developed for something that required untraditional means for its expression. I was using a text that would be deemed unrepresentable or untransmittable, as it were, just as I had used *Parsifal*, that most difficult of operas.

BC: What was the subject of *The Night*, and what work followed it in your career?

HJS: The subject of *The Night* was the world of conflicting scenarios produced by the devastation of Europe during World War II. Next came work based on the character of Molly Bloom, from Joyce's *Ulysses*, and on Fräulein Else, from Arthur Schnitzler's novella of the same name. Then, at last, I found Kleist's *Penthesilea*, the Prussian tragedy of a sacrificial love so absolute in its expression that it shames the gods into rescinding their own inflexible, murderous laws. (Interviewer's note: Syberberg refers, in this sentence and the previous one, to the following films of his: *Edith Clever Reads James Joyce* [1985], *Miss Else* [1986], and *Penthesilea* [1987]. After directing Kleist's play *Penthesilea* [1808] on film as well as on the stage, Syberberg adapted Kleist's novella *The Marquise of O.* [1810] to the cinema in 1989. This novella had previously been adapted to the screen by the French director Éric Rohmer in 1976.)

BC: Why do you say "at last"? I share what appears to be your esteem for this relatively unknown play by a playwright who deserves to be better known; still, I'd like you to expound.

HJS: Certainly I will. This work succeeded where others had failed in eliciting a certain kind of visual response from me. That is, it stimulated me to express my inner worlds and thoughts and configurations in images and tones from another artist's work. And again it stirred me to defy the existing order: the real world, which resists its immortalization in art, and its art forms, which instead of doing justice to the world's complexities devote themselves to chronicling its ever-changing superficialities.

I would defy the existing order, moreover, in a form whose richness was not an artistic substitute for material wealth or religious surety, each of which sells itself as the ultimate answer to life's difficulties. I would create my art for the sake of human life, whose ancient nature has led to its ruin. I mean ancient in the simplest sense: human. And as if for the first time, to the few who were still in a position to bear its sight, I would present the human as it incorporates the whole of mankind in every aspect and particular.

BC: Wasn't it after returning from your "journey" with *Penthesilea* that you read Adolphe Appia for the first time?

HJS: That's right. I read of Appia's struggles and his pronouncements, as close to me as they were far away. "Scenic illusion is the presence of the living actor." And also, as he again underscores the primacy of the actor who alone provides the key to the mise en scène: "It is imperative that we base a production on the presence of the actor, and in order to achieve

this, that we clear the stage of everything that is in conflict with him."
Here we see the primacy of the actor in the master's blueprint for the
stage, which he empties in order to enhance the actor's powers. And the
man who uttered those words had to work with amateurs, who obviously
did not have the talent of the great actors of his time, and with a poorly
outfitted stage apparatus. But he also knew about music and its power
once it took hold of someone who could respond to it. Thus, I was
reading, and reading of, one of those revolutionaries whom you simultaneously push to the side and start curiously taking nibbles at, the heritage
of whose experiment will produce great new riches.

BC: Surely you must also have read of light as the soul of direction.

HJS: Yes, but I read too that even at that time the electric light had
produced a technical revolution whose wires and switches and lamps
threatened to engulf the stage. And I read Appia's thoughts about the
three-dimensional versus the two-dimensional representation of a forest
onstage. For him the question really was, Did you try to create a two-
dimensional representation of a human being in that forest? (This question doesn't apply to film, of course, which in its two dimensions can
record the real world.) I read, in addition, how to use objects and stage
levels, together with light changes, to reveal the meaning of this facial
expression or that body movement. And I thought of the cradle of dramatic representation, the ancient theater, which was set in the earth and
under the sun instead of in some cave in the city, where our plays are
staged. I thought of the self-knowledge that the ancients achieved through
their plays, and of how hard it is for us to do the same. And the music
beneath the surface of the scripts I've read lately tells me that out of the
fragments into which our world has split—a fragmentation or atomization of which film is one expression—we must build the world up again;
we must make it whole; and we can do this through renewed emphasis on
the living actor, to the exclusion of everything on stage that does not bear
on his art and his revelation.

BC: In Appia's day, as you have pointed out, there was an attempt, aided
by the advent of new lighting techniques, to cleanse the theater of historicism by clearing the stage and concentrating on essences. There were also
clashes between the theater and the new medium of film—clashes that
were not taken seriously because film wasn't recognized as an art form.

HJS: Today, however, as we live under the threat of the world's destruction, we will have to decide whether we want an aesthetic of protest that

lives by the soiled and lame ideology of technical supply and demand, or whether we want once again to clear the stage, to concentrate our thinking on what enhances nature, not on the technological consumption and the ideological colonization that destroy it. It will take very little to complete this destruction.

BC: Well, knowing how much has been lost already, an artist must find it difficult to carry the burden of protest on his shoulders.

HJS: Yes, but whether the burden is carried by the film's succession of flat images or the theater's three-dimensional stage, by pictures or by words, by music or by the human beings who make it, isn't the most important thing, finally. What is, is the point at which the imitation of nature starts thinking of itself as a substitute for nature. This practice should be avoided. Nature will achieve immortality only through art that is true to itself, that stands out authentically from the density of the whole and acknowledges the tragedy of our time, that stands fast and takes root in the firm knowledge of whence it has come and where it is headed, to what heights it is striving.

So we have the old confrontation between the audience's desire for realism and art's guilty longing for immortality, which its descendants alone can grant it in the very process of continuing the species, which is to say, mankind. And we have the confrontation between artists themselves, between the ones whose ritual is dying out and the ones whose new ritual will replace it.

BC: In the early twentieth century, this was a struggle between old and new forms of theater.

HJS: For me, it was already a struggle between old and new kinds of film. In that sector of Europe's subsidized theater that is committed to art, the struggle lies elsewhere. It is a headlong, absolutely destructive struggle between the community of intellect and the forces of the banal, the obscene, and the trivial over whether the genuinely serious stage, which always seeks ideal truth, shall be permitted to survive. We can call this theater "utopian," "paradisiacal," or "Arcadian" if we want, but we shall endure as a civilization only so long as we take up the mandate, issued to us by a protean reality, to find ourselves in art, in the high art of the theater as well as the other forms. If we do not, our culture's decline will be mirrored by our own. We can angrily tear the mandate up, if we wish; or, in frustration, we can just walk away and refuse to acknowledge its existence. On the other hand, we can zealously urge it on the public. But first it must at least be formulated as an expression of society's better judgment, if only to be consigned to our unconscious. For without such a mandate for art, society is dead, and in time even its echo will die.

BC: Adolphe Appia clearly did his part in this struggle.

HJS: Appia fought in art's behalf, and his successors have done so, too. We have come quite far, but we have unintentionally run up against the business of art and its museums for tourists. Still, in our refusal to collaborate with the merchandisers, we do not run the risk, like Appia, of never realizing ourselves in the practice of our art. Like the late Glenn Gould, like the monks of old, we are still able to employ our skills to the extent that our memory will be preserved, that future generations will know why we lived.

BC: Whether or not Appia realized himself in the practice of his art, one can regard the rebirth of electric light in his theater as the event that made possible the fusion of all visual elements into an artistic whole, with the director as its overseer.

HJS: But one can also regard this rebirth of electric light as the event that ultimately made film possible: film, the form that shined light on celluloid and thereby gave rise to the mass-produced living *image*—in contrast with the unique occurrence of *live* theater—the form that through the easy availability of its prints (its color prints, eventually) was mass-consumed in the movie house and then was mass-consumed in the isolation of the home, first on television and then on videotape.

BC: Moreover, film's disciples greeted the theater's loss of aura as a victory over its obscurantism of the soul, its obscurantist metaphysics of the avant-garde.

HJS: True, but in reality the theater's "death" was the birth of dead light and dead images, the birth of a plastic art on film that split the nucleus of the world into a series of views and angles, much as scientists split the atom and thus disturbed the world in ways we all know. Only the human spirit, like an echo of cultures past, has been able to cohere in the face of environmental destruction and the threat of nuclear holocaust.

BC: Even with a bad production in the theater, as we all know but which we must recall, one is still guaranteed the sight of human life—be it evil, miserable, or ordinary.

HJS: Unable to present us firsthand with the grace of pure life, film has become, by contrast, evidence for the death of culture. Film's play of dead light represents the destruction of the world, the director as demiurge without the power to love and without the power to create, who has turned the stage into a studio where the dark light of the image is more important than the living light of human beings. And this same director, in a television studio for the taping of a show, becomes preoccupied with nothing so much as the lamps over and among the heads of his live audience, which in this era of network audience shares achieves only a symbolic existence for its trouble and is finally dispensable, like the king at his court theater. The consumers of the media are the new audience, and they confirm the death of the old, live one.

BC: Like the death of certain kinds of light in the theater.

HJS: Yes, exactly. Light belongs in the theater just as fire belonged on the altars of the ancient gods. One can even say that theaters exist for the purpose of letting light shine. The ordinances in Germany that, in the name of democracy, proudly prohibit the use in our best subsidized spaces of certain kinds of light in favor of the other, more technically advanced kinds, and do so without any inkling of the artistic damage done—these ordinances are signs of self-government's own extinguishment under a mountain of official decree. They are signs as well of the extinguishment of the human spirit, which for centuries in Germany has had the freedom to challenge and to extend itself. These ordinances seal off our theaters from life and even from death, from the risks attendant in art—an art that is replaced, as a result, by protest ideologically founded on the Promethean gift of fire, that wellspring of life out of which art itself is fashioned. The loss to our stage of such domesticated fire as the living light of candles and gas signifies yet another gain for the cult of bureaucracy.

BC: And what about the light that film took from the theater? Can film give the theater something in return?

HJS: Good question. Let me follow it with another: Could this gift be the very forbidden fire from which films live, and could it be in the form of a metaphor for the radiant or electronic impulses printed on those artificial substances celluloid and videotape? That is, can film's visual freedom and its visual provocation—the ability that it has to set free in the viewer's unconscious a quiet profusion of images that flow unchecked into the depths of his heart—can these qualities be adapted to the theater, where they would become only one more leaf on the tree of artistic knowledge?

BC: How would that happen? The offstage events reported in the theater by messengers, for example, are realized on film in action.

HJS: Film does cut up these dramatic word pictures into a kaleidoscope of sights and sounds and deeds from all over the world. But these can themselves be transformed back into the palpable motion of imagined worlds in the monologue of the representational self, the single human being onstage who becomes synonymous with the world and taps the selves of his spectators. The ancient dream of the poet would thus be fulfilled: to write poetry for the stage and have it realized there, this time in rhythms borrowed from film, the same rhythms that lend meaning to what otherwise would be an empty succession of images.

BC: So film in this instance would be sacrificing itself to the theater, not the other way around?

HJS: Yes, the film must learn that it is art which sacrifices itself, in the end, to civilization. Yet, living off its own demise, as it were, art continues its celebration of civilization. Is it possible that it does so as never before?

BC: Yes, if you're speaking in terms of the sheer quantity of (bad) artistic production throughout the world.

HJS: Well, Mr. Cardullo, it turns out that I am more hopeful or optimistic in this regard than you, which surprises me. Thank you for a stimulating discussion.

BC: Thank *you*, Herr Syberberg.

Filmography of Feature Films

Scarabea—How Much Land Does a Man Need?, 1968
San Domingo, 1970
Ludwig II: Requiem for a Virgin King (first part of the " German trilogy"); *Ludwig's Cook*, 1972
Karl May (second part of the "German trilogy"), 1974
The Confessions of Winifred Wagner, 1975
Our Hitler (*Hitler, A Film from Germany*; third part of the "German trilogy"; in four parts: *The Grail, A German Dream, The End of a Winter Fairy Tale*, and *We Children of Hell*), 1977

Parsifal, 1983
The Night, 1985
Edith Clever Reads James Joyce, 1985
Miss Else, 1986
Penthesilea, 1987
The Marquise of O., 1989
The Bad and Happy Lot of Art after World War II, 1991
A Dream, What Else?, 1994
Plato Cave Memory (a video installation), 1997

Index